SPOKE ELEVEN

Publisher and Editor:
Kevin Gallagher

Contributing Editors
Karina van Berkum
Marc Vincenz

———

spokeboston.com

———

ISBN: 978-1-952335-95-2

Copyright © 2025

———

Cover design by Marc Vincenz
Interior design and layout: MadHat Press

Published in the United States of America

by MadHat Press
PO Box 422
Cheshire, MA 01225

———

madhat-press.com

SPOKE ELEVEN

BOSTON, MASS.

TABLE OF CONTENTS

Kevin Gallagher and Karina van Berkum	On Your Left	vii

POETS
CID CORMAN

Daniel Bratton	Cid Corman's "Real-Theatre" Folder: Looking into Discovery	5
Guy Rotella	On or About Cid Corman	19
Jenny Penberthy	Tribute to Kamaike Susumu, Co-Translator with Cid Corman	27
George Evans	Afterbeat: Cid Corman	43
Bob Arnold	The Man Who Always Was	57
Burt Kimmelman	When History Gets Personal: Cid Corman and The New American Poetry	61
Gregory Dunne	"And Here Is the Silence, More Intensely Coming": On the Uncollected Kyoto Notebooks of Cid Corman	73

RON SCHREIBER

Ron Schreiber	January 1978	83
Mark Pawlak	Ron Schreiber 1934–2004: Poet, Editor, Gay Activist, Innovator, Rebel	85
Dick Lourie	No Ideas	91
Betsy Sholl	Remembering Ron Schreiber	94
Cornelia Venendaal	Letter From the Editor	97
David M. Eberly	A Militant Among Us: Ron Schreiber and the Good Gay Poets	99
Kevin Bertolero	"A Place for Me": On the Poetry of Ron Schreiber	101
Leslie Cagan	Remembering Ron	108
Linda Dittmar	Renegade	111
Mary Bonina	With Dignity	114

* * *

Mairéad Byrne	Sixteen Poems	117
Lee Bartlett	Twelve Poems	136
George Evans	Lands End	150
Olena Jennings	Sixteen Poems	199
Kirk Glaser	Cracks and Apertures	224
Tracy K. Smith	Patrick Sylvain	259
Patrick Sylvain	Invocation and Other Poems	261
Michael Franco	Songs of the Harper	283
Hoyt Rogers	Colors	314
Ron Padgett	September Song	335

PROSE

Peter Valente	The Alchemist of Language and Ideas: On Several of Herman Melville's Novels and Travel Writings	339
Jennifer Bartlett	Chapter Thirteen: The Bin	351
Michael Londra	Manifold Honey: The Phoenix Art of Delmore Schwartz	359
Lee Bartlett	"A Mad Night": Talking to Michael McLure about The Six Gallery	367
Jack Pulaski	In the Park	373
Peter Valente	Pliny the Younger: A Balance Between the Public and the Private Persona	385
Pliny the Younger	Letters (translated by Peter Valente)	393
Covered	*biographies*	403

On Your Left

The mission of *spoKe* is to advance a better vision of the world through poetry and poetics. Founded in response to the Boston Marathon bombing, we are strong to advance:

1. A global poetry that engages with or is from the world's places, cultures and literary traditions: past, present, and visions of futures.
2. American poetry that sees the English language and literary tradition as core but one of many roots and paths for poetry.
3. A poetics that attempts to innovate language, idiom, sensibility, and poetic form while maintaining a public presence.

In the tradition of one of Boston's greatest magazines, Cid Corman's *Origin*, we go deeply into a few poets, regions, and cultures in each issue. In *spoKe* 11 we finally pay homage to Cid Corman himself with essays, letters and reflections that introduce and go deeper into the most unsung but influential Boston–bred poet of the 20th century. We also pay tribute to poet, editor and gay activist Ron Schreiber in a feature guest-edited by Mark Pawlak. We are proud to exhibit the poetry of Mairéad Byrne, Lee Bartlett, Olena Jennings, Patrick Sylvain, and others. *spoKe* 11 has an incredible group of prose features, notably Peter Valente on Melville and his translations of Pliny's letters, Jennifer Bartlett, Lee Bartlett on McClure and the sixth gallery reading, Michael Londra on Ben Mazer's Delmore Schwartz.

Not letting up.

—*Kevin Gallagher and Karina van Berkum*

POETS

Cid Corman

Cid Corman and Susumu Kamaike at Doshisha University, Kyoto (c. 1960)
Collection of the Author

Cid Corman's "Real-Theatre" Folder: Looking into Discovery

Daniel Bratton

From 2005 to 2010 I belonged to the English Department at Doshisha University in Kyoto, where Cid Corman had himself taught during the 1960s. Cid had died just the year before my arrival, but I was able to enjoy and learn from close friendships with Susumu Kamaike, a retired Doshisha professor known for his collaborations with Corman in translating Japanese literature into English, and Shizumi Corman, Cid's grieving widow. One day, during a meal in a restaurant, Shizumi-san produced from an old carryall an item that on first appearance seemed anything but a remarkable literary artifact, a battered brown folder that exuded the musty aroma of humid Kyoto summers. Its faded cover bore Cid Corman's handwriting, the upper left corner reading "REAL-THEATRE," under which were written the titles of what proved to be three plays contained therein. Centered at the bottom was a quotation in Greek by the Stoic philosopher Gorgias, reminding one that Corman and his two brothers attended Boston Latin School, which to this day has an elective in Greek. These words were followed by an English translation: "Putting aside the honours that most men seek, I shall try by looking into discovery, to be as excellent as my power permits both in my life and, when I am to die, in my death." Inside, giving the folder the feeling of an old scrapbook, were what I eventually counted as twenty-seven items, all but one on tattered and fading yellow or yellowing paper of various sizes: a mimeographed excerpt from a letter by Corman on oral poetry, postcards (including diagrams of real-theatre staging), a letter to Gael Turnbull, correspondence from Will Petersen, statements of Cid's conception of theatre, some literary fragments, and drafts of seven plays, including complete drafts of the three titles on the cover of the folder.

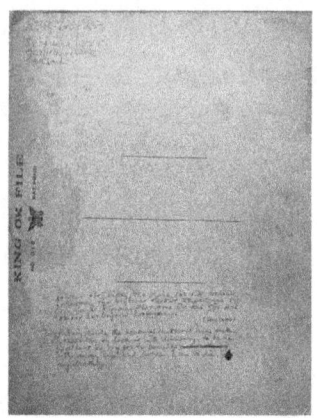

Corman's Real-Theatre folder

Although this folder is very much a Kyoto artifact, the roots of real-theatre were in Boston.[1] In fact, it is no coincidence that the first item, titled "FROM A LETTER, November 1959," is concerned with oral poetry, for behind Corman's conception of "real-theatre" are his formulations on the oral foundation of poetry, dating back to his activities in Boston during the late 1940s and early 1950s, prior to a Fulbright scholarship that took him to Paris in 1954.

In 1949, Corman began "This Is Poetry" on Boston's WMEX radio station, near Fenway Park. He observed in *The Gist of Origin* that these weekly broadcasts, generally fifteen minutes long, "ran for three years without a break … [and] included many poets in the Boston area, whether visiting or living there, reading their own work, poets like Archibald MacLeish, John Crowe Ransom, Richard Wilbur, John Ciardi, Theodore Roethke, Stephen Spender, and Richard Eberhart" (Corman 1975, xvii). From the beginning, Corman's broadcasts were not aimed at an elite audience. He emphasized this in a contribution to *Poetry* magazine written during this time titled "Communication: Poetry for Radio": "Intelligence is by no means restricted to academic circles, nor is it the special property of poets. There is an affection for poetry around and waiting to be encouraged. I am not idealizing; my experience is too broad and too precisely convincing in this medium for me to have to theorize. There are people who listen to us and who want to hear" (Corman 1952, 214–215).

The valuable contacts that Corman made through "This Is Poetry"

---

1. Corman and Will Petersen capitalized real-theatre on some occasions and did not always hyphenate it; however, I am following its most common iteration in lower case and with a hyphen, with the exception of direct quotations.

not only created a sense of community but also contributed to his founding of *Origin* magazine in spring 1951. He had met William Carlos Williams and his wife Florence ("Flossie") during his residency at Yaddo, the well-known artists' community in Saratoga Springs, in July 1950 and already knew of Charles Olson through Robert Creeley and Vincent Ferrini, who had read on his radio program (Corman 1975, xix). Creeley had planned a little mag and, when this fell through, Corman picked up the gauntlet, showcasing this ever-expanding literary community in one of the groundbreaking magazines of the alternative poetry, an endeavor that would continue through four and one-half series over a half a century.

Cid's involvement in community through his radio broadcasts was complemented by the poetry groups he organized. In an interview with Philip Rowland, he recounted, "Before I left Boston, I had three groups going simultaneously—of course no money involved, nor was there any for the radio show—the first radio show in the history of modern poetry—and it was only with modern poetry I dealt, usually work which was not yet in book form, out of magazines, the latest work that I found interesting" (Rowland 2013, 3). He was emphatic that these gatherings were not workshops. "All these groups you see today, they're poetry workshops. Never entered my mind to have a poetry workshop; and I've had groups in Europe and here [Japan], over the years, and, never a workshop" (3–4). These poetry groups tie in with Corman's conception of real-theatre as being "at home," unrehearsed, creating community.

It was also at this time that the Poets' Theatre was established in Cambridge. "The History of The Poets' Theatre" records that at the time of its formation in 1950 there were few staged performances of poetry and poetic drama in the area:

> Working out of a small Cambridge theatre (over a hardware store), always on a shoe-string, the theatre brought the world's leading poets and dramatists to town for readings and performances. The animating force of the Poets' Theatre in those days was an unforgettable Irish woman, Dublin-born Mary Manning (aka Molly Howe), who had been a playwright and actor at the Abbey and Gate Theatres.... Other founding members included Thornton Wilder, William Carlos Williams, Edward Gorey, and Alison Lurie.[2]

---

[2]. History Cambridge indicates that the Poets' Theatre "was originally held in parlors and church parish houses," venues that would suit Corman's conception of real-theatre performance spaces: https://historycambridge.org/?s=the+poets%27+theatre. Also see https://www.poetstheatre.org/our-history .

Corman's unpublished play *The Center* was performed at the Poets' Theatre in May, 1951, under the direction of V.R. Lang, who also starred in verse dramas there. Tim Woods observes that at this time Cid "busied himself with promoting, disseminating, educating himself in, and constructing a poetic community and poetic practice that he envisaged as the future of poetics." Central to this was a "deeply engrained conviction of poetry's democratic and public value," along with an abiding interest in poetry of other languages and exploration of new trajectories that would challenge the effete aesthetic tendencies of much of the American poetic canon.[3]

A clear connection exists between Corman's passionate involvement in these communities and his specific concern with the oral tradition of poetry. In fact, Corman repeatedly claimed to have been the *inventor* of oral poetry, though here he was referring to his improvisations of poetry: "The poems are immediate: they are not planned in advance and there is absolutely no text" (Corman 1977, 84). He began recording oral poetry just after his time in Boston, during his year in Paris. He had borrowed a wire recorder from the American Embassy (or the American Fulbright Commission, according to another rendering of the story), which he took back to his squalid room—he lived in a broom closet with no window and had to use the sink as the toilet!—to record William Carlos Williams' *Paterson* Four. However, he ended up inventing his own spontaneous poems, a natural progression from what he'd been doing on his radio program where he never used a script. Corman continued making tape recordings of oral poetry throughout his years in Kyoto; in fact, Shizumi Corman gave my wife and me a file box containing old cassettes that includes Cid's recordings of oral poetry, sometimes made in the dark hours of the morning as an occasional dog barked or car went by their house in Utano. These occurrences influenced the content and direction of the poems.

Still, Corman also wrote of oral poetry in the larger context of the oral roots of poetry, and in his letter from 1959 at the front of the folder he articulates a central aspect of his poetics, "that the fundamental act of poetry, as of everything else, is the affirmation of breathing, the act of living in dying." He added that the old, honored notion of the poet as inspired by the Muse is not inaccurate, as "inspiration is the breathing into the poet of that energy which he translates into poetry in releasing it, realizing the sense in the words he uses."[4]

---

3. Tim Woods, "Cid Corman: Editor, Translator, Poet," *Paideuma*, vol. 41 (2014): 52–56.
4. Permission for all textual citations from the real-theatre folder is given by Bob Arnold, Literary Executor of the Estate of Cid Corman.

This letter follows on the heels of his recent arrival in Japan, on March 28, 1958, his preoccupation with oral poetry rapidly expanding into a passion for Noh theatre—and real-theatre. Though Gary Snyder had extended the original invitation for Corman to come to Japan, he was not actually in the country at the time of Cid's arrival: it was the American artist, writer, translator, and later editor Will Petersen, already teaching in Kyoto, who initiated Corman into Japanese ways, finding him a teaching job and, more importantly, sweeping him up into the world of Noh. Kamaike-sensei, to whom Petersen introduced Corman within a week of Cid's arrival, once told me that he found Will Petersen to have the deepest understanding of Japanese culture of any *gaikokujin* in Kyoto at that time. Petersen actually danced on the Kawamura Noh stage as a shimai performer. Although Cid did not immediately study utai, the singing component of music in Noh, upon his arrival in Kyoto—he was not physically suited to shimai—he would go on to practice it for a period of approximately ten years: these weekly sessions involved the copying of voicing intonation as precisely as possible from the teacher, who allowed the use of a tape recorder. According to Kamaike, Corman was sharp in grasping the essential elements: "maybe he wasn't able to reproduce it right away, but he *understood* it—he knew he would be able to reproduce it soon."

Corman's utai practice books from the mid-1960s

Kamaike-sensei shared with me an article from the *Kyoto-Shinbun* (February 23, 1970) on abdominal breathing as essential to utai. It argued that because traditional Japanese structures were made of wood, paper, straw, and earth or clay, they absorbed sound, so a particular elocution was devised in response: abdominal breathing. Corman learned through Petersen and Kamaike that this controlling of utterance produced by inhaling as deeply as possible and exhaling little by little was likely introduced by Noh performers back to the fourteenth century. Exhilarated by this new influence on his poetics, he later put this technique into practice when he studied utai. Kamaike also told me that what attracted Corman most to Japanese classics, including Noh, was the aesthetic sense of *wabi* and *sabi*, which spoke to his own predispositions.[5]

Not surprisingly, at the heart of Corman's real-theatre folder we find correspondence emphasizing the relationship between breath and his poetics. A three-page letter he wrote to Gael Turnbull, dated November 12, 1959, begins: "my concern for oral poetry and my work with it has only accentuated a growing realization that the fundamental act of poetry, as of everything else, is the affirmation of breathing, the act of living in dying. To put such emphasis on breathing may strike you as being on par with yoga exercises. Perhaps it is; that would hardly disqualify it." He concludes with a peroration of sorts:

> Read some of the piddling stuff that passes for poetry these days. Why you choke on it. It is either breathless or so choppy that no living soul can possibly live with or by it—including the authors.
>
> If your words do not have the spine of breath in them, no plotted or pieced structure will do any good. The body is dead and you are simply painting a corpse.
>
> To breathe words is to breed words. To know that every breath, and thus every word, IS a matter of life and death. Until this act is recognized and entered, no poetry exists. But when it happens, everything happens; it is all, as it is, poetry.

However, it is not until we get to Will Petersen's letters to Cid in the folder that we begin to fully appreciate how the centrality of breath to his poetics broadened into a full-blown conception of theatre—a real-theatre—under the influence on Noh.

Petersen's letters cover a broad range of subjects, but much of their content anticipates several essays that Corman composed on real-theatre, explorations that link what Cid and Will envisioned as an alternative theatre to the Living Theatre, Jerzy Grotowski's Poor Theatre, Peter Brook's Empty Space, and other revolutionary challenges to the theatrical status quo.[6] However, in exploring the possibilities of

---

5. Interviews with Kamaike Susumu, Kyoto, December 21, 2005 & January 18, 2006.
6. Petersen's correspondence indicates a keen interest in Grotowski, though at a later date. He wrote Scott Johnson on January 12, 1970: "At once get 3 Jan issue of the NEW REPUBLIC and read STANLEY KAUFFMAN on GROTOWSKI'S theatre….

theatre, Corman was staking out a distinctive territory where Noh and oral poetry exerted a dominant influence.

Included in the folder, just before Petersen's letters, is a two-page statement on theatre that Corman wrote between August 1959 and December 1960. It begins: "Theatre, as it concerns me, refers to a place where people, of their own accord, gather to recognize the concurrence of art and the dying that is life. The drama relates to us as performance, a realization in and of itself, of particular moment, expressed through the various conjoined poetries of speech, motion, accoutrements and instrumental sound." Corman then explores what he means by "real-theatre," employing a phrase that recurs in his musings on theatre, the "act of realization." In "The Theatre of Commitment," for example, he wrote that real-theatre "refers to the theatre of realization"—not mere intellectual apprehension but a coming to one's senses so "as to live anew" (Corman 1977, 34-35). It is an "essential theatre." The stage is to be without curtains, without props, with "no lights switched off to hide the audience." This act of realization is conveyed through the text, performers, and place.

The attributes Corman assigns to this theatre of realization in his two-page statement coalesce with his poetics: "When I say this theatre finds itself in poetries, I mean that language where every word weighs, as it must in theatre, is poetry." Here he returns to the centrality of breath: "From the center comes the breath, flows out through every pore, every edge, makes time in all directions and finds accord in us, if we stay open to it." He goes so far as to say that "no theatre that is not poetry can endure."

Corman expounds upon many of these ideas in "Notes Toward 'Real-Theatre,'" an unpublished manuscript from 1959.[7] Once again he observes that the theatre with which he is concerned is one of realization, "in which the drama occurs at every step, every breath, is event." He contends that such a theatre cannot be "popular," in the sense of receiving wide economic support, and cannot provide mere entertainment, being a theatre of participation. At a time when Grotowski was eschewing the conventions of traditional commercial theatre and laying the groundwork for a "Poor Theatre," Corman was envisioning a theatre without "stars," with "no make-up, no fancy costuming, no special lighting or trick effects."

Grotowski—anything you can find on, by, about him, please send on. Needless to say, Noh surfaces & deepens in me." Letter quoted by permission of Scott Johnson.

7. Cid Corman, "Notes Toward a Real-Theatre" (unpublished manuscript, August 28, 1959), quoted courtesy the Lilly Library, Indiana University, Bloomington, Indiana.

However, to note such similarities also invites one to determine what distinguished Corman's real-theatre from other experimental theatre actively seeking to demolish the "fourth wall" between actors and spectators. Once again his poetics provides a partial answer. He notes in the same manuscript, "Such theatre essentially requires poetry. It has nothing to do with anti-naturalism or of stylization or what-have-you....And by 'poetic' I clearly do not mean lambent or flowery. I mean root-language, root-event, response of action to action, word to word, in the most aware way.... No enduring theatre is possible that is not poetry. No exceptions have occurred or can occur."

As well, in theorizing his poetic theatre of realization, Corman describes its physical setting in a manner that at once reminds one of what Peter Brook and his contemporaries were doing with "empty space," yet again sets real-theatre apart. By way of illustration, a friend of mine, Sandra Philips, recounts how, leaving Canada back in the early 1970s, she travelled to Grotowski's Teatr Laboratorium in Wroclaw, Poland, apprenticing there for a year in a stone building without windows before heading to Peter Brook's Théâtre des Bouffes au Nord in Paris, its floors covered in dirt, with mud everywhere and no curtains. Here she interviewed Brook, who told her to visit El Teatro Campesino in San Juan Bautista, California, where he had recently taken what he categorized as "Rough Theatre" directly into farm communities. Sandra eventually returned to Canada to act in Toronto's Factory Lab; one is reminded of the humble origins of the Poets' Theatre above a hardware store in Cambridge, for Factory Lab began in a former candle factory above an auto garage. As this global revolution in the staging of theatre was occurring, Corman, who would have heartily concurred with Brook's term "Deadly Theatre" to describe the commercial stage, was harking back to his days of organizing poetry groups in public libraries and people's homes in Boston in advocating that real-theatre be taken *completely* out of a theatrical setting. Emphasizing the non-commercial and communal nature of his proposed theatre, he posited "it becomes clear that theatre must be enacted in the HOME. It must reach the individual as individual and allow him to be PERFORMER."[8]

---

8. Cid Corman, "Realtheatre" (unpublished manuscript, August 3, 1966), quoted courtesy the Lilly Library, Indiana University, Bloomington, Indiana. In fact, several items in the folder suggest that Corman and Petersen gave a good deal of thought to staging real-theatre. These include a colored diagram titled "Real-Theatre," a second diagram in pencil, and final notes that indicate they had conferred with Ohno Hidetaka, a well-known Kyoto visual artist who collaborated with Corman on several books, about possibly doing away with the traditional Noh back panel and "working

In this respect, Cid may have been more radical than some of his contemporaries: such a theatre actually eliminates the need for a producer and director; it needs no stage directions.

His emphasis on "home" theatre without a money-motive complicated my quest to discover whether Corman and Petersen ever publicly "staged" any of their plays. I picked the brains of a few old friends and contacted Corman scholars and *Origin* poets who had known Cid and Will Petersen during the 1960s and 1970s—Scott Johnson, Scott Watson, David Miller, John Levy, Cynthia Archer (Will's wife), and Daphne Marlatt, who would go on to write the first Canadian play written and staged in the formal tradition of Noh— but nobody had any recollection of real-theatre productions. (David alerted me to Petersen's *Moby Dick as Noh*, published in *Japan and America* in 1984, but this was never staged and appeared nearly twenty years after Will had returned to the United States— and distanced himself from Cid Corman.) Of course, several people recalled readings and talks hosted by Cid on the second floor of CC's, the coffee shop in Kyoto that he and Shizumi opened in 1973. Although these events do not seem to have included any dramatic productions, they epitomized Corman's mission to create community though poetry, with customers, friends, and writers, many of them international, forming a unifying circle on tatami mats. John Levy, who worked at CC's in exchange for room and board in 1974, taped some of these events, recalling that Cid would often give a lecture about a specific poet, sometimes give a reading of his own work, and occasionally play a tape of himself doing oral poetry.[9] Prior to this, Corman had shared some of his oral poetry tapes with an audience at the University of California San Diego, attempting to address its members "at the most naked and penetrating possible" (Corman 1977, 97). As well, cassettes given to us by Shizumi suggest that Cid cultivated the same sense of community when, in the early 1980s, the Cormans ran their ill-fated kaiseki restaurant at 132 Newbury St. in Boston, before returning to Japan for good in 1982. These tapes, some also recorded at 89 Dartmouth St., where the Cormans lived with Cid's younger brother and his wife, confirm that he organized multiple events showcasing spontaneous oral poetry, sometimes generating fifty or more poems in one session.

---

out of triangular floor-boards (easily transportable)" along the lines of the previous diagrams.
9. John Levy, email message to the author, June 19, 2024.

Cid and Shizumi at the opening of CC's in 1973 (collection of the author)

So why, given the abundant evidence of Cid's performances of oral poetry, are there apparently no records, recordings or memories of performed real-theatre? As early as 1960, writing Will Petersen from where he was staying in San Francisco, Cid acknowledged the difficulty he faced in promoting his vision of theatre. Commenting upon several poetry readings he'd recently given, he mused: '"And my thoughts keep wandering to real-theatre. I realize the difficulties more acutely, apart from the writing and theory. In this country it will be very tough. But I'd like to take a shot at it. It's just possible that as I travel around and talk, some opportunity will turn up. I'd like to rig it for both of us together.... Still, I don't figure anything for a couple of years. Which gives us 'time.'"[10] Other letters reveal that he shared with Petersen an idea to turn one of Philip Whalen's poems into real-theatre, but nothing seems to have come of this, either. However, though my quest to discover whether Corman and Petersen staged real-theatre events continues, what we *do* have are the dramatic texts in the folder, three fragments and four complete drafts, all commingling Japanese and Western dramatic traditions.

A twelve-page manuscript not mentioned on the cover of the

---

10. Letter of 16 August 1960 from the Will Petersen Papers, quoted by permission of University of Connecticut Archives and Special Collections.

folder is arguably the most intriguing of these texts. Titled *Noh or: The Poets (Shijin)*, its cast is assigned the roles traditionally given to the actors in Noh: *shite* (the main character, traditionally masked); *waki* (a supporting actor, generally unmasked, who interacts with and draws out the *shite*); *waki-tsure* (who accompanies the *shite*); *nochi-shite* (the *shite* after a change in scenery or when the actors have left the stage for a short time); *kyōgen* (comic actor); and chorus. Real-theatre is already evident: the *shite* plays Shakespeare; the *waki* Zeami, the greatest playwright of Noh theatre; the *waki-tsure* the famous shogun Yoshimitsu, Zeami's patron; the *nochi-shite* King Lear; and the *kyōgen* (as one might have guessed) his Fool.

East meets West when, after an opening in which Zeami and the Emperor engage with the chorus, Shakespeare enters, followed by the Fool. This encounter, in lines redolent of Noh in their lofty poetic cadences, leads to an interlude, echoing the traditional *ai-kyōgen* in Noh, the Fool delivering a long soliloquy. A second act follows in which Lear enters the scene, both he and the chorus playing upon well-known lines from *King Lear*, the *shite* and *waki* contributing to this intertextuality. The conclusion has Shakespeare delivering Kent's final lines from Act V.

In the three plays cited on the cover of the folder, all with Western settings, the characters continue to function in roles approximate to those assigned in Noh. However, there are fewer actors and Noh terminology for the players has been replaced by Western equivalents. For example, the cast in *Samson+Real* comprises an "affirmer" (Manoa, Samson's father), a chorus, and a "performer" (Dalila), with a comic interacting with the affirmer in a Kyōgen-like interlude. *Oedipus-Real* has an affirmer (the blind priest Tiresias), performer/poet (Oedipus), assistant (Antigone), and chorus, its two acts framing an interlude with two comic actors interacting with the performer and assistant. *Sycamore West* also has an affirmer (Caleb West, an old man), performer (his son), and comic, who interacts with the other two players during the interlude. Also, while *Samsone+Real* and *Oedipus-Real* draw on archetypes deeply engrained in Western culture, their themes reflect the authors' particular concerns.

Samson+Real, from 1959, is vintage Corman: it opens with the affirmer, Manoa, now an old man mourning the death of his noble son, tending the fire in a mean dwelling the description of which suggests Cid's account of his broom closet on the Left Bank. He welcomes to his hearth a visitor, Dalila, of all people—"she who stripped thy son of his powers,/ she who suffered him to have his eyes gorged at Gaza, / she who was honored for her bravery with eleven hundred gold coins." Now abandoned by the Philistines, "no longer their whore," Dalila tells Manoa that she is not seeking his pity, rather bringing him the one golden hair of his son that she still possesses. The intensity of their exchange is interrupted by the arrival of a comic (Kyōgen) old serving woman, appalled to find Dalila at the fire. Manoa eventually tires of her histrionics, asking the old woman to leave, the play returning in the second act to its powerful theme of transcendent compassion, conveyed in flowing Noh-like cadences.

Oedipus-Real opens with Antigone witnessing a heated blame-game between her now-blind father/brother and the blind prophet Tiresias (continuing the theme of blindness from the archetypal stories of Lear and Sampson). A difference between this real-theatre text and the others is that the interval that follows is closer to traditional Kyōgen, featuring two comics. These two clowns are incredibly nasty, viciously ridiculing the players as "two stray sheep / and a tattered ewe lamb" before finally being rebuffed by an angry Antigone. The second part ends with commentary from the Chorus the poetry of which seems at once from Greek tragedy and Noh.

Sycamore West (Real-theatre), on the other hand, has a contemporary postwar setting, the prodigal son returning to savagely enlighten his aging father about the horrors he's experienced serving his country. Here the dialogue seems far closer to Allen Ginsberg's declamatory style than Noh:

> Men rolled, men shafted, men dug out of ditches.
> Men crated away, men locked up in staightjackets
> Men who explode like petroleum
> and others who croak like frogs in a muffled swamp …
>
> And I've come from between the legs of whores
> from the mouths of bottles
> from the smoky end of dreams
>
> from war your war
>
> we fought your war
> remember
>
> you should come for the picnic.

Indeed, we should not forget Will Petersen's having been in attendance at the famous 6 Gallery on Oct. 7, 1955, when Ginsberg drew a line in the sand with his first reading of "Howl." Although Corman always distanced himself from the Beats, Petersen freely associated with them in Berkeley and San Francisco—photographs of him practicing calligraphy appeared in Beat books and magazines. Cynthia Archer has written, "Cid made a big deal to [her] that Will was not a Beat," but who was he to say?[11] After all, Will was the model for Rol Sturlason in Kerouac's *The Dharma Bums*, which even alludes to his recently published article in *The Evergreen Review* on the stone garden at Ryōanji.

Will Petersen performing shimai on the Kawamura Noh Stage, Kyoto
Photo Courtesy Cynthia Archer

This passage, seeming to be much more in Petersen's voice than Corman's, raises the issue of authorship. Clearly the plays were collaborative, but who wrote what? *Noh, or the Poets (Shijin)* seems more Petersen's work, given the deep knowledge it displays of Noh at a time when Corman had only recently arrived in Japan. The second draft of *Samson+Real* has Peterson's initials at the top, but he may have been responding to Cid's first effort. Perhaps it is best to simply see the plays as intensely synergetic.

In the end, the folder's greatest value may be its confirmation that Noh profoundly influenced not only Corman's conception of theatre but also his poetics. He found the Noh theatre a sacred place, in contrast to what he saw as the spiritual vacuity of the commercial Western stage. Accepting that Noh theatre is too rooted in its place to be copied, he suggested that through Noh those who feel the power of stillness can learn the "economy of spirit" and the "ecology of poetry"

---
11. Cynthia Archer, email message to the author, June 27, 2024.

(Corman 1970, 34). Noh inspired Cid to develop a poetic practice that allowed him to be as excellent as his powers permitted.

BIBLIOGRAPHY

Corman, Cid. "Attending the Noh," *Kyoto Monthly Guide*. Eds. Cid Corman and Richard P. Leavett. Kyoto Association of International Culture & Tourism, (Dec. 1970): 24–34.

—. "Communication: Poetry for Radio." *Poetry*, vol. 81, no. 3 (Dec. 1952): 212–15.

—. Letter to Will Petersen, 16 Aug. 1960. Will Petersen Papers, Box 1:2. Qtd. by permission of Archives and Special Collections, The University of Connecticut.

—. "Notes on Theatre: 13 Dec 65," *Surviving: Essays by Cid Corman*, introduced by Scott Watson. Tohoku Gakuin University Faculty of Liberal Arts Review (2004): 245–278.

—. "Notes Toward 'Real-Theatre'," 28 August 1959. Corman mss. III 1943–2004, Box 60, 4 pp. Courtesy Lilly Library, Indiana University, Bloomington, Indiana.

—. "Realtheatre," 8 August 1966, Corman mss. III 1943–2004, Box 60, 3 pp. Courtesy Lilly Library, Indiana University, Bloomington, Indiana.

—. *Word for Word: Essays on the Arts of Language*, Vol. 1. Santa Barbara: Black Sparrow Press, 1977.

Corman Cid, and Will Petersen. "Translators' Note: *Yashima*." *Origin*, series 2, issue 3 (October 1961): 17.

Rowland, Philip. "Cid Corman in Conversation." *Flash Point* (Winter 2001). Web issue 4, September 20, 2013. https://www.flashpointmag.com/corman1.htm

Woods, Tim. "Cid Corman: Editor, Translator, Poet," *Paideuma*, vol. 41, 2014: 49–78.

On or About Cid Corman

Guy Rotella

To muck up a metaphor, *spoKe* wears fealty to Cid Corman on its sleeve. It's an apt ornament. There's the Boston connection. Corman was born in Dorchester, went to Boston Latin and Tufts, lived in town off and on when he wasn't living abroad, and published his magazine there; even so, he was as loyal to foreign poets as to domestic ones. Like Corman's *Origin*, *spoKe* also inhabits Boston and is at the same time worldly, printing poets from around the globe in translation. More pertinent still, Corman made editing, publishing, translating, promoting, discussing, and writing poetry a lifelong labor and love.

Corman is best known as sole editor of *Origin*, a journal of poetry and poetics pivotal to a dramatic literary shift in the 1950s and 60s: the swerve away from the academic poetry that was both derived and in retreat from the modernist experimentation of the nineteen-teens and –twenties, and that then dominated the 1930s and '40s. Of course, swerves away are always also swerves toward. *Origin* helped initiate the shift toward the Projectivist, Objectivist, and other alternative modes and models that have led to the wide range of companionable or competing practices which, with additions, continue to characterize the U.S. poetry landscape today. A list of names associated with *Origin* can illustrate the claim: Charles Olson, Robert Creeley, Paul Blackburn, Louis Zukofsky, Lorine Niedecker, Robert Duncan, Ted Enslin, Paul Carroll, Ed Dorn, William Bronk, Gary Snyder, Robert Kelly, Denise Levertov, Larry Eigner, Philip Whalen, Clayton Eshleman, and Ian Hamilton Finlay. (An appendix to Corman's *The Gist of Origin* provides a complete list of the writers he published in the course of the journal's twenty-year run.)

The shift away from academic verse *Origin* helped vitalize has commonly been described as a victorious revolution, one in which the manacles of a supposedly moribund tradition (meter, rhyme, inherited forms, regular stanzas, and conventional—read timid, or just wrong—subject matter, attitudes, and so forth) were shaken off and replaced by freedom: freedom as variously defined in a flurry of manifestoes and polemics and in many divergent practices (again Projectivist and Objectivist ones, along with Black Mountain, Confessional, Deep Image, New York School, and race-, gender- and class-based, as well as breath/oral/performance/slam/rap, and concrete poetry and poetics, among them).

Polemics, by the way, are fine for poets, who properly treat their druthers as rubrics. They're less good for editors, since force and focus can narrow impact and scope. And they're all but anathema for literary historians: distorted surveys make lousy maps. Hazlitt, Collingwood, and many others affirm that art doesn't progress, but develops. In her "Rethinking Models of Literary Change," Mutlu Blasing argues convincingly that literary change is not simply a revolutionary or evolutionary matter of new forms making new meanings but rather an intricately improvised dance or, better, set of dances in which forms change functions and functions change forms. The steps of those dances are (in potential, at least) infinitely variable. At the extremes, so-called open forms can enforce closure, while so-called closed forms can be wholly open-ended. If this isn't something Corman ever quite said, his mixed accommodation of and resistance to, for instance, Charles Olson's more narrowly targeted proselytizing (for details, see George Evans's edition of the Olson-Corman letters), along with his wide-ranging editorial practice, suggest that he held a similarly eclectic and inclusive view. In addition to the poets listed above, for instance, *Origin* published such moderns as Williams and Stevens, and such less experimental, arguably academic or formalist poets of the next generation as Richard Wilbur, James Merrill, Richard Eberhart, and Samuel French Morse, as well as such other "independent," less easily categorized or "schoolable" poets as William Bronk, who, with Olson and Zukofsky, was a major beneficiary of Corman's magazine.

All of that said, Corman's major interest was in the avant-garde poets of his moment, and he took every opportunity to promote those writers and their work. He not only published them, sometimes devoting an entire issue to a large selection of a single poet's work, or printing their books under his Origin Press aegis: collections by Snyder, Bronk, Niedecker, and Zukofsky, for instance. He also included their prose arguments and explanations, publishing letters or related documents (although he drew the line at manifestoes). He also printed negative as well as positive responses to previously published work, on the principle that such exchanges benefit both writers and readers. Meanwhile, he organized poetry discussion groups, often at public libraries, and, taking advantage of another medium for promotion, he broadcast poetry readings and conversations on a Boston radio station.

Corman also engaged in extensive correspondence with both successful and failed submitters to his magazine, offering encouragement, frank assessment, and that vital thing for actual and would-be poets:

sustained readerly attention, a rarity in a world where submissions are many and responses few and mostly *pro forma*. In addition, before the Deep Image poets' recourse to Spanish and Scandinavian examples as a way to revivify American verse, and before terms like global and world poetry became commonplace, internationalism and translation were significant aspects of *Origin*'s project: Corman published work by Canadian, Scottish, and English as well as American writers, and he included work brought over into English from French, Italian, Spanish, Japanese, Chinese, and even Latin (Zukofsky's versions of Catullus). Corman translated many of those poems himself, and, characteristically, did so from languages he did and didn't know. It might be said that Corman took seriously Frank O'Hara's famous half-joking, friskily punning reference to buying "an ugly NEW WORLD WRITING to see what the poets/in Ghana are doing these days."

Cid Corman was no academic, in the professional as well as the poetic sense, but he contributed to literary history in his typically clear, self-abnegating, self-congratulatory, quirky, and candid introduction to *The Gist of Origin*, which is also a tutorial in the aims, pleasures, and quicksands of journal editing. It includes a typically bold maneuver in which Corman corrects Eliot's version of Sanskrit principles in *The Waste Land* in order to summarize his sense of both a poet's and an editor's proper attitudes and tasks, or, better, behaviors: for Eliot's "give," Corman substitutes "offer," since he considers acts of giving hierarchical impositions without proper humility and appreciation; for "sympathize," he proffers "respond," thinking it displaces Eliot's word's implied and arguably high-handed pity; and for "control," he puts forward "let be," arguing that the phrase erases a damaging presumption of authority in favor of a modest awareness of every writing and reading self's inevitable limits. However impertinent or pertinent these all but religious strictures may be, Corman often lived up to them. They also begin to demonstrate his capacity for making cases, and so suggest as well that in addition to being an astute editor, wide-ranging translator, indefatigable literary promoter and correspondent, and prolific, sometimes powerfully affecting poet, he was also a first-rate literary critic, a skill reflected in his editorial choices and in his illuminating brief book on Bronk and two volumes of collected essays.

A major and unconventional aspect of Corman's critical prose is his extensive use of writers' own words to characterize their work and to ground his usually trenchant assessments of it. In selecting and stitching passages drawn from his *William Bronk: An Essay* and from his collections *Word for Word* and *At Their Word*, I'll try appropriating a bit of that method to exemplify the qualities he admired as well as the quality of his admiring.

Writing on Bronk, Corman quotes extensively from Bronk's poetry and letters, using his (Corman's) own words only here and there to effect a transition or highlight an essential feeling, thought, or expression. His intent is not to judge but to exemplify. This generosity in letting writers speak for themselves, without "explication," is, to repeat, one of Corman's great qualities as a critic as well as an editor. His selections from Bronk are smartly chosen, and his rare accompanying comments are crisply observed and pointedly expressed; in a word, they're foundational. Here's Corman quoting Bronk on Bronk, "'My poetry is about all of those things of which we have concepts but which we find non-existent or unapproachable, and about our experience of finding them so.'" This places Bronk precisely among those postmodern poets for whom the modernist sense that all inherited forms of cultural order have collapsed remains palpably true, but for whom the solutions of such moderns as Eliot and Pound (religious revival; art as substitute church) seem false and evasive. Underlining such matters (although he saw things differently), Corman defines Bronk as "half wishing to yield to the [attendant] nothingness—half to be absolved from it," calls him "Acutely direct," describes his poetry as "without concessions," notes "his ear for the way language thinks and feels its way into and out of thought," and (quoting Camus) praises Bronk for "a lucidity that repudiates itself." Such terse exactness illuminates; it can hardly be improved on. I know, having tried.

Corman's essay collections also deploy well-honed critical skills. *Word for Word: Essays on the Arts of Language*, Volume I, is largely devoted to Corman's vision of oral poetry. "Devoted" and "vision" are the right words for it, since he believes the liberation of poetry from the tyranny of print will, by way of increased spontaneity, sincerity, and authenticity, help heal divisions in the self, between selves, and in society. This strikes me as more wishful than likely, but Corman, writing as an aesthetician and critic and as a poet promoting his own predilections, makes his case with clarity and passion. It merits the hearing his own rule implies: "A man's sentiments ... are not disputable." Let's hear him. "When one makes a poem immediately via his voice, the voice is an exact immediacy. No interpretation interferes ... In short, the word spoken and given the cogency of poetry, its concentration and all of the nuances of inflection (which are always immediacies, snatched from the air, as it were, and hot) has a power in communication that the written word cannot hope for." "[T]his new possibility brings poetry back into the full stream of current human life. It becomes at once [by way of audio recording, apparently] available to all." "Its fire is clear and real. The ear can sense itself being touched and the air made warm." This is in keeping with transformational, often transcendental ideas supporting Beat, and other speech- and performance-based poetics. Corman puts it this way, "[t]he breath is the unit of poetic immediacy."

Well, it's one such unit. That's snide. But if Corman makes salvific claims for poetry in general and for oral poetry in particular (thus his quarrel with Bronk: Corman retained a portion of the modernist hope that poetry could replace religion to order lives and make a world; Bronk didn't), he also (for all his idealism) remains refreshingly alert to the limits of his own nearly mystical claims ("shared" is not "divided," for instance). As to those limits, "My own practice may give me some insight ... but it can never be ground for any system or prescription." As with his inclusive editorial choices, a willingness to "entertain," to consider and reconsider, ballasts both his aesthetic and literary critical commentaries. He seeks, he says, "to forget all alleged hierarchies." He nearly succeeds. While denigrating the extraction of literary "meaning," which he considers as based on a false analogy with chemistry or mining, and while insisting with many of his contemporaries and their followers that a poem is an event, not an object, he affirms again and again that, while it's "clear that any of the traditional approaches must be weighed anew in usage," those traditional ways *can* be used and may be efficacious; furthermore, by implication, any new approaches used must also be weighed and found either wanting or satisfactory. "There is no ONE way."

Other parts of *Word for Word* address the theatre and a small subset of prose. In keeping with his communitarian ethos and his only seemingly paradoxical preference for an art of unfiltered one-to-one exchanges, Corman (sometimes crankily) decries American commercial and subsidized theatre and prefers the transformative, ritualistic character of ancient Greek drama and the Noh. (For long stretches, Corman lived in Japan; he married a Japanese woman, and, as pragmatic as he was idealistic, ran an ice cream store with her; his historical and descriptive introduction to Noh is a fervent primer).

Corman's discussions of prose by Beckett, Bronk, William Carlos Williams, and Zukosfsky employ strategies and address matters we've met before. Beckett "refuses every opiate"; he assumes that dualism, whether liked or not, is a given; as in Joyce and Proust, his only paradise is a paradise lost; his situation is the human one: "seeking endurance in the face of a palpable non-enduring nature"; "stubbornness is the...pap of his work." Though none of this is news, Corman's expressive energy refreshes his report, and whatever his dis-ease with Beckett's views (Corman only half-credits Beckett's conviction that art fails along with all the other anodynes, for example), he doesn't allow himself to refute or spin them. Bronk, too, Corman observes, rejects the transcendent or ecstatic stance Corman yearns for: for him (Bronk), "uniqueness is not a value, but a plight"; "want" indicates desire and need, but always also indicates a lack. To his credit as a critic, Corman faithfully describes what he wishes were otherwise. That "otherwise" (call it hope) he finds confirmed in Williams's *The Farmers' Daughters* and Zukofsky's *Bottom: On Shakespeare*. Corman praises the sometimes tattered, always tough bulwarks art can set against nihilist temptations, however lucid those temptations are. He encounters in the doctor-poet's stories, for instance, "A love for the weak and the strong, respect for the offbeat, for the independent soul, for dignity, for sheer cussedness and spite, for a thin body holding out for life, for candor, for generosity, for care," and finds in Shakespeare, and in Zukofsky's effort to treat the Bard's entire canon as a single work, evidence that, if decay is organic to growth, "growth is organic to decay"; he finds there, too (against prevailing views of words as nothing more than the arbitrary, oppressive tools of power, surveillance, and control) proof of a language in which "words of the deepest meaning adhere still to the things of the world."

The second gathering of Corman's commentary, *At Their Word: Essays on the Arts of Language*, Volume II, testifies further to his critical chops. He offers this advice for making judgments of comparative quality when reading poems: ask, "which is freshest, which is most truly inventive (unpredictable and yet true)." But having championed newness (not to say novelty), he then (and quickly) quotes Zukofsky to this alternative effect: "A valuable poetic tradition does not gather mold; it has a continuous life based on work of permanent interest." Discussing Zukofsky's radical renderings of Catullus, Corman provides (and demonstrates) this useful distinction: "Where Virgil sounds for orotundity, Catullus plays and nips." He schools, of all people, Robert Penn Warren in how to read Robert Frost (at the time, Warren's *Understanding Poetry*, a textbook created with his fellow New Critic Cleanth Brooks, was all the rage for teaching literary interpretation).

Similarly, in the years when Marianne Moore was still regarded as a feminine oddity rather than, as now (thanks to the aid of feminist and postmodern criticism), one of the great modernist poets, Corman responded to her work with the rigorous attention she demands and deserves. "[N]o thing is irrelevant to her," he writes. "She finds manifestos in everything. Seasoned moralities, thanks to her unfailing wit." He flatters (and slyly imitates) her "retarded [that is, delayed] not-at-all halfhearted rhymes," saying of her poem "The Jerboa," "I'd like to see someone match the music she has gotten out of a hop skip and a jump." He adds, "she is restrained (not *constrained*), sensing that 'deepest feeling' lies that way." Furthermore, Moore has "in her speech, which is robbed of none of speech's probity, a voice and ear for melody." In her habit of quotation, there is "thrift, not drift." Her language, "if precise, is not parsimonious, no more than Thoreau's." He concludes: "she might be considered as Quaker baroque. In such a frame ... she has refined the ear of rhyme with almost every conceivable kind of byplay; she has extended, along with others like Pound and Williams, the possibilities of the prose line in poetry; she has enriched the life of metaphor with unexampled resourcefulness and perception; she brings an elegant restraint into successful wit." This may not say all there is to say of Moore, but it would take twenty years for mainstream literary criticism to catch up with it.

There are many more examples in *At Their Word* of Corman's critical penetration, as he explores Creeley's poems, Stevens's letters, and work by Hart Crane, Dylan Thomas, Frank Samperi, Eigner, Whalen, Snyder, and Niedecker. Most characteristically, he reviews Olson by doing nothing but quote his subject directly for twenty-nine pages. That's putting the poet and the poetry first.

It's time I do (somewhat) likewise. Corman was a prolific poet himself. And whether it was Zukofsky or Corman who said it, these words affirm his position: "No one can make poetry who doesn't live it every day." Corman did live it every day, writing poem upon poem upon poem, often descrying the extraordinary within the mundane. His all but uncountable books, chapbooks, pamphlets, and broadsides, many of them from presses so small and fleeting as to be fugitive, his bewildering array of old, new, revised, repeated, and translated or imitated poems (their implied character or status only rarely marked as such) will require an indefatigable bibliographer for sorting out. I've already said enough indirectly to imply his thematic and technical values, but a good further characterization is one he provides himself.

As Marianne Moore said, describing others describes one's self. Here, Corman on Niedecker can serve as Corman on Corman: "[s/he] understood [poetry] as preciseness and conciseness brought to the pitch of music." And if Corman's output is mixed (sometimes the ordinary and daily overwhelm him, leading to work that seems merely diaristic, too casual, even sentimental), at its frequent best his poetry affects and impresses because it's so insightfully observed, powerfully felt, and effectively expressed. At this point, it would be ideal to follow his example and exemplify rather than analyze or judge. But to avoid confronting the problems of space and permissions, let this instruction serve as both an argument in his favor and a goad to further exploration: read Corman's *Livingdying* and *Sun Rock Man*, then sample Ce Rosenow and Bob Arnold's *The Next One Thousand Years: The Selected Poems of Cid Corman*. Meanwhile, here's a poem to start with, about, say, setting an example, about influence and succession

> The father
> cuts the wood—
> the child's truck
> stands waiting.

Post Script:
In the early 1970s my teacher and mentor, later colleague and friend, the poet and Stevens scholar Sam Morse, took me to visit his old friend Cid Corman, then resident in Boston. Two old campaigners, they spoke in a code my grad student ears could hardly decipher, but they burnished the air with lofted (not to say lofty) talk of poetry and poets. It helped confirm my vocation. Many years later, two of my students, taken with innovative poetry and poetics, and influenced by Corman, among others, began a Boston journal called *Compost* (its title speaking, as Corman did, of growth and decay; decay and growth). Ten years or so ago, one of them, Kevin Gallagher, founded *spoKe*.

Tribute to Kamaike Susumu, Co-Translator with Cid Corman

Jenny Penberthy

> Cid crossed the Barrier
> with Bashō
>   and Kamaike Susumu
> did he not?[1]
>
> "Niedecker, C.C., Akutagawa, Bashō—four big names."[2]
>
> Niedecker—Cid was our go-between.[3]

I arranged to meet up with Kamaike Susumu in Kyoto in May 2015 knowing that he had been a crucial intermediary in Lorine Niedecker's exposure to Bashō and other Japanese writers who had influenced her last two decades of work. Daniel Bratton, Canadian scholar and friend of Kamaike-sensei—both had at different times been faculty at Doshisha University in Kyoto—put us in touch. Kamaike-sensei, 85 years old, met me at my ryokan and drove me around Kyoto and to Arashiyama pointing out sites central to traditional Japanese culture and aesthetics and other sites relevant to Cid's long life in the city—the location of the home that he and Shizumi had shared; their business, CC's coffee shop; the location of the former Muse café/club where Corman, Kamaike-sensei, and others would meet—Clayton Eshleman remembered it as "in effect, [Corman's] office."[4] We visited the Ryoanji Temple with its spare rock garden, and the following day we took the train to Nara and visited the Todaiji Temple with its immense statue of the Buddha. While we strolled, the sprightly Kamaike-sensei pointed out the steep, wooded hill that he and friends had climbed the week before.

Kamaike was more than eager to talk about Cid and their collaborations. First, he explained to me that he had met Will Petersen as a student when he went to a Zen Temple in Kyoto for an English lesson. Kamaike was among a few students at his university selected

---

1. Lorine Niedecker to Clayton Eshleman, postcard, Dec 31, 1967. Fales Library, New York University.
2. Kamaike Susumu to the author, July 25, 2015. I'm grateful to Kamaike Yoko for her permission to quote from her husband's letters and publications.
3. Kamaike to the author, May 31, 2015.
4. Clayton Eshleman, "Cid," *Cipher Journal*, https://www.cipherjournal.com/html/eshleman_cid.html

to visit the temple where monks gave English lessons for a day or two. Will Petersen was the English teacher at the temple and he and Kamaike became friends.

Cid arrived in Kyoto in 1958 wanting to learn Japanese, and Will introduced him to Kamaike. They had a few lessons, Kamaike recalled, but Cid was not an eager student of the language. Instead, he would question Kamaike in English about Japan, the culture, the literature. They continued to meet and, no doubt, Kamaike's English was helped by the regular contact. After a while Cid began to talk about translation, and he'd bring Japanese texts that Kamaike would discuss with him and provide equivalents for. Then Kamaike would look over Cid's versions and suggest alternatives.

They would meet once a week and Kamaike said he often worked late into the night on the translations. He spoke with no trace of judgement about the fact that Cid, the renowned translator, had never learned to read or write fluent Japanese. Because Cid had mastered the Latin-based structures of several European languages, Kamaike told me, the challenges of the Japanese language proved to be more than he had time for. Kamaike described the unspoken understanding they reached in 1958:

> Cid and I started for a quiet temple (Shodenji), about 1 mile north of Kinkakuji. Probably it was one day when he had spent a few months in Kyoto, probably in May. Afterward, Cid made a poem with a title "THE LESSON" for S.K. (my initial). It appeared in his book *Descent from Daimonji* in 1959. The poem is two pages long, showing how and where our lesson began and came to the end. We were completely dipped in nature.[5]

The experience recalled obliquely in "THE LESSON" saw an end to Japanese lessons and the start of a working relationship where Kamaike would provide both a word-for-word translation of the work in question along with its literary historical background, classical variants, etc., drawing on his own knowledge and scholarship. Cid's composition of an English version would emerge from intense exchange and discussion. Daniel Bratton tells me that Cid, freed from the work of translation, would "devote himself to nuance and what worked poetically: Kamaike told me on several occasions how he and Cid would spend hours discussing etymology, Japanese literary conventions, and cultural significance."[6]

---

5. Kamaike to the author, June 21, 2015.
6. Email from Daniel Bratton, Sept 2024.

On a postcard Kamaike sent to Cid on Nov 19, 1960 during Cid's two-year sojourn in the US, he included his translation—word for word perhaps—of a haiku by Bashō:

> With a visit
> Of
> Pine-winds to the eaves
> Autumn fading

Cid's skilled response was:

> pine winds
> visiting eaves
> autumn passing[7]

In Kamaike's first letter to me he said, "Through our co-translation work I learned many things from what he said and wrote" (April 28, 2015). This gracious statement may certainly have been true but there is no doubt that Cid learned a great deal from Kamaike. Cid's major translations from the Japanese could not have occurred without Kamaike's enabling fluency in both languages, his deep knowledge of Japanese traditions, and his willingness to devote vast amounts of time to their endeavours.

Kamaike and I corresponded about the Japanese erasure of self, an essential, cultural trait that he dated back to the 14th century. He called it the "you first" manner, commenting further that "'to stand out' was underestimated"—his gentle way of saying that a self-promoting stance was disdained or scorned. "In Japan the frequent use of 'I' is regarded as a sign of 'self-assertion,' leading to underestimation."[8] Kamaike's contribution to Cid's widely and justly admired translations has been neglected because of his "you first" manner. As Carol Williams writes, "Kamaike Sensei has not until recently been given the credit he is due."[9]

Kamaike may well have been involved in Cid's first published venture into translation from the Japanese in mid-1959 when his own Origin Press published his two books of haiku—a selection of "Versions of haiku by Bashō" in *Cool Melon* and "adaptations from well-known Japanese poems" in *Cool Gong* with frontispieces by Hidetaka Ohno. The books bear no mention of the help that Cid might have

---

7. Cid Corman papers, Lilly Library, Indiana University, Bloomington, Indiana. For permission to quote, thanks to Bob Arnold, Literary Executor of the Estate of Cid Corman.
8. Kamaike to the author, August 24, 2015.
9. Carol Williams, "Response to Cid Corman in Kyoto," February 13, 2013, *Jacket2* https://jacket2.org/commentary/response-cid-corman-kyoto

received with the initial translation from Japanese. However, he did acknowledge the artwork by Hidetaka Ohno reflecting his engagement with the Yamada Gallery.[10] Kamaike credited the artists of the Yamada Gallery in Kyoto for their schooling of Cid in Japanese aesthetics. He noted that Cid "was very fast to grasp the points. I sometimes visited there as an interpreter."[11]

Corman and Kamaike's collaboration appears to have begun in earnest with Akutagawa's "Notes on Bashō" published several years later in *Origin*, a lengthy piece dense with explanatory notes.[12] Kamaike remembers,

> Some months after Cid began to live in Kyoto, I suggested, "You should read Akutagawa's 'Notes on Bashō' for understanding the greatness of Bashō and Akutagawa." And he began to read. So, we made the appointment 'once a week we meet at Muse'—the long travel [sic] of work then started.... I sensed Cid would be able to translate 'Notes on Bashō.'[13]

Kamaike was shaping Cid's introduction to Japanese literature and Akutagawa's "Notes on Bashō" would have had a formative influence on his developing poetics. After *Sun Rock Man*, Cid's poetry began to change. Kamaike said to me, "Japan transformed [his] writing." Niedecker said to Cid, "it wdn't be out of place for you to go down in Japanese literature!"[14]

Translating "Notes on Bashō" would have been a pedagogical exercise and quite different from the task of working with Kamaike's word-for-word translations of haiku.

> In the process of our work, various language problems gave us painful researches. I had to search their answers in Japanese references, sometimes some of them remained unsolved for many months. For verbs, adjectives and adverbs, their overtones often made trouble because they usually have very subtle differences....
> In most cases "sound effect" has priority. Our "Notes on Bashō" is

---

10. See Daniel Bratton on Cid's collaborations with the artists of the Yamada Gallery, "The Poetics of Cid Corman's Literary Collaborations with Japanese Visual Artists." Poetic Ecologies: Nature as Text and Text as Nature in English-Language Verse Conference, 15 May 2008, Université de Bruxelles, Belgium.
11. Kamaike to the author, May 31, 2015.
12. *Origin* ser. 2, 8 (January 1963): 32–64.
13. Kamaike to the author, May 31, 2015.
14. December 12, 1964 in *"Between Your House and Mine": The Letters of Lorine Niedecker to Cid Corman, 1960 to 1970*, ed. Lisa Pater Faranda (Durham, NC: Duke University Press, 1986), 49.

> given 32 pages in *Origin*. Our translation [took] about one year in total. It may sound too long, but I had my occupation. Before Oku-no-hosomichi we had tried to work on other translations, such as haiku, Man'yōshō, Noh plays, etc.¹⁵

To Jonathan Williams, Niedecker wrote, "Weren't the *Origin* 8 Notes on Bashō lovely?"¹⁶ Niedecker herself was published in *Origin* 8. In a letter accompanying his copy of the issue, Kamaike said, "Niedecker, C.C., Akutagawa, Bashō—four big names."¹⁷

Here are samples of Akutagawa's Notes that would have resonated with both Cid and Niedecker.

> "Haikai are nothing but weeds along life's way and a nuisance," is what Bashō told Izen. And frequently with his disciples he'd poke fun at *haikai*.... However, no one but Bashō could have treated "weeds along life's way" with such care.

> Bashō ... said with unabashed assurance, "The life of haikai resides in the precise use of the colloquial." Nor by "precise use" is he referring to the grammarian's pedantic literality. Rather is he evoking the vitality of common speech when felt and brought in "on the wing" ... Bashō used the colloquial not because of any intrinsic merit in it, but because it yielded to him fresh poetic dimension. Needless to say, Bashō felt free to draw on any language possibility, so long as it intensified and trued the expressiveness of a poem, whether it was a Chinese term or a phrase from polite conversation. Into every word he used he instilled new life....¹⁸

Niedecker was no stranger to minimal forms and colloquial language or indeed to Bashō and haiku. In 1956, she would write to Jonathan Williams, "I'll be working in the direction of the short Japanese-derived poems"¹⁹ and to Zukofsky, referring to her five-line stanza with its rhyming third and fourth lines, "did I create a new form ... influence of haiku I suppose ..."²⁰ Haiku, some of them Bashō's, had begun to transform her poetics beginning in the mid-1950s.²¹

---

15. Kamaike to the author, May 31, 2015. "Notes on Basho" includes very extensive footnotes most likely researched and written by Kamaike.
16. February 3, 1963. The Poetry Collection, University at Buffalo Libraries.
17. Kamaike to author, July 25, 2015.
18. "Notes on Bashō," *Origin*: 35 and 39–40.
19. December 19, 1956. The Poetry Collection, University at Buffalo Libraries.
20. December 1956. In Niedecker and the Correspondence with Zukofsky 1931–1970, ed. Jenny Penberthy (Cambridge, UK: Cambridge University Press, 1993), 230.
21. We know Niedecker read the Kenneth Rexroth anthology, *100 Poems from the Japanese*, when it appeared from New Directions in 1955. She may well have read other

Cid's primary contact in Kyoto was Will Petersen and Will's devoted study of the Noh immediately engaged Cid. As Cid told Zukofsky,[22] he too was inspired by the Noh and he began writing his own Noh-influenced plays. Alongside these, he embarked on the translation of the Noh play, *Yashima* by Zeami. Cid, a man of countless projects, would no doubt have engaged in this translation simultaneously with his work on "Notes on Bashō." Cid, Will, and Kamaike all appear to have been involved in the translation of *Yashima*. Its first published form is in *Origin*[23] with an anonymous "Translators' Note" and an appended note by Cid, "from *Notes Toward Realtheatre*."

According to Kamaike, their translation of *Yashima* strictly follows the breathing of the Japanese original. We learn from his English synopsis of his essay, "A Study on Rhythm and Ambiguity in Translation" (1980), that he discusses "… the method of our translation of *Yashima* … which is quite different from [Pound & Fenollosa and Waley], coming very close to that of the style of some modern American poets, such as Louis Zukofsky, John Taggart and Frank Samperi.[24] Regrettably the essay itself and its discussion remain untranslated from Japanese. The instruction of Cid clearly went the other way too: Cid familiarized Kamaike with the American poets whose work Cid admired and published in *Origin*.

The Noh script received a careful reading from Niedecker. She wrote to Zukofsky whose "'A'-13 iii" occupied the first half of the same issue: "So beautiful, *Origin* 3, I sit in silence. It wouldn't be better for me if I were way off somewhere on a great height—peace.… The Japanese Noh of Zeami, silence—some sounds are silent, becoming something else: Mary Garden said Melba's high C 'was like a ball of light.'"[25]

Kamaike told me about the "Program Notes" that he and Cid subsequently prepared for English audiences of the Noh play *Motomezuka* (The Sought-for-Tomb) at the request of the Kyoto Kanze Kaikan Noh Theatre in 1970. He had documented the process in his article in *Doshisha Studies in English*:

> We made efforts to track down the allusions and reproduce the intricacies of style and rhythm in order to make the Noh more accessible.… For this purpose we employed an unusual style in

haiku collections at this time too.
22. The Corman-Zukofsky correspondence, held at the Harry Ransom Center, Austin, Texas, was particularly steady during Cid's early years in Kyoto.
23. *Origin*, ser. 2, 3 (October 1961): 15–64.
24. Kamaike Susumu, "A Study on Rhythm and Ambiguity in Translation—Synopsis," *Doshisha Studies in English*, 1980: 47. From a copy provided by Kamaike.
25. October 17, 1961. In *Niedecker and the Correspondence with Zukofsky 1931-1970*, 293.

> translation, free from the traditional English syntax—almost word by word and line by line translation—with notes telling, for example, what every step and beat, every drummer's cry means.
>
> In the process of translation I found it possible to sing in English the opening passage of the sashi utai in the same rhythm—with almost the same length of time—as the original. The sashi utai resembles a recitative, taking the form of a dialogue. The utai (singing) has two types, tsuyogin (strong-pitched singing) and yowagin (weak-pitched singing), in which two kinds of rhythm "on the beat" and "off the beat" are used. It is "off the beat" rhythm where I found it possible to sing the passage in English.[26]

The centrality of breath and pace to the Noh would have resonated with Cid's long-standing commitments to oral poetry and the performance of poetry. Breath, silence, space on the page were also priorities of the new American poets. Breath in Noh theatre was the fundamental animating force of the art. "You breathe with all your life," Kamaike told me. Nevertheless, he adamantly resisted Cid's desire for a performance of their English translation of *Yashima*. He was also dismayed by Cid's zeal for the public reading of poetry. "Cid was mad about readings. There was no real audience for them in Kyoto." After Cid returned to Kyoto in the early 1980s he held readings upstairs at CC's. According to Kamaike they attracted very few people.

> I know he continued poetry reading before only one audience [member]. Regardless of the number of audience, he could check the sound effects of his poetry—the length of lines and stanzas, whispering them in his mouth, busily moving his lips. Sometimes stopped, changed some words for others. His concentration on this checking was amazing.[27]

Cid's practice would match Bashō's advice to his followers: "Pronounce the word(s) of your choice on your tongue one thousand times before you use it."[28] Niedecker certainly sounded out her poems as she composed them but only in private and once completed, she wanted them left to the printed page.

"Notes on Bashō" was, of course, a preliminary exercise before tackling the classic, Bashō's *Oku-no-hosomichi*. Kamaike and Cid's co-translation was published first in *Origin* as "Back Roads to Far Towns"

---

26. Kamaike Susumu, "A Study on the Noh Theatre in Translation—Synopsis," *Doshisha Studies in English*, n.d.
27. Kamaike to the author, June 21, 2015.
28. Kamaike to the author, June 21, 2015.

in 1964, then in book form by Mushinsha/Grossman in 1968, and by White Pine in 1986.[29] The *Origin* introduction is dated Jan. 1963–Apr. 1964, but Kamaike told me that the translation itself took five years. Translating from 17th-century Japanese was far from easy for Kamaike and those five years would have included a significant amount of research. Clayton Eshleman regarded this as "the finest translation of haiku (and haibun, which is prose accompanying haiku) that has ever been done in English."[30]

Kamaike and Corman arrived at a method where "a literal rendering of the Japanese syntax is not impossible, but rather very effective to create, to some extent, the rhythm and ambiguity of the original." [31] He told me that Cid was wary of too much discussion of the nuances and historical resonances of an individual haiku. "Cid would say that 'If we get involved in this problem too much, we might lose the poetry this particular haiku has.' When we had this problem, Cid stopped my farther insight, saying 'That's enough.' Cid was afraid 'what remains unsaid' might be lost."[32]

There would have been many successive drafts as they worked towards a final version. Here is the first page from one of those drafts—given to me by Kamaike. The handwritten edits and annotations are Kamaike's:

---

29. It occupied the entire issue of *Origin*, ser. 2, 14 (July 1964).
30. Bashō's *Back Roads to Far Towns*, Cipher Journal, n.d. https://www.cipherjournal.com/html/eshleman_basho.html
31. Kamaike Susumu, "A Study on Rhythm and Ambiguity in Translation—Synopsis," *Doshisha Studies in English*, 1980: 47.
32. Kamaike to the author, 21 June 2015.

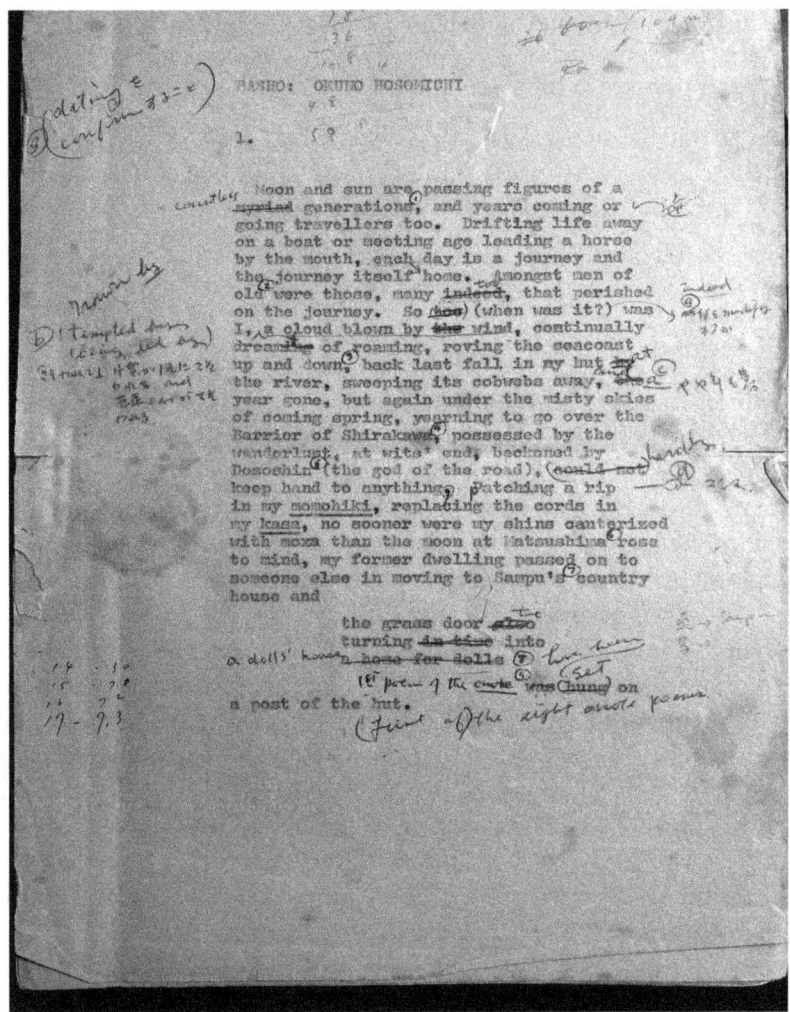

I commented to Kamaike on Cid's repeated use of the present continuous tense.

> ... As you say, I also noticed Cid's preference. His frequent use of –ing form year by year increased, as if indispensable for sound effects. In *Oku-no-hosomichi* he used –ing form 17 times in the opening paragraph. Maybe Bashō's philosophy "Life is travelling" weighed on mind.

Returning to our exchange about the place of the "I" pronoun in Japanese, he said,

Let me give you one more notice: in *Oku-no-hosomichi* translation we used the word "I" only once, which appears in the opening paragraph. We faithfully followed Bashō's style—only once.[33]

This translation had a lasting impact on Lorine Niedecker. "Your Bashō . . . o one of my great things."[34] Several of her poems after 1964 would reference Bashō. Here's the first stanza of one:

In the transcendence
of convalescence
the translation
of Bashō[35]

When Kamaike and Corman's translation was published again in 1968, she wrote to Bob Nero that this was "The ultimate in exquisite condensation."[36] To Cid, she said, "Here —I think this is it—the ultimate in poetry. The hard and clear with the mystery of poetry — and it's done largely by the words omitted. Stark, isolated words which must somehow connect with each other and into the next line and the sense out of the sound."[37]

Her 1966 journey around Lake Superior was made with Bashō's journey in mind. His carefully researched "pilgrimage" is matched in her own scholarly preparations for her trip, and the consequent poem "Lake Superior" was published in a collection of her longer poems titled *North Central* in 1968. I've always been puzzled by the term "North Central" which seems not to be widely used locally or more widely in the Midwest. My hunch is that Niedecker discovered the term on the map at the start of the *Origin* edition that traces Bashō's journey through "North Central/Honshu":

---

33. Kamaike to the author, 24 August 2015.
34. Niedecker to Corman, May 18, 1967, "Between Your House and Mine," 124.
35. *Lorine Niedecker: Collected Works* (Berkeley, CA: University of California Press, 2002), 204.
36. Niedecker to Bob Nero, November 8, 1968. Private Collection. For permission to quote, thanks to Bob Arnold, Literary Executor of the Estate of Lorine Niedecker.
37. Niedecker to Corman, January 10, 1968, "Between Your House and Mine," 145.

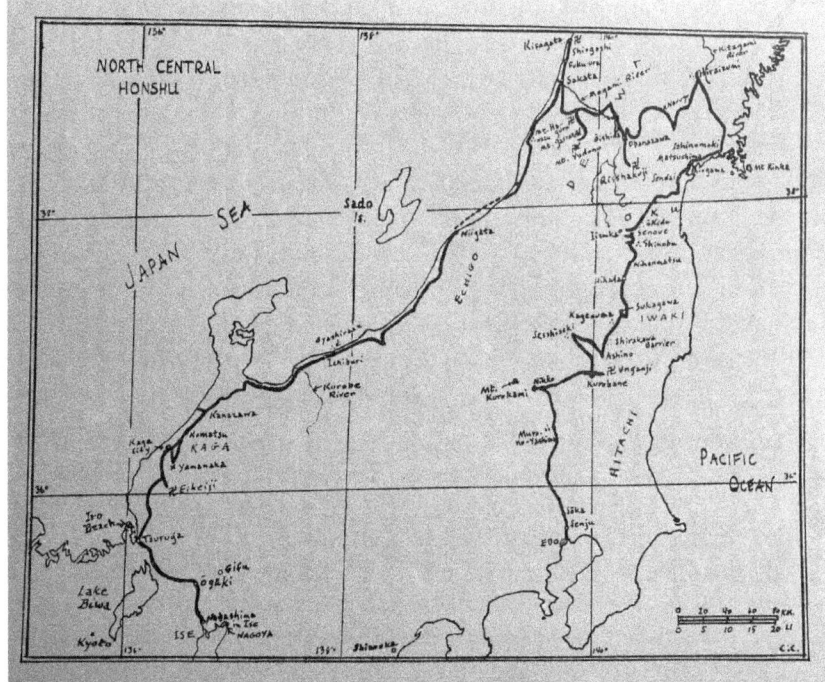

When I told Kamaike about the journey that I did around "Lake Superior," following Niedecker's route,[38] he wrote: "I'm envious of your long wonderful car journey from Wisconsin—back to the starting place: modern Canadian style of Oku-no-hosomichi."[39]

The Kusano Shimpei translations were happening simultaneously with Oku-no-hosomichi. Remarkably, Cid discovered Kusano in Ian Hamilton Finlay's 1961 publication *Glasgow Beasts* dedicated to Kusano.[40] It was Niedecker who had introduced Finlay to Cid and Finlay, eager to be published in *Origin*, had sent Cid recent poems along with a copy of *Glasgow Beasts*. Kusano's frog poems were widely

---

38. With Karl Gartung, Anne Kingsbury, Chuck Stebelton, Cathy Cunningham in 2018.
39. Kamaike to the author, December 23, 2018.
40. Daniel Bratton's essay "The Poetics of Cid Corman's Literary Collaborations with Japanese Visual Artists" alerted me to the Corman-Finlay-Kusano connection. *Glasgow Beasts* is dedicated "tae Shimpei Kusano / whae writ / a haill buik o poems / aboot puddocks / 'The Hundredth Class.'" (*To Shimpei Kusano /who wrote / a whole book of poems / about frogs/ 'The Hundredth Class'*). Finlay learned about Kusano's book of frogs, *The Hundredth Class* (1928) from the introduction and contributor's note in the anthology *The Poetry of Living Japan*, eds. Takamichi Ninomiya and D.J. Enright (London: John Murray, 1957). "The hundredth class" is likely the lowest of low classes, well below the Roman proletarian "fourth class." John Murray was the revered Scottish publisher, possibly Finlay's route to the anthology.

admired in Japan, and together Cid and Kamaike embarked on a translation project that would lead to successive publications.[41] The first substantial selection appeared in *Origin* ser. 2, 8 (January 1963) followed soon after by a small Origin Press publication *selected frogs*.

Before they embarked on the Kusano translations, Kamaike and Cid visited him in Tokyo. Kamaike acted as interpreter. After *Origin* and *Selected Frogs* in 1963, Cid received a postcard from Kusano, which he summarizes and then quotes: "[Kusano] didn't think it could be done, taken over into, brought across, trans-lated. And himself, in a language exotic, many years unspoken, writes: "Dearly big joy. Thank you."[42]

Kusano's surprise is justified. His frog poems pose multiple challenges for translation, some of them identified here by Kamaike:

> It is generally accepted that the use of onomatopoeia and mimesis is one of the unique qualities of the Japanese language. From cries of animals, chirps of birds or insects to mental or emotional movements of humans, they are so rich in variety and so special in the way they are used that it is not easy to find English equivalents. However, the life or death of a poem with a particular onomatopoeia or mimesis is often in the translator's hands who succeeds or fails in finding an English equivalent to it.
>
> Another problem is that the onomatopoeia or mimesis employed in the original sometimes carries an unalterable quality, for example, a dog's bark, "no-o-a-a-ru no-o-a-a-ru ya-wa-a-a" in Hagiwara Sakutaro's poem "Heredity". This is not mere mimicry of barking, but transformation of dogs' nature into particular sounds."
>
> Another difficulty in translating modern Japanese poetry is the Japanese typography—*kanji*, *hiragana* and *katakana*. Modern Japanese poets often enjoy the variation of this typography according to language level, overtone, context, length of a poem and so on. For example, in one of his frog poems Kusano uses only *katakana* to describe the frog's 'baby talk', which is very successful in the original. Thus, the Japanese typography gives very peculiar functions to poetry, but there is, needless to say, no equivalent to it

---

41. "Rainy Season," *P.O.T.H.* 2 (1962); "Four frog poems," *Origin* ser. 2, 8 (January 1963): 21–25; *Selected Frogs* (Kyoto: Origin Press, 1963); Kusano Shimpei Feature, *Origin*, ser. 3, 4 (January 1967): 11–64; *Asking Myself Answering Myself* (New York: New Directions, 1969); *Frogs &. Others*. (New York: Grossman, 1969); Kusano Shimpei Feature, *Origin* ser. 4, 13 (October 1980): 1–26.

42. "Jan. 63," typed note from the Corman papers, Lilly Library, Indiana University, Bloomington, Indiana. For permission to quote, thanks to Bob Arnold, Literary Executor of the Estate of Cid Corman.

in English. In translating Kusano's poems with Cid Corman I have been trying to find access to the effect of this Japanese typography to be produced in our English version.[43]

Here's a representative frog poem, this one from selected frogs:

conversation : under a full moon

> kikikiki kilkilkil kiki
> ki ki ki kiki ki
> kyulkyulkyulkyul
>
> pebbles stranded.
> cliffside eddies'.
> but in this valley.
> full moon an hour too.
>
> kikikiki kilkilkil kiki
> ki ki ki kiki ki
> kyulkyulkyulkyul
>
> shallow riveredpebbles ghost wavering.
> dark sword ascending.
> daytime purple-stippled trout belly.
>
> hi. hi. what's dying.

Kusano's frog poems fascinated Niedecker. She had many of her own frog poems and many theories about Kusano's signature end-stopped lines. "The frog book by Shimpei Kusano—so very nice, so frog-green. The periods (dots) are the frogs singing silently. We have frogs here now and sora rails giggling."[44] When Kusano's poetry was featured in *Origin*, ser. 3, 4 (January 1967), Niedecker once again noticed his periods:

> He uses periods to mark very small sound units; a few words or even a single word may be followed by a period. The periods emphasize the dimensions of meaning created by the silence between words, and in this way they are "singing silently."

The silent singing is a striking observation by Niedecker given the noisy Black Hawk Island frogs in her poems with their "frog-clatter,"

---

43. Kamaike Susumu, "A study on Onomatopoeia, Mimesis and Typography in Poetry Translation"—Synopsis," *Doshisha Studies in English*, 1986: 66. From a copy provided by Kamaike.
44. Niedecker to Corman, May 13, 1963, *"Between Your House and Mine,"* 63.

"frog bickering," "frog rattle," etc. In the same letter she notes, "Those periods—as tho the frog jumps and then sits a moment to allow us to meditate."[45]

In my correspondence with Kamaike, I queried the prominent dots/periods/full stops. He referred to them as "Kusano's symbol mark, far from the traditional Japanese style."[46]

> It is very natural you have been curious about his method of punctuation. It had already appeared in his early poems. When Cid and I began to translate his works, we soon noticed his unusual style and looked for the reason, but in vain.
>
> Kusano had naturally had his own reason, but we did not ask him about this point....
>
> Some one said, "It's a kind of Kusano's poetic overflow," it is not good enough. Kusano's old friend says, Kusano did not like the habitual use of punctuation, but wanted to add a poetic, strong exuberance to each line."[47]
>
> I'm afraid you may have more questions about Kusano, so do we Japanese, as far as we keep our sense of value in our modern civilization.[48]

When we met in person, Kamaike told me that "Cid would ask 'why' a great deal. This is not a question typically asked in Japan."

Judging by Kamaike's letters to Cid in the US and his reflections between 2015 and 2018, there was warmth and affection between them. Most of these letters provided local baseball news and inquiries about the Red Sox along with sumo wrestling info. When Kamaike showed me a typescript for Oku-no-hosomichi, he noted with humour, "Cid was a very unique typist—he used only his right hand forefinger for typewriting. His every key touch was so strong that it often made holes on the carbon paper. However, the old typewriter "ROYAL" had been indispensable for him all his life."

The duo collaborated on the translation of many other texts too—the introduction to one of Kusano's books of calligraphy, one of Akutagawa's stories, "Cogwheels," and hundreds of tanka from the Man'yōshō, the 7th and 8th century Japanese court anthology.

Kamaike put untold hours into our four years of correspondence, not to speak of my visit to Kyoto. Many of my questions had him searching through his files, contacting friends, reading criticism, etc. He

---

45. Niedecker to Corman, March 2, 1967, "Between Your House and Mine," 114.
46. Kamaike to the author, July 19, 2017.
47. Kamaike to the author, September 3, 2017.
48. Kamaike to the author, December 28, 2017.

was as diligent as I can imagine him being with Cid. He exemplified the "You first" manner. Cid was careful to include Kamaike's name on the covers and title pages of their joint translations. Nevertheless, we tend to remember those translations as Cid's—I count myself among the negligent.

Both Cid and Kamaike worked at these translations with the deepest reverence for Japanese culture. They brought a crusading zeal to their projects as they worked to bring Japanese literary works to a wider readership. In the *Origin* feature on Kusano in 1980, Cid began his introduction, "Kusano-san—still scarcely known outside of Japan (despite my years of effort)—is a poet for whom it is hard to find a parallel …"[49] Kamaike's generosity during our meeting in Japan and in our correspondence displayed his intense desire to communicate the nuances and complexities of a rich and often obscure culture. His typical modesty is present in this expression of care and respect: "No translation will ever be perfect, whatever that might be. [These are] our efforts in search of the point of convergence between the two languages."[50]

Bibliography

Akutagawa, "Notes on Bashō." *Origin* ser. 2, 8 (January 1963): 32–64.

Corman, Cid. Corman mss. III 1943-2004. Courtesy Lilly Library, Indiana University, Bloomington, Indiana.

—. "Some Notes on Kusano Shimpei." *Origin*, ser. 4, 13 (October 1980): 1.

Bratton, Daniel. "The Poetics of Cid Corman's Literary Collaborations with Japanese Visual Artists." Poetic Ecologies: Nature as Text and Text as Nature in English-Language Verse Conference, 15 May 2008, Université de Bruxelles, Belgium.

Eshleman, Clayton. "Bashō's *Back Roads to Far Towns*." Cipher Journal, n.d. https://www.cipherjournal.com/html/eshleman_basho.html

—. "Cid," *Cipher Journal*, n.d. https://www.cipherjournal.com/html/eshleman_cid.html

Finlay, Ian Hamilton, *Glasgow Beasts*. Edinburgh: Wild Hawthorn, 1961.

Kamaike Susumu, "A study on Onomatopoeia, Mimesis and Typography in

---

49. *Origin*, ser. 4, 13 (October 1980): 1.
50. Kamaike Susumu, "A Study on Rhythm and Ambiguity in Translation—Synopsis," *Doshisha Studies in English*, 1980. From a copy provided by Kamaike.

Poetry Translation"—Synopsis," *Doshisha Studies in English*, 1986: 66.

—. "A Study on the Noh Theatre in Translation—Synopsis," *Doshisha Studies in English*, n.d.

—. "A Study on Rhythm and Ambiguity in Translation—Synopsis," *Doshisha Studies in English*, 1980: 47.

Kusano Shimpei. *Selected Frogs*. Kyoto: Origin Press, 1963.

Niedecker, Lorine. *"Between Your House and Mine": The Letters of Lorine Niedecker to Cid Corman, 1960 to 1970*. Ed. Lisa Pater Faranda. Durham, NC: Duke University Press, 1986.

—. Letters to Clayton Eshleman. Fales Library, New York University.

—. Letters to Jonathan Williams. The Poetry Collection, University at Buffalo Libraries.

—. *Lorine Niedecker: Collected Works*. Berkeley, CA: University of California Press, 2002.

—. *Niedecker and the Correspondence with Zukofsky 1931–1970*. Ed. Jenny Penberthy. Cambridge, UK: Cambridge University Press, 1993.

Williams, Carol. "Response to Cid Corman in Kyoto." February 13, 2013, *Jacket2*. https://jacket2.org/commentary/response-cid-corman-kyoto

Afterbeat: Cid Corman

George Evans

One thing I miss about the latest gone world (pre-digital, pre-internet, pre-laptop, pre-social media) is personal mail—typed and handwritten letters, postcards, and aerograms daily dropped through the mail slot or into the mailbox of everywhere I've lived. Physical correspondence is all but obsolete now, its objects antique, and generations exist that would have trouble understanding or imagining what I'm talking about, or even care, so it's safe to say that particular form of communication is, as we used to say, dead as a doornail. There are things I miss about the past, though excluding a once unimaginable multitude of friends lost to time and circumstances, mainly death and relocation, there are whole categories of things and people I do not miss, would never wax nostalgic over, and in some cases wouldn't wish upon anyone. But handmade mail I do miss, unabashedly.

I'm a pre-internet being, and though no Luddite, maybe cyber troglodyte would be accurate, one who knows the usefulness of online research (unreliability and all), and the value of online radio music stations, access to music in general, and the internet's universe of newspapers. Nonetheless, I can't avoid the conviction that without a pre-internet life and human-based apprenticeship, the cyber world would be worth far less to someone like me. I'm not an academic, I'm an educated autodidact, and a pre-internet being, like all of the serious writers I've known best or been closest to, which dates me, although some, unlike me, later became cyber-wizards. But I shuddered the first time I received an e-mail from my late friend the poet, editor, and translator Cid Corman (1924–2004) because his physical letters were grounding elements in my often peripatetic, unpredictable life. Still, I intuited he would never go full electronic, and as far as I know he did not. Physical correspondence was too important to him, he treasured its physical presence, just as he did the intangible contact with his many correspondents, his conduits to and from the outer world—it was a form of socializing once as ubiquitous as social media.

I met him only three times (once in Kyoto and twice in San Francisco), but he was a force in my life for decades as an epistolary friend. Our letter exchange began in 1977 in Kyoto right after I met him, and ended with a last aerogram arriving in 2004 not long before his death, shorter than usual, but classic-Corman with a brief spontaneous handwritten poem on the outside.

In my experience, he was open-minded and unblinking in his support and promotion of those he published, as well as his international array of literary friends and acquaintances past and present, young and old, met and unmet, agreeable and disagreeable, even in the face of occasional criticism from those who perhaps felt he failed to publish them adequately, if at all, or were offended that he ignored, dismissed, or breezed by them in formal criticism. He could be devastatingly frank but not willfully cruel, and was quick to apologize or rephrase if he misread or was misread. Although he could appear hardheaded and stubborn at times, he worked with a steady hand and calm demeanor. Editing can generate disagreement—ask anyone who's edited an anthology or literary magazine, usually acts of love or passion—but Corman did it with vigor, commitment, and an open mind. Beginning in his mid-twenties he worked hard at it for little reward for the rest of his life.

His refusal to be retributive or vindictive was a character trait made all the more remarkable in recollection during these dark times, two decades after his death, the world again rife with autocrats, wars raging in Europe and the Middle East, the U.S. ragged from civil and political strife, and Japan—his beloved, adopted country—going through major changes, domestically and in the midst of shifting Asian power struggles.

*

There is no concrete definition of what committed poets spend their lives doing, but they must do it alone, outside the mainstream, under their own spell, and although the effort leads to nothing specific and lands nowhere in particular, it costs a whole life if one takes it seriously, which Cid Corman did without fail and with absolute dedication.

Nonetheless, writing poetry is universal (we're born to it, like singing, dancing, and drawing), plus it makes a perfectly good hobby, one that many take up while falling in love, after heartbreak, after the death of a loved one, after war or failure to experience war, after seeing the wilderness or some intense detail of the natural world for the first time (being eyeballed by a wild animal, getting caught in a desert windstorm, peering into the Grand Canyon), or something as mundane and common as the loss of a pet. Unless left to its own devices to find its own natural measure (like floodwater or wildfire), it can be dressed up in measured meters and syllabics, sonnets, villanelles, ghazals, limericks, presented as odes, elegies, aubades and the like, enhanced by line breaks and wild enjambments, or decorated with rhymes. One thing for certain, I've never met anyone who has not written a poem at one time or another, categorized or not, because it's an innate part of life, and common as air. Just ask around. Even boxers do it.

The terror and beauty of poetry as an art is that its results, its objects, poems, are not fungible, cannot be commodified, traded on any market, viewed as an investment or converted to money, and do not appreciate in value. A poem is born full-fledged. If it's relevant, it is; if it's not, then not. It may be useful for the moment, then useless for a century, or an era, or forgotten altogether (not uncommon), if not completely unread (also not uncommon). It keeps no promises, meets no expectations, cannot be bought and sold, yet cannot be lived without, even by those who claim it has no use. Its ostensible uselessness is a fact or reality that can't be denied, yet in that uselessness lies its power, along with the fact that not all poems are equal—anyone can create them, but the process is not egalitarian and the results are not equal.

It's the most common art and most esoteric art, the most down to earth and most rarefied art, the most flawed and most perfect. It very often satisfies its creator alone (at least it should), and that thrill more often than not is its primary function and value, which is completely acceptable. The results are usually ephemeral, but poems can contain the history of the human universe and natural world, the phenomenal and emotional, the scientific and historical, the mysteries and complications of life itself, and any manner of catalogue or list of surprisingly similar or contrasting things. The history of any given poem reflects the essence of life itself: to be born is to die, with the beginning comes the end, and (not meaning to be sarcastic or facetiously profound) what more can we expect?

*

Corman's definition of poetry was simple: it's a religion. He noted it offhandedly in a letter once, and although we failed to discuss it beyond that, it struck me like a bell clapper or Zen whack (though neither of us were practitioners). In a way it sounds flippant, but he was a very serious man, and didn't have that sort of humor, plus he wrote poetry constantly. If indeed poetry is a religion, as I believe it was for him, I would add it's an all-inclusive one. It lacks a specific creation myth but is nonetheless filled with countless saints and devils, every imaginable heaven and hell, revelations, prophecies, the usual unknown, the known unknown, the neo-unknown, fabulous creatures and monsters, every genre of music and drama, miracles, romance, sex, plus advice and misadvice of every stripe on any possible topic. It's also a vehicle for angst, brutal confession, self-adoration (frequently narcissistic), and addresses race, politics, the family, the mall, the freeway, sex, drugs, rock and roll, hangovers, horse races, painting, jazz, gambling, and, well, you name it and you can find it or include it. It's a universal container for human life experience, the natural world, the universe, and whatever else you can think of. Everything fits, from bluesy folk art to paeans from lofty towers, from the halls of academe to the halls of Montezuma. It is a high art and a low art, but a pure art with many levels, and an extraordinary history that tracks and maps, measures and records all life on earth, possibly beginning its written manifestation on the walls of caves and with petroglyphs, and most definitely with ancient Mayan, Chinese, and Greek poems, ranging from stone carvings and scrolls to refrigerator magnets and song lyrics.

*

Our lives became entwined through *Origin*, the influential, almost mythical literary magazine he created, edited, and published on a shoestring through five series for thirty plus years, from 1951 to 1986, beginning in Dorchester, Boston, and ending in Kyoto, Japan. Poetry was his lifeforce, and *Origin* the primary vehicle for his visionary editing, along with books published under the Origin Press imprint, which included, for example, first poetry collections by Robert Creeley and Gary Snyder, collections of his own work, and books by William Bronk, Ted Enslin, Gael Turnbull, and Louis Zukofsky. For decades, Origin published vital non-mainstream writing that helped define, shape, and influence modern U.S. American poetry irreversibly, and always without institutional support that I'm aware of except for brief involvement by the National Poetry Foundation at the University of Maine, Orono, near the end. A few names from the contents of *Origin*'s first issue, Spring 1951, indicate where he was headed: then unknown poets Charles Olson, William Bronk, and Robert Creeley, Corman translations of Catullus, appearances by William Carlos Williams and Richard Eberhart, work by the Boston poet Katherine Hoskins, and Massachusetts poets Samuel French Morse and Vincent Ferrini. One can detect twenty-six-year-old Corman's youthful enthusiasm in the clumsy humor of the bio notes on the contents page, a detail pared away in future series. He was reportedly planning a print and digital sixth series of *Origin* when he died in 2004, three months shy of his eightieth birthday.

*

One of his main objectives in life was to fish for poems that could make a difference to their times, their cultures, their contexts, and speak for them, sometimes in ways not previously spoken, and to bring them to public life the best way he could—first via radio, then with *Origin*—and as a man of limited means (often no means) he had to be innovative to survive in a world founded on poetry, and he was. A Boston native, Corman, born in Roxbury to Ukrainian parents who later moved the family to Dorchester, was a natural innovator. In 1949, feeling his way around as a young poet and budding editor, he created what I've seen noted as the first modern poetry radio program in the U.S., *This is Poetry*, a weekly fifteen minute broadcast on WMEX Boston, established courtesy of introductions by a high school friend of his from Boston Latin School, Nat Hentoff, the great jazz critic and aficionado, who deejayed a jazz program at the station. Corman embarked on his broadcast efforts reading a wide range of poems (and occasionally fiction by poets) to a receptive audience, but quickly converted the presentation to live, unrehearsed conversations and readings by poets he invited to the program. His guest list reads like a who's who of the poetry world at that moment. The segments could be international in scope, and the readings sometimes bilingual—a native speaker would read the poems in the original language, and he would read English translations, his own among them.

*

He saw no end to financial struggles during his life except for brief intervals, but he had the practical and spiritual support of his loving Japanese wife, Shizumi (nee Konishi) Corman, and at least one stable financial resource, her family's Kyoto café named CC's (his initials), which, from what I observed, she was firmly in charge of. I assumed his daily life was one of respectful treatment in Kyoto because not only are the Japanese unerringly polite and accommodating to foreigners in general, but they hold serious poets and writers in high esteem no matter where they're from. I also assumed his marriage and permanent residence (if not additional citizenship) took the edge off the usual Japanese reluctance to fully accept foreigners (gaijin, literally "outsiders") into their society at large, a cautionary cultural trait dating from ancient times in spite of genuine friendliness towards strangers and unlimited enthusiasm for adapting innovations from the rest of the world.

Although I lived in Kyoto for a year the first time I went to Japan in 1977, I kept very busy with writing projects, Japanese language and history studies, daily martial arts commitments, attending cultural events, and visiting temples and places of cultural-historical significance in the city and nearby, all while making a subsistence living with a patchwork of jobs teaching conversational English. Something new came up every day, the year went fast, and when it came time to leave I did so with great reluctance, a departure I still regret with a poignant sense of nostalgia. Because of my busyness and preoccupations, coupled with the fact that he lived in another part of town and my main mode of transportation was shank's mare, Cid and I met there only once, and that for a few hours drinking coffee at a table in CC's, but we hit it off right away. I liked him, and Shizumi too, strongly sensing they felt the way I did about the city, very positive. As a matter of fact, I don't recall him ever complaining about Japan or the Japanese over the years, though he knew I would have been the wrong recipient for that sort of thing because I was quite happy there, even living hand to mouth that whole year. Because they lived relatively far away from the tiny but ancient and beautiful Japanese house I rented for a song, we started corresponding back and forth across town right after my visit.

The second time I lived in Japan, two years later in 1980 for just over a year, it was as a research fellow invited by the Japanese government to study classical and modern Japanese poetry, assigned to a university in Kyushu, far south of the glittering ancient capital that often left me wonderstruck by its history, architecture, and unique inhabitants. I always meant to get back there, but never did, and these days I understand it's so swamped with tourists one can barely see the rocks in Ryōan-ji, the famous Zen rock garden I lived near and often visited.

As I recall, Cid and Shizumi were temporarily living in Boston during my second residence, so I wouldn't have been able to see them at any rate.

*

In addition to Shizumi and her family, Cid had concerned friends who looked out for him at times. His life and spirit were reminiscent of the Bohemian tenor of Ezra Pound's poem "The Garret": "Come, let us pity those who are better off than we are. / Come, my friend, and remember / that the rich have butlers and no friends, / And we have friends and no butlers." Corman, however, lacked Pound's sarcasm on the subject, and where one man might spend a windfall on a pair of shoes or a night on the town, he would spend it printing the next issue of his magazine, on something else he was publishing, maybe send it to a needy friend, or to buy a stack or aerograms for his vast correspondence.

I wasn't privy to details of his finances, nor was it my business to be, but we discussed general money realities in our exchanges, just as I did with another long-term correspondent, Cid's good friend the ever-resilient Maine poet Ted Enslin (which in his case included how to harvest clams and cranberries, and choosing the right roots to make walking sticks for sale among other forms of survival, not to mention his general condemnation of credit cards). But most such topics focused on surviving penury, which Cid and Ted were both experts at. As the eldest son of chronically strapped orphans (an ice and coal man/truck driver and a homemaker/part-time theater janitor) with a large family to feed, and as one who left home at a young age to drop out of school and figure out how to survive on his own without any financial support, there wasn't anything anyone could teach me about poverty or hard work, yet it was a subject we each knew something about and could relate to. But because such talk unavoidably begins to sound like poormouth script, I'll leave it at that, noting the subject of survival is hardly foreign to any artist in any medium, especially those born without means, though a life in poetry is particularly and naturally challenging.

*

I've read somewhere that he couldn't speak or read Japanese, and although I didn't spend enough time with him to confirm or contradict that with any confidence, I find it very hard to believe. All Japanese have English skills ranging from functional to fluent (it's part of their compulsory education system), but it's inconceivable that one could live among them, especially as the member of a Japanese household, and not learn the language, even on a rudimentary level. On top of that, his work translating Japanese poetry, and the exquisite results in a number of cases, which I confirmed to be correct (certainly accurate) as my own knowledge of Japanese expanded, back when I still studied it, belies claims that his Japanese was non-existent. Criticism of his work on that level (especially when I've heard it from the source) always struck me as cultural territorialism and sour grapes, if not outright jealousy, which is, I'm sorry to say, rife in the poetry world if only because there's little to gain from a life in poetry but poetry itself. Cid knew that better than anyone, and not once during our years in touch can I recall him expressing even a drop of such irritating rancor towards any poet. Dismay and dismissal, yes; jealousy, no.

*

Cid published my work in *Origin* a number of times, twice as the featured poet, allowing me thirty four pages to work with each time. Both features were substantial events for me, resulting in new writing directions and cross-cultural friendships. The initial feature, in 1980, eventually resulted in a first book, *Nightvision*, published in 1983 in Durham, England by British poet Ric Caddel and his wife Ann, co-publishers of the fabled Pig Press, who would see the book through three editions. Its publication led to a brief reading tour of England (for which the second edition was published) sponsored in part by the British Arts council, including, among other venues, the second floor of a rowdy London pub, a deconsecrated church (floor crypts and wall cenotaphs intact) in Colchester (reputed birthplace of Old King Cole and Humpty Dumpty), and the storied Morden Tower in Newcastle upon Tyne, where the reading took place in an acoustically flawless, minimalist circular top-floor room in a surviving turret of the medieval town wall.

In Colchester, the one British city George Orwell destroyed in 1984 with a nuclear weapon during the novel's reported third World War (circa 1950), only one audience member and two organizers turned up for the reading, but it was raining, so I asked the main organizer to wait a bit before starting. I thought of it as an act of courtesy, but not so him—turned out he was U.S. American with a faux accent, and courtesy be damned, I was obviously being vain, but he then confessed he'd forgotten to advertise the reading (which was his only actual job there), and implied he didn't care for my work at any rate, though he hadn't actually read it.

I wondered where the one audience member had come from, and found out when it was announced the reading was to be cancelled. "The hell, you say," she said, abruptly standing up. She was wearing muddy Wellingtons, a work skirt, heavy outer clothing, and a woolen cap of sorts over wild graying hair, identifying herself as a farmer who'd come from hell and gone to hear George Evans, and by god she was going to hear him. She'd read about the event somewhere in a paper, though one that had nothing to do with the organizer—it was certainly Ric and Ann's doing.

I stepped to the podium, taking in the stained class and empty pews. "Good evening," I said looking at her all alone front row center. "I'll be happy to read to you."

"And who might you be, sir?"

"George Evans," I said.

She laughed, surprised. "Younger than I imagined. What's this all about then?"

"Poetry," I said.

"Poetry?"

"Yes."

"Well, get on with it then."

I left the podium and sat near her, waving the organizer's friendly young assistant over, and she came and sat with us.

"Feel free to read us your own poems," I told them. "I won't mind."

"I'm a farmer not a poet," the woman said, "and farmers don't write poems."

"Some do," I said.

"Name one."

Instead, I read her a poem about a vineyard where I'd worked, and the evening went on that way until the rain stopped and I stopped.

She'd mistaken me for the Welsh writer George Ewart Evans, a good writer of a different stripe who wrote about rural life. He lived only sixty plus miles northeast of Colchester, so her mistake was understandable, but it was the actual 1984, so he would have been in his late seventies, hence her surprise.

In the end I invited her to join us at a pub, but she had to get up at the crack of dawn, thanked us for a good evening and left. While the gringo locked the church, his assistant and I watched the old farmer expertly rock her jeep out of a deep mud ditch and roar off. I had to get up with the chickens too, if only to walk around before catching the train out to see if I could sense what it was Orwell so disliked about Colchester, and by the time we reached the pub I'd lost interest in the company, peeled off and went to bed, The Clash blasting like pied pipers inside the pub.

*

My association with Cid and *Origin* held me in good stead throughout the trip, a trip that resulted in new friends and vital experiences. One of those was a hike with Ric, who shared my interest in Neolithic mysteries and cross-country hiking, to a remote prehistoric fire circle near the Scottish border where we sat contemplating infinity and the beauty of the vast rolling, untrammeled fields of heather disappearing then as in the unknown past into Scotland. A naturalist, Ric knew all the ancient footpaths of northern England, if not of the whole country (an interest he shared with a mutual friend, poet, mountain climber, and fellow trekker, Lee Harwood of Brighton).

Another leg of that journey included a trip north to a small Northumberland town to visit Ric's long-time mentor and friend, the renowned British poet Basil Bunting, whose Poetry Archive Ric co-founded at Durham University where he was a librarian and co-director of the Basil Bunting Poetry Centre. Along the way we paused to explore nearby Hadrian's Wall, where Ric marveled at my gringo half-knowledge of Britain's Roman occupation and expertly endeavored to fill in the blanks, which I was grateful for, decades before discovering possible paternal ancestors in Northumberland among the British, Vikings, and Scottish, possibly among the barbarians who so threatened the Romans with incursions from the northern wilderness beyond Hadrian's Wall—at least I hope so.

Bunting, a wry and lively old man, lived in the aptly named Fox Cottage in Hexham, near or next to a pub, and after a hearty welcome said he'd read *Nightvision* (a copy of which was on his table with a cracked spine), referring to it as "your volume" in his rich Northumbrian accent, stretching the L and seeming to grimace at the thought, but delighted that I was even more amused than he was by the quip, after which he regaled us for a few hours at that long wooden table in his bare, bright cottage slowly going dark as we sat with a bottle of single malt I brought as a gift while the old poet chain-smoked Players cigarettes, of which he had an endless supply neatly packed in a large cupboard he humorously swept open to display, explaining how he'd just laid in his annual supply purchased every year using the entirety of a Queen's Pension (or some such), received annually in cultural recognition of his *poetry* (pronounced with a humorously dramatic, biting accent). By the time we wobbled out of there (me from the scotch and asthmatic Ric from the smoke), we'd enjoyed, among other things, a wide-ranging conversation about poetry and mutual friends, a graphic lecture on the art of his friend French painter Balthus (which neither of us expressed any particular interest in, and which to this day I have no interest in); a couple of playful visits from compatriots trying to pry him loose to come to the pub; and at least one final anecdote about his former domestic life, answering a question about why he lived alone, ending with a beloved wife's parting words: "Basil, I'm leaving you now because you're pickled in alcohol and tobacco and will never die. I'm not waiting around." Intending an anecdote, he was laughing as he said it, but his heart was clearly broken. So were mine and Ric's. We hated leaving him there alone. He died about six months later.

There was also a remarkable mushroom hike in the Peak District with Ric's firm friend, the tremendously talented low-key poet, editor, mycologist, and musician Tony Baker, whose young family welcomed me into their cottage in the tiny village of Winster, Derbyshire without hesitation, making me feel so at home it was as if I'd been there all my life. Tony first read my work in *Origin*, contacted me via Cid, and was first to publish my work in England, in his hand-stapled magazine *Figs*, which his wife Liz helped collate and put together.

I also met and spent time in London with the British-Australian poet and scholar David Miller, a long time friend and correspondent of Cid's whose work I knew from *Origin*, and with whom I was already corresponding. The conversation never stopped while he patiently accompanied me to at least one museum (possibly to see the Elgin Marbles as I recall), and pointed out local details while we walked around parts of the city. In addition to poetry, we shared an interest in the works and lives of Malcom Lowry and W. H. Hudson, and he was a true expert in both. Our time together sped by and there was not enough if it. He might have been with me when I finally located the site of William Blake's house, which was difficult to find and turned out to be pizza parlor on a busy street, with no trace of Blake but a blue commemorative plaque on the storefront.

Taking advantage of an open-ended train pass Ric generously secured via the Arts Council, I traveled venue to venue and everywhere else I could in the short weeks I'd patched together with barebones funding, supplemented in part by an unexpected U.S. National Endowment for the Arts poetry fellowship that allowed me to hang up my toolbelt and walk off a construction job that kept me in coffee, burritos, typewriter ribbons, and with a roof over my head. I was armed with a fistful of contact addresses gathered from new friends there (Ric especially), plus some from Cid and friends in San Francisco, particularly poet Carl Rakosi, a close friend and mentor two or three years younger than Bunting, and a fellow Objectivist well-known in England.

Cid had introduced us during his first visit to San Francisco when he read his work for the San Francisco State Poetry Center, a venue that paid well and had a reputation for presenting cutting-edge work by cutting-edge poets, resident and passing through, prominent and not. After Cid's reading at a theater on campus, he introduced me to a number of poets in the audience, some from *Origin*, some simply friends, including Carl (whose work I'd known for years with no idea he lived in San Francisco), George and Mary Oppen, Robert Duncan, Anselm Hollo, John Levy, and Jack Marshall, all of whom would become friends, adding new dimensions to my life. Carl and George gave me their numbers, urging me to contact and visit them, which I did, and we stayed in touch to the end. Duncan I would meet again at Carl's apartment, where I met a number of traveling and resident poets over the years. I'm still in touch with John, a long time friend of Cid's and Carl's who was visiting from out of town that day, and who still produces solid poetry distinctly his own. I sadly lost track of Jack somewhere along the way, and the others have all passed. It's a poignant memory, but was a typical experience with Cid. When he sensed potential connections, he put poets in touch (as he also did for me with James Laughlin, Donald Allen, Vermont poet Bob Arnold, and Australian poet Clive Faust among others). It was a habit begun in early Boston days that lasted his whole life. His model was Ezra Pound.

During his second visit, stopping in the city to see friends and do a reading at a gallery while on his way to events and a short residence in the east, he asked me to accompany him to the San Francisco Zen Center where he'd set up a visit with an old friend from Kyoto, Philip Whalen, who lived at the Zen Center and whom he hadn't seen for years. The three of us sat on tatami mats in one of the main halls, and after introductions I quietly listened to them reminisce about people and places, fully aware, as they were, that they would probably not meet again, and they did not. The next time I saw Philip was when I took Carl to visit him under similar circumstances, though he was clearly dying, a resident at the center's hospice. He was a large man, more so the first time we met, quite diminished the second, but each time his demeanor was impressively calm, his sense of humor fully intact, and his affection for both poets, and theirs for him, was obvious. The conversations were different, both were complex and engaging, and I listened quietly each time. With Cid it was serious, of lost friends and past times. With Carl it was more playful, of consolation and stalking mortality. I had one major thing in common with each poet outside of poetry—a city. With Cid and Philip it was Kyoto, with Carl and Philip it was San Francisco, their versions and mine. In each case I sat and listened in two places at once, and now I sit in a third: the world without them.

The Man Who Always Was

Bob Arnold

breath never left off

I'm of two minds about selecting Cid Corman's poems, and no wonder, given the man!

On the one hand we all know his output was tremendous, but I don't necessarily believe that means we have to measure our own scale by his dimension. Cid could be redundant in his explorations, and I find no fault there; it merely meant he was ever cutting away, searching, drawing, sketching. Think of a skilled woodcutter shaping a forest. It brings up for a great deal of wonderful reading.

At the same time, he was a sharp editor, razor-sharp, and would produce his own journal *Origin* at an even 65 pages each issue. The majority of his books were backpack marvels—packed light for the long-distance traveler and the narrow trail. Scaled down. Plus his domain and mind was Kyoto, and his practice amongst the natives was humility, silence, space, less is more. He wasn't always wise with it and would blabbermouth into wholesale marketing of thousands of poems, but he meant to be wise. And quiet. I'd like to think we are not making as much a representative selection here, but a philosophical one practicing the less is more and at the same time presenting the highest quality of Cid's poetry summing up that force of goodness. It's definitely an edgy approach. What's 500 poem-pages of expanse, compared to the experience of reading Cid Corman in one warm flush sitting. As a poet, he would forever advocate how one poem can be enough, providing space around that one poem, so *resonance be allowed*. We, as editors, are simply allowing Cid Corman to practice what he preached.

Cid Corman lived the last forty years of his life, last days, last very seconds in Kyoto, Japan, with his Japanese wife, Shizumi. They resided in a tiny and marginal location that others who visited knew much better than I—having never visited, myself, except by letter, and quite often Cid and I exchanged letters two to three per week for years on end. This was long before email correspondence, which Cid only learned to use sparingly. He was already a massive correspondent and daily writer of poems, and one day more of the world will know this through his vast unpublished and printed works. The books range up to two hundred titles (peanuts for a man who claimed to write a book a day), and the unpublished works are scattered amongst fine libraries and institutions. Get in on the secret: Cid Corman was a major poet, translator and editor of the twentieth century. He was well over six feet tall, generally out of shape physically but immense with energy, strength, and character. His bald head was often capped with a beret which looked quite bohemian on him, and this was correct since Cid spent some of his early years in France and Italy living out of a suitcase, slumming with poets and artists and sometimes souls of poetry who wrote nothing, but *lived the poem*. These were Cid Corman's people.

Cid Corman was raised in Dorchester, Massachusetts, in a now-dangerous neighborhood he would barely recognize. All his life he adored his parents, Abraham and Celia, and his two brothers Harvey and Len; strangely, his sister Sylvia is less spoken of in his poems and autobiographical prose. Nonetheless, they all played a major feature in his development as a poet. They each kept him alive, often financially, and particularly with his two brothers there was a shared existence. His one wife for life, Shizumi Konishi, would inherit the same love Cid gave to his mother and father and siblings and closest friends, and despite the often shabby treatment of Cid by some of his colleague—if Shizumi was by his side, all was well.

Cid could be difficult, or at least singular, like all fascinating critters. Complex and simple. Grainy and smooth sailing. One moment ornery and glacial, the next moment pacific and nectar, it all depended on his axis. He seemed to think in the old Japanese tradition of the apprentice and the master—Cid of course being the master to many of the younger poets that arrived in his mailbox or at his door after the loudest wave of Asian influence came crashing the shores in the 1960s via the works of Gary Snyder, Kenneth Rexroth, Alan Watts and the Vietnam War. There was something gem-like and sparkling to a Cid Corman poem, learned himself from the myriad of poems he translated from enriched world poets. He never stopped finding known (but made *new*) and unknown poets to bring to English.

Things to know about Cid Corman are that he never conceived any children, but he wrote wondrous poems completely fathered onto others' children, so made his. The woodcutter and his son with waiting wagon in this book is one of Cid's quick-sketch beauties taken from one of my letters to him and shared from my family work scene. He was quite capable of receiving love and returning it just the same. He much enjoyed his Boston Red Sox throughout his life, Japanese baseball, and sumo wrestling. He never learned to drive a car. He hitch-hiked, he walked, he waited. Almost every part of our letters had something to do with the Boston Celtics, world cinema (he enjoyed Bresson, much respected Meryl Streep and Shizumi has a thing for Jennifer Jones), and so many differing steppes of books to love. We papered our letters and conversation walls with books; one or two or three always in hand, we may as well have worn books as deep fluffy boots and shoes. One time we stood together in Scribners Bookshop in downtown Manhattan during an impossible dream visit that was true (he from Kyoto, I from Vermont) and just flocked for a hen house flurry hours flapping our wings over tons of books. What luxury. Two guys in from desert islands. He cared nothing about the books he already knew in that part of the conversation—he wished to know more and more about the new and younger poets he hadn't read. He was the opposite of grandpa: everything fascinated Cid, if but for a few seconds. The ingredients may all reappear in a letter from him in a year, so best keep on your toes.

For a man who never wore a tool apron, broke a woods trail, connected down down into a soft stump with an axe or snarled with a chain saw, Cid managed to attract himself to some of the wilder portions of a poetry life. He translated old trail guide Bashō one of the best. He published Gary Snyder's first book of poems, *Riprap*. He was friends for over a half century with the woodland & coastal Theodore Enslin. Louis Zukofsky was his own frontier, and Cid literally preached his poems to audiences traveling across America in 1960, about the same time Jack Kerouac was giving up on the road. Lew Welch, Philip Whalen and Will Petersen were friends; so was Robert Creeley (despite more sensational rumors), who once raised pigeons in backwater New Hampshire. Cid wanted my book *On Stone* about stone building and woods life and made it an Origin title, then he asked for two more books until it was a trilogy. And perhaps the wildest part about Cid—the pioneer of the man, the wagon master and pathfinder—was his work as editor with *Origin* from roughly 1950 to his dying moment 31 December 2003. Same dying day (but different year) as his discovery and friend Lorine Niedecker. And though it is true Cid hung on in a coma for three more months ... he was *elsewhere*. He walked into the hospital a very sick man, and never walked out. The very last place on earth he ever wanted to die, that's why he was *elsewhere*.

When Cid wrote letters to me it was sometimes the only letter of the day in my rural mailbox, and there might be two in the bargain from him. Cid told me it was often the same case for him on his end:

just my letters in the mailbox that day. What's this—two lonely guys? Or two guys fully involved. "About *what?!*" you might ask. I can just see Cid's beaming face coming through loud and clear and answering with the drama of a whisper: "it's about *poetry.*" Like Orson Welles' "Rosebud." It was all about poetry. *Breath never left off.*

When Ce Rosenow kindly asked me to join her in preparing a selection of Cid's poetry I offered two ideas: let's make this collection for the poets who don't yet know they're poets (check yourself out, you may be unaware), and that I might work best traveling along as her passenger. The sidekick who asks, "Did we miss our turnoff?" or, "What a beautiful day for a drive!" And, of course, a passenger may just want another passenger and that's just where you, dear reader, fit in.

Cid was but one man, one neighbor, one friend. The last thing he cared about was recognition—it was either the Nobel Prize / or nuthin'. So truly: read these poems as yours. Share them with someone else to make them theirs. See if you can be nearly as generous.

When History Gets Personal: Cid Corman and The New American Poetry

Burt Kimmelman

I started counting syllables. The summer of 1998, drafting haiku-like impressions of a pond in Cape May, New Jersey, I paired them with black-and-white watercolor paintings Fred Caruso was making. Our families shared an old mansion across a road running along the pond's shore.[1] I mailed my lyrics to Cid Corman who quickly replied, bragging he'd once written an entire book of poems without a single adjective or adverb.

Pound had warned: "Go in fear of abstractions" ("A Retrospect" 51). Reading Cid's response, I thought of this passage in Charles Olson's "Projective Verse" (1950):

> The descriptive functions generally have to be watched, every second, in projective verse, because of their easiness, and thus their drain on the energy which composition by field allows into a poem. Any slackness takes off attention, that crucial thing, from the job in hand, from the push of the line under hand at the moment, under the reader's eye, in his moment. Observation of any kind is, like argument in prose, properly previous to the act of the poem, and, if allowed in, must be so juxtaposed, apposed, set in, that it does not, for an instant, sap the going energy of the content toward its form.
> (Originally published in *Poetry New York*; cf. Poetry Foundation online)

Donald Allen, editing *The New American Poetry: 1945–1960*, assigned Olson pride of place. His poems inaugurate the anthology, his essay first of the book's commentaries. Faculty and students of Black Mountain College were later Modernist/early Postmodernist inventors of art, music, dance and poetry. In his own way, Cid—especially through his long-running magazine, *Origin*—was key to this efflorescence.

He had never been to the college and he withdrew himself from Allen's consideration. Cid's friend William Bronk was the last poet to be eliminated. They were indispensable to the zeitgeist then, yet neither fit sufficiently within the book's ultimate organization into

---
1. My collaboration with the artist Fred Caruso was published (and is still available) as *The Pond at Cape May Point* (Marsh Hawk Press, 2002).

stylistic divisions like "Black Mountain," "New York School," and "San Francisco Renaissance."

Allen sat before his typewriter, Olson's hand resting upon his shoulder. Could Olson have viewed Corman as a rival? The Olson-Williams enmity (John Taggart once explained) was simple: "They were fighting over Creeley." The Cid Corman I met in the sixties was warm, a bit larger than life, and perhaps out of Olson's control. Cid read at my college. This was about when I met Bronk, Olson, Robert Creeley, and many other "New American" poets, like Joel Oppenheimer, Diane Wakoski, Paul Blackburn, Allen Ginsberg, Ray Bremser, and Gregory Corso.

Most of these poets had appeared in *Origin*. There was in Corman—as in Olson—something forthright: a genius and drive not to be circumscribed. In a 2000 interview with Philip Rowland, Corman offers this tally:

> I'm the first person to organize poetry groups.... Before I left Boston, I had three groups going simultaneously—of course no money involved, nor was there any for [my] radio show—the first radio show in the history of modern poetry—and it was only with modern poetry I dealt, usually work which was not yet in book form, out of magazines, the latest work that I found interesting. And I would present—I.A. Richards fashion, without any author's name—unidentified, unknown to the groups. Three groups met every week. ("A Conversation [etc.]," online)

He sensed the coming poetry wars. The revanchist *New Poets of England and America* (edited by Donald Hall, Robert Pack and Louis Simpson) appeared in 1957. No poet in the one anthology was in the other. Corman wasn't in either. He lived and worked in eclectic ways. His spare, syllabic lyrics were highly regarded.

There were his legendary radio broadcasts; and there was Origin Press as well as *Origin*. He followed his own star. Still, why choose to stay out of the limelight? Was he neglected amongst his peers, despite his poems' apparent similarity to Creeley's verses[2]—starkly different, on the surface, from Olson's massive excursions? In *Call Me Ismael* (1947), Olson theorizes his still emerging poetics: "I take SPACE to be the central fact to man born in America, from Folsom cave to now. I spell it large because it comes large here. Large, and without mercy." In its very nature, Olson's proclamation strikes me as anathema to either Creeley's or Corman's poetic impulse. Olson's precision is a marvel—yet he had no abiding interest in the ephemeral lyric.

---

2. Both Corman and Creeley blurbed *The Pond at Cape May Point*.

Alicia Ostriker has characterized Corman as "a poet's poet" whose writing contained "[t]he pure language, in minimal lines like those of Williams or Creeley." (Ian Hamilton thought Corman "less mannered than Creeley, less anxiously naïve.") Hayden Carruth lauded Corman's "brief lines—measured by syllable count," which created deft "interplay of tones and accents" that turned "on a point of acute perception." Michael Heller commented on how "the meanings" in Corman's lyrics adhered to [his] language at [a] depth and complexity" that sustained his "visionary nature" ("Cid Corman 1924–2004," Poetry Foundation online).

Cid could rub people the wrong way. He was, George Evans recalls, "opinionated" to the extent that he "drove some to fury ([while he] made and lost friends regularly, [he] had a steady base of devotees)" ("Bashō's Pheasant," online). Bob Arnold remembers how, simply, "difficult" Cid could be and how "singular"—a person of self-contradictions:

> Complex and simple. Grainy and smooth sailing. One moment ornery and glacial, the next moment pacific and nectar, it all depended on his axis. He seemed to think in the old Japanese tradition of the apprentice and the master—Cid of course being the master to many of the younger poets that arrived in his mailbox or at his door [...].
>
> ("The Man Who Always Was," online)

My initial glimpse of Cid was of someone who was heartfelt. I've kept my sense of this affable, enthused man, who could be laconic in offering his readers the essential expression of a percept.

Here's Cid's "Memento":

I still
have a
wild
flower

between
leaves of
a
day-book

minute
yellow
crushed
in thought

not ro-
mantic
though
rescued

from the
annals
of
those fields

where we
brooded
and
dreamt of

lives we
could not
then
escape

except
into
by
this death
(1964, Poetry Foundation online)

In "Memento" we can find Creeley or Williams easily enough, yet Cid's sense of lyric—like his back-handed, boastful advice—derived from a personal understanding of language and art that rendered his unique spareness. (He was "was ever cutting away," Arnold writes, "searching, drawing, sketching. Think of a skilled woodcutter shaping a forest.")

Does the relative neglect, today, of Corman's presence originate in the extravagant recognition of Black Mountain College, its institutional heft? Olson was the institutionalist *par excellence*; Corman was the loner. This contrast, I find, to be the greatest irony: he was intrinsically gregarious—but this propensity, weirdly, explains his falling out with Bronk in the late seventies, after decades of friendship.

Charles Tomlinson recalls dining with Louis and Celia Zukofsky at their Manhattan apartment in 1966. He needed Louis' participation in an anthology he planned to title *Seven Significant Poets*. The five principal Objectivists were to be featured with James Laughlin (New

Directions' founder) and Bronk. Zukofsky, taking in the plan, fired back, snarkily dismissing Bronk's work as nothing more than "All that Stevensian bothering." (The condescension extended to Stevens, albeit Zuk's final essay, "For Wallace Stevens," glorifies him—a *mea culpa* that goes so far as to present an elaborate juxtaposition of their verses.) By the evening's end, Tomlinson secures Zukofsky's promise to allow his poems to be reprinted (later, however, faced with having to sign a permission-to-publish form, Zukofsky balks [Tomlinson 444]).

Bronk and Tomlinson—who'd begun with him, as had George Oppen, a correspondence after reading him in *Origin*—were friendly then. Corman's *The Gist of Origin* (1975) describes Bronk's work as the "thread that binds all the issues together" (xxxvi). Both Corman and Bronk were integral to the larger experimental climate of the time. They affected other poets who'd be published with them in Creeley's *Black Mountain Review* (Stevens also turned up there).

Olson had spoken harshly about Bronk. He chastises Corman: "I am sick of this sort of thing you show me from Bronk—the green of it, the green-sick, too—the bad-headedness, as well as the manners" (31 July 1951). But Olson's blurb praises Bronk's *The World, the Worldless* (1964)—"I may have, for the first time in my life, imagined a further succinct life"; Olson is insightful, also full-throated. The book gained Bronk a wider readership, eventually major awards. (Oppen had edited the manuscript his half sister, June Oppen Degnan, acquired for New Directions.)

*

Bill's and Cid's friendship unraveled once his adulatory book, *William Bronk, an Essay*, was released in 1976.[3] It contained long passages from many of Bill's letters, whose faith in their relationship was shaken. Bill was offended by what he called their seemingly mutual "exhibitionism" (letter to author, 17 April 1993).[4] The relationship between them never

---

3. The prior year, Corman's book, *Once And For All; Poems for William Bronk*, was brought out by Elizabeth Press.
4. Nearly twenty years later, the memory has remained fresh; here's the start of a letter from Bronk to me (dated 17 April 1993):

Dear Burt,

Years ago Corman wrote a little book about me and that was the end of our friendship. It wasn't that the book was hostile. He said indeed that it was all an act of love. But it was almost all quotes from my letters to him and gave the impression to me and I thought it would seem the same to any reader that we had written it together and was on my part a kind of exhibitionism.

quite came to a stop. (Was the nature of their schism more emotional than anything else?)⁵

They continued on as fellow poets, or as editor and poet, except with less enthusiasm—the fun replaced with wizened acceptance. (Bill repeatedly brought up Cid's betrayal to me—he'd circle back to it in my visits.) Was Cid's generosity, ebullience, artistic and critical brilliance what drove the wedge between them?

Looking through their extensive correspondence, I can track their course. The warmth and security of their alliance was enough enticement for Cid to take liberties. A letter from Bill starts out congenially enough ("Frost now for several mornings and many leaves down but not nearly the bulk of them") before turning to the breach:

> I have been thinking a good deal about the Truck [press] which distressed me when I first looked at it. You know how I have always felt about the privacy of intimate letters and the publication of those in the book seemed a ruthless coarseness on your part if I had not authorized it or an equally coarse exhibitionism on my part if I had authorized.
>
> The aim of any decent writer should be to be bare in the world except as some have used that bareness as a costume, — there is that danger also. If we aim to be a plain man how plain can we afford to be? Doesn't it entail a natural modesty which is lost if we are seen to be plain? Let anybody think what he wants to think. [...] I think your motives were not inimical.
>
> (14 October 1976)

---

5. A slightly different interpretation of the relationship between Bronk and Corman, as well as Olson's complicated feelings toward Bronk, can be found in David Clippinger's introduction to an edition of the Corman-Bronk correspondence (archived at the University of New Hampshire):

> [T]he early letters between Bronk and Corman mask a layer of tension that seethes beneath the surface and would come to a head in the first letter of this selection, Bronk's letter dated the 1st of June 1961. The tension was fueled by Charles Olson's professed disdain of Bronk's work and, by proxy, Corman's commitment to publishing Olson and Bronk in *Origin*.

("A Faithful Account of Where I Live: The Letters of Cid Corman and William Bronk—an introduction, by David Clippinger," *Titanic Operas: Poetry and New Materialities*, Emily Dickinson Archives, 2001)

Clippinger's edition of their letters for the years 1951–1973 doesn't include a very small number of these letters. (N.B. My use of this correspondence doesn't rely on Clippinger's, nevertheless superb, editorial work, while his opinions about the poets herein under discussion, and within the socio-artistic context of the New American Poetry in these years, need to be heeded, such as the following passage of Clippinger's].)

He goes on in what might be described as a stiff congeniality, returning to their routinely casual banter. Another letter, that December, advises against Cid's idea to revise *Origin*:

> Things can't be repeated twenty years later anyway. To have something again at all equivalent to ORIGIN something quite different would have to be done by some quite different person.
>
> It is a bitterly cold winter but the skies and clouds, the white ground are often lovely. [...] I am writing almost nothing.
>
> Love,
>
> B.

Cid's reply is fulsome and self-searching:

> Utano
>
> 20th October 1976
>
> Dear Bill,
>
> of course—your word saddens me—since it means so much to me. And there is no way I can deny being responsible—assuming I wanted to. At the same time—you would be profoundly mistaken if you imagined anything but love as my motive.
>
> It is clear—for better or worse (or both?)—that we read things in different ways. Perhaps I ought to have sensed your being unhappy with my openness (though I put care into drawing only what seemed to be essential matter and NOT exhibitionistic in either intent or possibility (that is—that wouldn't be construed so)—but there is a point—as in my publishing the Celan poems in ORIGIN—where the issue strikes me as being larger than personality—though not without personality.
>
> The letters as quoted may be "too intimate" in feeling and seem to reflect –as you put it—"a ruthless coarseness" on my part—but I doubt strongly whether readers will take it so. And it can only be obvious—I feel—that my exposing you so simply does make you feel such a response and my apology can only be an apology for that.
>
> I can say that the printers themselves were profoundly moved by the book—as they worked on it. And I think people will be moved—and not out of any coarse motives, etc.
>
> [....]
>
> The letters—as quoted—are honest to the core—that is their beauty and power—and they dont make more—or less—of you than is found in the poetry itself. But I feel there is mutual illumination involved. I admit I may well be mistaken—but it is

a mistake of heart's intelligence then and I know you will forgive me that beyond your ache. Just as I ask your forgiveness for having caused it—under whatever rationale.

The ^(new) poems are themselves more naked—more <u>intimate</u>. Impossible to look to them for cover.

Which only brings us back to where we are—insofar as we are.

[The balance of this letter is handwritten:] I am grateful to you for being so clear in your response—

Love always,

Cid Corman

[The superscript, above, is handwritten and inserted between "The" and "poems."]

Cid's next letter (4 April 1977) unwittingly discloses something about their vexed arrangement and, too, how they both have been relegated to the opera's chorus:

dear Bill,

we're complementaries: quitting is not like me. But I'm also not inclined to be foolhardy. I take calculated risks—when it seems worth it.

Cid was larger than life within anyone's history of American avant-garde poetry (as true of Olson), a history that has been, in its way, chronicled in the long-running *Origin*. I wonder, in hindsight, if his friendship with Bill—begun as reserved, polite, also brazen—made enough room for the big huggy-bear he really was:

Cid Corman   :   51 Jones Avenue   :   Dorchester 24   :   Mass

Friday evening
December 22nd, 1950

Dear Mr Bronk.

Pardon the formality from me. I just figure it would be too abruptly presumptuous for me to launch into the "Bill" or whatever at once, but I hope we get there soon. This leaves me uncomfortable.

[…] I prefer printing those I like in healthy sections: from 20-40pp at a crack. One poem doesnt give adequate feel of your range or potential. For me or the reader.

Theres no press on any of this. Provided you are going at writing with devoted seriousness. I am, however, receptive. And the more, the more.

[....] I'm so beat with writing and rewriting outlines of policy and position that anything I say now will seem like the too-grooved favorite record.

Suffice it to say the mag is to be well printed, run to between 75–100pp and be like nothing else this country (or any country) has seen—and yet it wont be eccentric or cute. In fact, I hope it will be central and acute.

Let me hear from you when you can.
The best of the coming and the present.

[Hand-signed as follows]

Yours——

Sincerely——

Cid Corman

Corman's 1976 monograph is a puzzle. His incisive but over-the-top indiscretions created an estrangement that never fully dissolved. The arc of their relationship, in their letters, traces Bronk's increasing trust (always Corman wooing Bronk, then his compliance; always Corman offering precise critical insights, then Bronk's "I am a little disappointed that I did not move you more" [1 June 1961].)

However much formality he required—eleven months later, his letter begins with a cool "Dear Corman"—Bronk slowly cleaved to an intimacy, though. He genially praises "Creeley's story" in *Origin*'s recent issue, swiping at Richard Wilbur (he "respected Wilbur's poem though [he] wouldn't have written it"). Corman and Bronk were always involving one another, as poets do, in mutual canon-building and -rebuilding.

Each exerted a powerful force on my writing, and I had my own bird's-eye view of how The New American Poetry was reshaping the pursuits of several generations of poets. Now, still bound to the question of American Modernism's bequeathal, I see each poet intuiting something to do with their shared artistic moment of which no one, then, could have been fully aware—now it helps to explain a deeper generational impulse emerging out of, basically, collaborations amongst poets.

25 September 73

Dear Cid,

Yes, it is almost all silence and almost no metaphor now.[6]

Tonight at Sherman's farm at hardly seven o'clock the west all aglow on the blue. White geese on the pond and groups of ducks flying over. Frost only in spots so far and the wild asters in all their various glory. Asteroids. Still a few of the earlier flowers lingering: black-eyed susans, Queen Anne's lace, chicory, clover, some of the golden-rods.

Is the <u>Partial Glossary</u> ready? I had a letter, finally, from Martin Booth. He says he would like to do a booklet or a broadsheet.[7] I said OK so do what you want to do.

The Conclusion

I thought
we stood at the door
of another world
and it might open
and we go in.

Well, there is that door
and such a world.

      emptiness, phantasmagoria

         B.

---

6. Bronk's *Silence and Metaphor* was published in 1975 (Elizabeth Press, New Rochelle, NY). His essay "Costume as Metaphor" appeared the prior year (Elizabeth Press, New Rochelle, NY). Corman assisted Bronk in preparing typescripts and the like.

7. *A Partial Glossary: Two Essays* was also brought out by Weill's Elizabeth Press, in 1974. Martin Booth was getting published by Jim Weill of Elizabeth Press in this period.

BIBLIOGRAPHY

Bronk, William. Letter to Burt Kimmelman (17 April 1993), not as yet archived.

Corman, Cid. *The Gist of Origin*. New York: Viking, 1975.

———. *Once And For All; Poems for William Bronk*. New Rochelle, New York: Elizabeth Press, 1975.

———, and William Bronk. The Cid Corman–William Bronk correspondence, as represented in this essay, unless otherwise indicated, is housed in, respectively, the William Bronk Papers and the Cid Corman Papers, respectively, at the University of New Hampshire.

Clippinger, David. "A Faithful Account of Where I Live: The Letters of Cid Corman and William Bronk—an introduction, by David Clippinger." *Titanic Operas: Poetry and New Materialities*, Emily Dickinson Archives, 2001.

Evans, George. Ed. *Charles Olson and Cid Corman: Complete Correspondence*. Vol. 1. Orono, ME: National Poetry Foundation, 1987.

Pound, Ezra. ["A Few Don'ts" *Poetry* 1913. "A Retrospect." *Pavannes and Divisions*, 1918. *Literary Essays of Ezra Pound*. New York: New Directions, 1954.] Repr. *Literary Essays*. Ed. T. S. Eliot. [1954.] New York: New Directions, 1968. P. 5.

Rowland, Philip: "A Conversation with Cid Corman." *Flashpoint* Winter 2001, Web Issue 4 (online).

Tomlinson, Charles. "Objectivists: Zukofsky and Oppen, a memoir," *Paideuma: Modern and Contemporary Poetry and Poetics* 7 (Winter 1978), pp. 429–445.

"And Here Is the Silence, More Intensely Coming": On the Uncollected Kyoto Notebooks of Cid Corman

Gregory Dunne

In 1957, Louis Zukofsky (1904–1978) was told by Jonathan Williams and Gael Turnbull that, while visiting Italy, he should look up the young poet Cid Corman. At the time, Louis Zukofsky was fifty-three years old; Corman (1924–2004) was thirty-three. Why, one might ask, would an elder poet of signal achievement, be encouraged to meet with a relatively young man, whose main distinguishing feature was his founding and editing of *Origin*, a small literary magazine? One suspects that it was related to the issue of publication as Zukofsky, despite his strengths as a poet, was finding it difficult to locate reliable publishers. Williams and Turnbull were correspondents of Corman's and knew of Corman's interest is publishing, his dependability as an editor, and his poetics. They likely felt that there might exist between the two men a productive relationship that would prove fruitful in the publication of Zukofsky's poetry. As it turned out, their judgement was correct. The meeting between Corman and Zukofsky in Florence proved to be a most fruitful one. Mark Scroggins, in his masterful biography of Louis Zukofsky, *The Poem of a Life*, relates the story of the poets meeting in the following manner:

> Both Jonathan Williams and Gael Turnbull had told Zukofsky that he ought to look up this young man, and Turnbull wrote Corman to tell him that the Zukofskys were on their way. Corman had been reading *Black Mountain Review*, in which parts of "A"-12 appeared, and he was eager to meet the poet whose lines had such a "delicate strong music." Their day together was cordial; ... Corman would become one of Zukofsky's closest correspondents, and his most loyal publisher. (281)

Corman would go on to publish a beautiful edition of *"A"* 1–12 in Kyoto under his Origin Press imprint in 1959. The two poets corresponded throughout the length of Zukofsky's life, and when Corman published his first book *in good time* in 1964, he sent a copy to Zukofsky, who responded in turn with a laudatory word that spoke of Corman's "quiet accomplishment." (Dunne 120–121)

Corman's deep connection with Zukofsky is noteworthy for the role it played in getting Zukofsky's work into the world, but it is also worthy of notice for what it indicates about Corman himself, namely that even as a relatively young man, Corman had the trust and confidence of an elder poet such as Zukofsky. Zukofsky must have found something of substantial merit in the younger man: a trustworthy, dependable, fellow poet—a confidant.

Zukofsky was not the only elder poet who found something in Corman that was worthy of admiration, interest, and trust. Paul Mariani, in *William Carlos Williams: A New World Naked*, the definitive biography of Williams, reports on the correspondence between Corman and Williams, and in particular how it involved their discussions on poetics. Corman first met Williams at Williams' home in the '50s, and. As with Zukofsky, the meeting was cordial. Corman would go on to correspond with Williams throughout the elder poet's life. Corman, ever interested in the theory and practice of poetry, found ready kindship with Williams. Mariani recounts a letter Corman wrote to Williams while Williams was involved with his composing of *Paterson 5*. Mariani provides background before quoting directly from the letter of the thirty-two-year-old Corman:

> Writing from Matera, Italy, in August 1956, Corman centered his interest on the question of mimesis in poetry ... the poet hard at work on his craft, willing to quarrel with the master about the inexactness of such terms as "imitation," "realization," and the unacceptable passivity of the poet as "recorder." A poem should not represent at all, Corman insisted; rather, it should present, make present. To dance, that is, to create a poem, was a specific "I-function:" "It is not nature that dances, but we, each one of us, that 'dances' it into 'being.' A poem is a presentation, or an introduction, if you will, into being. Of being."

Mariani goes on to sum up the saliency of Corman's remarks and how he imagines that they were received by Williams:

> It is clear, that Corman engaged Williams' critical mind in a way that not even Olson or Ginsberg did, and one can see how this letter would have chimed with many of Williams' central concerns with technique in *Paterson 5*—the dance, the presentation of a present world." (Mariani 439)

A short time after these exchanges with Zukofsky and Williams, Corman would, in 1958, finish living in Europe and move to Kyoto, Japan, where he would reside permanently, except for some years back in Boston in the '70s. Settling into Kyoto in 1958, he continued his busy life with poetry. He revived *Origin* magazine and began his editing and publishing work anew. He continued writing poetry, translating poetry, and corresponding with various people from all walks of life. In the midst of his activities, he established a small cake and coffee shop in Kyoto (C.C.s), which remains in operation to this day. Furthermore, throughout this period of his life, he managed to maintain a journal (notebook) and keep daily account of his activities, his reflections upon his life, poetics, and thoughts concerning subjects related to poetry: religion, politics, education, philosophy, culture, and his voluminous, ever ongoing, engagement with correspondences. In short, the notebooks might be understood as the seedbed out of which his poetry springs. At this time, most of his notebooks have been collected and placed in various research libraries in the United States but there are some notebooks from the years 1960 through to 1975 that have not been collected yet. These journals are currently in Korea under the safe guardianship of the poet Fred Jeremy Seligson.

Fred Jeremy Seligson came into possession of the Corman notebooks when Corman gifted them to him, as a token of his appreciation to Seligson for the later's having provided financial support during difficult times. Seligson and I refer to the notebooks as the "Uncollected Kyoto Notebooks" for they were left uncollected at the time of Corman's death twenty years ago in March of 2004. Over the past several years, Seligson and I have worked with the notebooks and organized selections from them.

What makes these notebooks of specific interest and value is that they can be seen to detail and chronicle the manner in which Corman as a young poet, and as one of the "chief architects of the New American Poetry," according to Stephen Fredman, made his way into his own poetry and into his own life as an American poet in Japan. (Dunne 150) By 1960, the thirty-six-year-old Cid Corman had lived in Kyoto for two years. As one reads through the notebooks, one becomes acquainted with a poet of prodigious talent, and a poet fully dedicated to the art of poetry, a poet who had already garnered the attention, respect, and trust of both Zukofsky and Williams. The uncollected notebooks give us a way into Corman's poetic world and help us to appreciate and understand the poetry that Corman was creating and the way in which he was helping to ushering other poetries and poets into the world.

The fifteen years of notebooks present a large amount of material to make one's way through. The impression that I am left with, at this stage, is one of understanding how central the notion of community was to Corman's poetics. He was aware that he was building a community. Over and over again, we see him reaching out, and communicating through correspondence, through his magazine *Origin*, and through the books he published under the Origin Press imprint. The notebooks are replete with references to letters received and to letters sent. He communicates with equal interest to family members, close friends, esteemed poets, and to people who are unknown to him, or barely known to him. He responds to everyone who writes to him, and almost immediately. His outlook is supremely democratic. Here, in a 1963 notebook, for example, he makes notes on his communications with his brother Harvey, Louis Zukofsky, and a person whose relationship with Corman is less well known: Virginia Coroma:

From letter to H: (15 Dec)

One thought is clear throughout. That each man who comes to the age of awareness. Must confront the absolute knowledge of his own impending death. Out of this knowledge, each man I feel must and does somehow alone and through others compose a meaning that will cut the gross impact, not of that event.

And then to Zukofsky:

From letter to LZ (Louis Zukofsky) (26 Dec)

... for accord at the heart. Well here when touched. As if the string that a fiddler plays when suddenly left alone, in vibrating, listens to its own sound more intensely. And here is the silence, more intensely coming. There is much to be known in this world, but there is also not a little not to be known. How much more each of us has yet to learn how to be felt? To be sounded of our music ...

And then to a person perhaps less well known to him:

From letter to VAC (Virginia Coroma) (30 Dec)

—one of the things about making poetry. As in making life. It doesn't, as it may seem it does, or should to others, get easier. But only, if the man becomes, simpler ...

One reads the above entries and sees that Corman is not only in touch with a variety of people but that each correspondent is brought into relation within his developing sense of his poetics. In his correspondence, Corman is never far from his central concern of poetry, and his constant interest in thinking philosophically and theoretically on the topic. We see this above in what he wrote to Zukofsky. In Kyoto, living in relative isolation, he would have had that opportunity to hear the quiet that he speaks of, a quiet that "... when touched. As if the string that a fiddler plays when suddenly left alone, in vibrating, listens to its own sound more intensely. And here is the silence, more intensely coming." Here, Corman seems to indicate in his letter to Zukofsky that the experience of being in Kyoto will be fruitful for him as a poet, for "here is the silence, more intensely coming."

*

I had once asked Corman about what aspect of the Japanese culture he was attracted to and he replied:

> All cultures (Peoples/histories) stories interest me. Kyoto is a good city for a poet to work in. Relatively quiet—the largest village in the world. The Japanese have a deep interest in poetry—even if they don't read it much. It is a natural (now) part of their lives. This may not remain so—but during my lifetime it will.

In reading the notebooks, Corman's wide range of interests becomes manifest. In speaking with Bob Arnold about his editing and publishing the final two volumes of *of*, Volumes 4 and 5, Arnold commented on how Corman's interests were manifest within these final two volumes of this masterwork:

> The poet here is showing us his education, and it's vast: from the cinema, baseball, sumo, literature, television, the street, media, politics, history, philosophy, psychology, other poets left and right of him, music, utterings, animal life, mystical life, no life, Noh. You had best be ready. In these last two volumes there is a porthole to an animated and spirited world, much like the ancient sutras, which this transplanted soul (Corman) of the Far East was well acquainted with. (Fully a Book, *Jacket2*)

It will take some few years for Seligson and I to complete reading and making selections of passages from the notebooks. We hope that, within good time, we will have a body of essential selection from the notebooks that will prove ample enough to comprise a book to be published and made available to readers interested in the life and poetry of Cid Corman, a man whose belief in poetry was without bounds, as he eloquently expressed:

> Poetry is the most important thing that human beings can be aware of. Poetry is life itself, a central thing. It is the most important

element in the world and even beyond the human world because it give us respect for everything else. It is taking every-thing into account and bringing it to point. (Dunne 71–72)

*

Selections from the Uncollected Kyoto Notebooks of Cid Corman, late December 1963 to first days of 1964

The excerpts are from *The Uncollected Kyoto Notebooks of Cid Corman, Selections: 1960 to 1975*. Selections were made by Fred Jeremy Seligson and Gregory Dunne and submitted with the permission of Bob Arnold, Literary Executor for the Estate of Cid Corman. Inquiries concerning Corman can be sent to longhousepoetry@gmail.com and copies of Corman's books are available for purchase at longhousepoetry.com.

From letter to FS (Frank Sampari) (31 Dec)

one must. Learn to dance. With event. With place. With people. With everything living and dead. And everything is living and everything and is dying. How can you feel less than that?

*

They sense children have of a profound correspondence between any two things, words that have the same name title.
    Poets invariably feel words of the same sound enjoy a "sympathy" of meaning. They flow into one another, can usurp each other's power (ambiguity).
    The verbal is so implicit in our natures as to constitute man's deepest "magic"—for it is most invariably and widely employed.

*

The only way, however, to confront death adequately (i.e. completely) is to confront life wholly.

*

The artist wants to and must see from WITHIN AND KNOW THAT. Or have it be known through the words—as experience—given.

*

Letter to VH (3 Jan)

In art, as in life, to offer anything less than ALL at every moment is to offer NOTHING.

*

Letter to MS (8 Jan)

Everybody is great and nobody's anything. It's enough to breathe day and join the rhythm of night.

Works Cited

Corman, Cid. *in good time*. Origin Press, 1964.

Corman, Cid. *of*. Edited by Bob Arnold, vol. 4 & 5, Longhouse, 2015.

Dunne, Gregory. *Quiet Accomplishment*. Ekstasis Editions, 2014.

Arnold, Bob. "Fully a Book" | *Jacket2*. Jacket2.org, 2015, jacket2.org/interviews/fully-book. Accessed 21 Oct. 2024.

Mariani, Paul. *William Carlos Williams: A New World Naked*. Trinity University Press, 7 Mar. 2016.

Scroggins, Mark. *The Poem of a Life*. Shoemaker & Hoard, 1 May 2010.

RON SCHREIBER

Ron Schreiber photo by Bill Zavatsky

Ron Schreiber

January 1978

every day is Sunday, now.
Monday it snowed &
Tuesday everything stopped.
the trains stopped, the buses stopped, the
factories stopped, the hospitals almost
stopped & every day for a whole week
there was no traffic & people walked in the streets.

today is Saturday & the traffic is stopped.
tomorrow will really be Sunday.
the next day will be Monday &
it will snow again, &
just like last week it will snow again
all day Tuesday & everything will stop.
only this time there will be no place to put the snow.

this is the second winter of the apocalypse.
last winter was very cold.
this winter there will be more snow than ever.
Tom's mother said there is all this snow in Boston
because Tom is queer, but last winter
the orange crop froze in Florida.
& it snowed in Albany where Tom's mother called from.
& it will snow again Monday & Tuesday

& break record after record.
some people will say it snows because we are queer.
others will say it snows because the northeast
is a decadent part of the country.
but it is really snowing because
this is the second winter of the apocalypse,

which is coming in ice & cold.
this winter there are mudslides in California.
last winter there was drought.
& next winter the earth will open over the
San Andreas fault like it has opened in Turkey
& Guatemala City. the apocalypse
is not one gigantic tragedy.
it comes a winter at a time.

then a summer at a time & people don't say
—oh the world is ending. they blame the snowfall
on the queers, who are suddenly everywhere,
dancing on the rim of the earth,
making love while the sun still shines.

Ron Schreiber, *Tomorrow Will Really Be Sunday*, Calamus Book, 1984

Ron Schreiber 1934-2004:
Poet, Editor, Gay Activist, Innovator, Rebel

Mark Pawlak

Ron Schreiber arrived in Boston in 1967, a newly minted Columbia PhD, (his dissertation was on William Carlos Williams) to join the faculty at the University of Massachusetts Boston. The campus had opened in renovated Park Square office space in downtown Boston in 1965, only two years before he joined the English Department. Ron was there at or near the beginning of this and many other Boston enterprises, where he had a lasting impact on the city's educational, literary, and cultural communities. It's noteworthy that more than five decades later, many of the things he helped start persist and even flourish to this day, carried on by others.

In Boston, Ron served as unofficial ambassador for the "mimeograph revolution" in small press publishing centered in New York's Lower East Side. As Steven Clay and Rodney Phillips wrote in the introduction to their documentary anthology *A Secret Location on the Lower East Side: Adventures in Writing 1960–1980* (New York: New York Public Library and Granary Books, 1998), this "revolution" resulted from "[d]irect access to mimeograph machines, letterpress, and inexpensive offset [which] made these publishing ventures possible, putting the means of production in the hands of the poet. For the price of a few reams of paper and a handful of stencils, a poet could produce, by mimeograph, a magazine or booklet in a small edition over the course of several days." Begun in the 1960s in New York and San Francisco, this movement flourished and spread throughout the 1970s. An underground culture that gave voice to avant-garde and marginalized poets, it countered mainstream, establishment poetry venues and transformed American poetry in the latter half of the 20th century.

In Ron's New York years, he co-founded not one but two of these magazines that were part of the "revolution": *Things* (1963, 3 issues) and *Hanging Loose* (1966, still going). *HL* started off as mimeographed loose pages stuffed in an envelope with cover art—hence the name. With his move to Boston, the press became part of the poetry community here as well as New York.

In his other independent editorial work, Ron edited, in 1969, the Hill & Wang anthology *31 New American Poets*. The promotional material characterized it as "poems of 31 of the best of America's unrecognized poets. The New York, San Francisco and Black Mountain school, hip, pop, protest, concrete, and lyrical poetry are all represented in this brilliant, diverse, and dynamic collection." It included early poems by the likes of Jack Anderson, poet and NY Times dance critic, minimalist poet Robert Lax, feminist novelist and poet Marge Piercy, plus Keith Wilson, Besmilr Brigham, Jim Harrison, Dave Eggers, and John Haines, among others.

Ron's arrival in Boston coincided with the growing influence of the Vietnam era antiwar movement and the flourishing of the diverse, multifaceted American counterculture. Women's Liberation and Gay Liberation were in their nascent years. Ron embraced all the era's ferment. A gay, white man, he had been active in gay liberation in New York and continued to play an important role in that movement in Boston, joining with other gay men, many, like himself, poets. He was a founding member of The Good Gay Poets and contributed to *Fag Rag*.

Those late 1960s and early 1970s years were characterized by the youthful defiance of boundaries and inherited stereotypes: institutional, political, gender, etc. People with common interests, mostly young, gathered in apartments and living rooms to discuss, argue and, in the parlance of those times, "struggle" against received roles and ideas. In contrast to, and often in reaction against, traditional family structures, communal living arrangements were commonplace, arrangements which Ron documented and celebrated in his early poems.

He also played a seminal role in forming groups that found common cause and advocated for change. For example, with fellow poets Patricia Cumming, Marjorie Fletcher, Lee Rudolph, Betsy Sholl, Cornelia Veenendaal, and Jean Pedrick, he formed a writers' group to critique one another's poems and support each other in publishing their work. In 1973, this group formed the Alice James publishing collective, a literary enterprise whose mission was to provide an outlet primarily for women writers, woefully underrepresented at the time by commercial publishers. Like Hanging Loose, Alice James Press is a thriving, respected poetry publisher today, although no longer a collective. Ron's own first full poetry collection *Moving to A New Place* was one of the early books published by Alice James Press.

In 1971, as a supporter of women's liberation, Ron formed a discussion group with other men modeled on the women's consciousness raising groups prevalent at the time. Originally consisting of staff and professors at UMass Boston, it later expanded beyond the campus. (I was invited to join in 1978.) The aim of the group was to "struggle" with our masculinity, to confront how we behaved as men—not least in relation to women. For most of its existence, Ron was the only gay member of the group. An outspoken gay man never at a loss for words, he was also far from being a separatist. He had as many straight as gay friends. Speaking at Ron's memorial service Peter Weiler, representing the men's group, offered this distinction: "We looked with amusement and dismay at the later emergence of a so-called men's movement associated with Robert Bly, author of *Iron John*, which called for men to get in touch with their inner wild man through drumming and tree hugging. While we did try to get in touch with our inner feelings, Ron preferred that we connect with our gay feelings...." The men's group met weekly during its first two decades, today it meets once a month over dinners—yes, it's still ongoing, despite having lost several of its original members, Ron among them.

On another front, at UMass Boston in Park Square, and then after the 1974 move to its new harbor campus, Ron fought against the status quo. He was a charter member of the Socialist Column, a collection of adjunct and non-tenured faculty who supported progressive campus causes and antiwar activities, and who aided one another in their struggles to seek tenure in the face of a conservative administration. When Ron himself came up for tenure, he announced that he was proudly—and boldly—gay, declaring that "If they want me, they should want me as I am." English Department colleague Linda Dittmar described him as "a rebel with integrity, who was always challenging assumptions ... always pointing out that the emperor wore no clothes."

At UMass Boston, Ron taught creative writing, composition, and literature, but he also created several distinctive courses reflecting his personal interests and inspirations. One was "Visionary and Prophetic Modes in Literature," with readings from such sources as the Bible, Blake, Hesse, and primitive poetry; theoretical works about non-rational perception; Tarot readings and the I-Ching. Another, titled simply "Blake," consisted of close reading and discussion of *Songs of Innocence and Experience*; Blake's later lyrics; the shorter prophecies; and one of the major prophetic books, either *Milton* or *Jerusalem*.

But perhaps most groundbreaking was the survey course he developed and taught beginning in 1973—it was among the first of its kind—on Homosexuality in Western Literature. For a number of years, he invited the peace activist Leslie Cagan to collaborate in teaching the course. Described by the *New York Times* as one of the "grande dames of the country's progressive movement" and a "national figure in the antiwar movement," Cagan, a lesbian, complemented Ron in leading classroom discussions with diverse groups of students: men and women, straight, gay, and lesbian.

Well into the 1990s, UMass, Boston's only public university, remained a working-class commuter school. Our students were working adults, their average age 26, many of the males Vietnam veterans—not your typical college student body. A veteran of the Korean War himself, Ron's uninhibited openness about his own life experiences, beliefs, and sexuality gave students permission to bare their intimate selves and hidden insecurities. I observed this indirectly through my role as a lecturer in mathematics, specializing in remedial math and college algebra, courses most liberal arts majors needed to pass in order to graduate. Ron knew of my reputation for helping math-phobic students overcome their fear and hatred of math, especially women who had been made to feel dumb by their middle school, junior high, or high school math mis-education.

One day, a knock on my office door revealed a woman roughly my own age, mid-thirties, wearing cut-off jeans, a tank-top, and with short-cropped hair. "Ron Schreiber sent me," she announced. "He said you could help me pass my algebra requirement. He told me you were 'OK.'" In the course of our weekly tutorials, lasting more than a year, this woman revealed she had come out to Ron as a lesbian who supported herself through prostitution—confidences shared with me because I had gained her trusted and because Ron, never judgmental, had persuaded her she had nothing to be ashamed of. She was the first of many students he referred to me: English majors, male and female, straight and gay—oh, and she did successfully pass algebra. She did graduate.

All this while, Ron supported, influenced, and inspired other writers, both published and unpublished. He encouraged young writers to adopt a kind of professionalism, separating the creative from the bookkeeping aspects of writing. He acknowledged that early rejection often derailed aspiring poets and so he recommended they steel themselves against this reality. "You have to develop calluses," he advised, offering a method he practiced himself: "before you seal the envelope with your poetry submission to a magazine, have another envelope addressed to the place you next plan to send the poems. When the poems come back, just slip them in the ready envelope, seal, and repost—thereby avoiding dwelling on the rejection." This was at a time before electronic digital submissions, a time when simultaneous submissions were frowned upon.

Another thing he imparted was an insistence that poets hone their craft. He placed great emphasis on the importance of line breaks in poetry, frequently citing Denise Levertov's essay "On the Function of the Line." When workshopping poems, Ron was always empathetic and non-judgmental, but also critically insightful. If he thought you were being dishonest with yourself or others in writing poetry, or in conversation, he would call you out.

When fellow Hanging Loose editor Dick Lourie resettled in Somerville from Ithaca in the 1980s, Ron, Dick, and I met on an irregular basis to share and critique each other's poems. "Forget we're friends," he'd say, always insisted on honesty. Presenting his own poem, he wanted to know, "Does it work?" And if Dick or I pointed out a problem, Ron would demand to know, "Is it salvageable?" And if the poem was deemed too seriously flawed, he would accept our critique, abandon it, and move on.

From its inception, Hanging Loose proudly published a diverse range of poetic voices, beginning at a time when establishment journals were dominated by straight, white, male poets. Reflecting his anti-establishment *bona fides*, Ron advocated for the marginalized and underground writers, for women, gays and lesbians, and poets of color. The content of the magazine has always been presented in non-hierarchical alphabetical order, another reflection of Ron's beliefs. He personally encouraged gay and lesbian poets to submit their work. A partial list of those who did includes: Jack Anderson, Karen Brodine, David Eberly, Michael Lally, Joan Larkin, Michael Lassell, Audre Lorde, Ron Mohring, and John Ratti.

I had just joined the editorial staff of Hanging Loose when we received an unsolicited submission from Tim Robbins, a gay high school student from Cincinnati. I remember Ron's excitement at receiving the poems, finding them evidence that our magazine's reputation as welcoming such work had spread widely by word of mouth. Ron struck up a correspondence with Robbins, offering encouragement, guidance, and critical appraisals of his poems that lasted until Ron's death 25 years later. Tim's first poems appeared in issue #38; his latest in issue #114. He vies for the honor of author with most poems ever published in *Hanging Loose*.

At Ron's memorial in Cambridge 20 years ago, a large gathering of friends, fellow poets, social activists, and former students gave testimony to his brilliance, honesty, generosity, and importance as mentor and cherished friend. Of Ron's generosity, I was frequently the recipient. One tangible example: the weathered farmhouse in Truro he co-owned with Larry Mitchell. During the "off" seasons—fall, winter, spring—he would offer it as a get-away to friends for a small contribution toward the cost of electricity and propane. For several years, in late May, after I'd turned in my grades, I took advantage of his offer, occupying the farmhouse with my typewriter and pile of books during the week prior to Memorial Day, before Cape Cod was swarming with summer vacationers. There I was able to decompress from the academic year before my summer responsibilities commenced at the University. Alone, undisturbed, I always got a lot of reading done and made progress on writing projects that had lain dormant since the previous summer, or I started new ones. When I took my daily walks to the Pamet River and Ballston Beach, Ron's poems describing his treks along that same rutted dirt road through woods leading to footpaths cresting dunes, kept me company.

*

I could easily have doubled the number of contributors to this posthumous festschrift, but narrowed the scope to Ron Schreiber's poetry, teaching, and life in Boston in keeping with *SpoKe* magazine's focus. What follows are contributions by: Dick Lourie (Hanging Loose Press); Betsy Sholl and Cornelia Veenendaal (Alice James Press); David Eberly (The Good Gay Poets and "Fag Rag"); Kevin Bertolero (a critical overview of Ron's poetry); Leslie Cagan (Ron's coteacher of "Gay and Lesbian Literature"): Linda Dittmar (UMass Boston); and a poem about Ron's last days by Mary Bonina, poet, friend and neighbor.

No Ideas

Dick Lourie

When Ron died in 2004, we had been friends for almost forty years. This past January 25th would have been his 90th birthday. I don't want to use the old cliché ("I feel like he's still here"), but of course I just did. Anyway, it's not like a *presence*. It's the way that what you remember seems sometimes to take on form and dimension.

Before I met Ron, I was waiting to meet him. In 1964, I had become friends, in Denise Levertov's 92nd Street Y seminar, with Emmett Jarrett, a poet and Columbia graduate, who had started a magazine with Ron called *Things* (after Williams: "no ideas but ..."). Ron was Emmett's friend; they'd met at Columbia, where Ron was teaching and getting toward his PhD. In those more-or-less-letterpress days, the project had become too expensive; they wanted to kill it after the third issue and start over with something more "modest" (read "cheaper"). Emmett invited me to join up, in what became *Hanging Loose*. So we started planning to get going on it.

Ron, however, was not around at that moment. Gay and out, he was living with his Dutch lover Nico in Amsterdam but, again in those olden days—five years before Stonewall—it didn't strike me as odd that a gay guy would want to work with two (then soon after, with Bob Hershon on board, three) straight guys. Maybe an irony: before the powerful force of gay liberation manifested itself, this quartet didn't seem to us a big deal. OK, Emmett is transplanted from Alexandria, Louisiana; Dick and Bob are two Jews from New Jersey and Brooklyn respectively; and Ron is a gay guy from Ohio. Here we are, committed to poetry so, OK, kids, let's start a magazine. (As Bob famously said to his wife at the time, "It's only a poetry magazine, how much time can it take?") Ron returned (with Nico) to New York, and off we went.

My point here, I realize, is that *Hanging Loose* started as a magazine able to attract gay writers just, so to speak, in the natural course of things. Looking back, for example, I see poet Tim Robbins, who began publishing in our high school section in issue #38 in 1980. And didn't stop. Most recently his work appeared last year in #114 (That brought his total of poems to 100). Ron mentored Tim from the start, with correspondence and encouragement by mail. Of course he was a gay high schooler, but also a wonderfully prolific *Hanging Loose* poet.

Or Joan Larkin, who was, as one source puts it, "active in the small press lesbian feminist publishing explosion of the 1970s ... " and was at the same time an old and personal friend of *Hanging Loose* and its editors. Joan's work has appeared in the magazine starting with issue #48 in 1985. We've also published two of her poetry collections. Her own work appeared again in our #115, for which she was also guest editor.

As I look back now, I see that the bridge Ron created for us with the community of gay and lesbian poets was not some effort to "reach out": it just came from who Ron was. Who he was of course included being a strong, radical, gay activist and militant. And for Ron it wasn't having "a foot in both camps." On the contrary, being Ron, he was all in for each and both. For us, because the four of us seemed to have come together so naturally at the start, what he did was just part of what Hanging Loose became and remains.

*

Before I moved to Boston in 1981, I frequently stayed with Ron when I came for *Hanging Loose* meetings. I remember driving from New York, feeling that when I got to Museum Street in Cambridge, I was home, with Ron and Nico.

And those evenings at the house in Truro, where all of us (and maybe some who were unfamiliar with our customs), would sit on the porch with cocktails served by Nico (Nicolas de Ruijg), in some gorgeous dress, high heels, and pearls.

Abby and I got married in 1981, long after Ron and Nico had broken up and Ron was with the love of his life, John MacDonald. Among our recollections: John, always a gifted floral arranger (he worked for years at Boston's famous Winston Florists), did Abby's bouquet, and Nico arranged her hair. And the reading of our marriage vows, in which we said we were marrying under protest, because our gay friends were forbidden that right. A large part of that particular richness of our lives, we owe to Ron.

In the years after I moved to Boston, our Hanging Loose meetings around the editorial table were sometimes in Ron's North Cambridge apartment, or at our house near Union Square in Somerville. After so many years of being together, we had our rituals. All the manuscripts to be considered were piled in the middle of the table. Ron was in charge (why? lost in the mists of history) of picking one off the pile and handing it to the next person—clockwise around the table—to read aloud. He was himself a terrific reader—yes, if I want to, I can hear his voice. Then we voted, yes/no/maybe, on each poem. Ron also invented the "slight maybe," which he could deploy with skill, if (I think) he wanted to indicate that some, but not too much, discussion would be required.

One feature of Ron's apartment was the cheese on the kitchen shelf. He insisted that the Dutch never keep cheese in the refrigerator (like Chiquita Banana?). We always thought maybe the Dutch would refrigerate the cheese, then take it out to get it to room temperature. But Ron, as always, knew better.

Another feature of a Hanging Loose weekend was usually a Saturday night dinner out. Ron was not a big drinker, but he loved that cocktail with the cherry and the little umbrella. I think it was a mai tai.

Ron had a great laugh on him: loud, raucous. I recall one poet complaining to me about it, the way it might erupt at a poetry reading. I can hear that laugh, too, if I want to think about it.

I think one of Ron's favorite things was his—I think daily—walk to the Porter Square post office, that old worn cloth carry bag on his shoulder. And what we, Bob, Emmet, Mark, and I, got out of those trips were the sheets of yellow 8½ x 11 with Ron's carbon copy, typed notes. Maybe some things had to be itemized, maybe there were various comments, maybe votes on submitted poems. I hope I have a batch of those someplace. There could be a couple of these a week in the mail or, it seemed, a couple of them a day. These were pure Ron: press business updates about new magazine subscribers or books sold, or sometimes other "bulletins," sent with democratic indifference as to degree of actual importance. What mattered, we realized, was Ron being sure he stayed in touch.

After Emmett had retired from Hanging Loose and it was just me, Mark, Bob, and Ron, the three of us debated whether to tell Ron about email, in fear of what deluges might follow. Finally we had to.

Ron was a scholar and teacher and editor before he was a poet. When he did start writing he told me that my poems were in part responsible for showing him a way to write: the personal and the conversational and taking the plunge, the risk of being accused of "that's just prose with line breaks." I was always proud that I helped him get started. And in turn his work kept showing me that both of us had taken the right path.

Another old cliché I don't want to use: I wish we'd had more time together. But I've got what I've got.

Remembering Ron Schreiber

Betsy Sholl

As I remember it fifty years later, the vision for Alice James Books began with the seven people who met weekly to workshop poems. I was the newcomer to the group and one of the two youngest members, so I don't really know how that group first came together. It was 1971 when I joined, a time when sexism was still the norm in the literary world, but also a time when people sensed they could take over the means of production and create alternate systems. Ron, with his political savvy and his experience at *Hanging Loose* was a major voice of encouragement for the whole group, helping us imagine that a press with an emphasis on women was actually possible.

It's hard to remember specifics now, but I know that Ron brought to Alice James his experience at *Hanging Loose*, and the expertise that gave him. He also brought his belief in small presses, in alternate visions. He knew specific things, like how to acquire ISBNs, how long a print run should be, the number of pages needed for perfect binding, and how to work with a distributor. I'm not sure Alice James could have moved from concept to reality without Ron, his knowledge and his willingness to share.

Another thing Ron brought to AJB was a wider literary perspective. His poetry world included New York, not just Boston and Cambridge, his aesthetic was perhaps broader, more open. Being at *Hanging Loose* gave him a wide awareness of the literary world and a range of voices. Ron was generous in many ways, for one he was patient and even affectionate toward my sometimes-clueless youth—partly because of his good nature, and partly because we had similar politics and more alternative lifestyles. He was always kind and had the ability to detach from the disagreements that any group of people can fall into. Ron brought humor and a kind of evenness when crises occurred, remaining unflappable. He was also quick to encourage and congratulate others. When I happily ran into another "Alice" the other day and told her I was writing this, the first thing she said was how kind Ron was, how his belief in her work gave her the courage to go on.

One example of Ron's generosity was his willingness to reread my manuscript right before it went to press. I was such a new and untrained poet, I felt very unsure, and Ron took me under his wing. I went to his house, and we read poem after poem together. We got to one poem I was particularly unsure of. Ron saw that it fit the sequence but wasn't all that strong. He thought a while, then said, "Oh I don't know. Leave it in. After all, it's only a first book." "Only a first book," but it was *my* first book ... Still, that little comment has stayed with me all these years, and I tell the story to students, tell it again to myself before any new manuscript or book. It may have been an offhand comment, or it may have been a deliberate lesson. I'm sure Ron registered the effect. What he gave me was the idea that we commit ourselves to an ongoing writing life, to working beyond any one book. I saw the possibility of carrying that work lightly—one book is neither the beginning nor the end, not the entire goal. And a mistake, a failure? Well, that's not the end either. "It's only a first book"—I've carried those five words, minus the "first," all these years to help keep my head on straight. I'm not sure anybody else could have said that with the same lasting effect. It was Ron's light touch, his sense of a larger world and his affection that have helped me to cherish that little shock of insight. Moments like this made Ron a kind of poet guide for me, and I suspect all of us at Alice James.

Another lesson from Ron isn't particularly connected to poetry, but it is one that I have returned to more than once. My husband, Doug Sholl, was a community organizer working in Mission Hill and Jamaica Plain, and one of the kids asked him to negotiate coming out to his parents. Again, this was the early '70s, so quite a different time. I asked Ron for advice and he told me that we would be surprised to discover that this is something parents get over. Their child is alive, hasn't killed anyone, isn't strung out on drugs. They can still have a child. Ron gave us the confidence to meet the family without fear or defensiveness, and it turned out much as he said it would. That assurance about families and matters of sexual identity has remained a comfort to me as members of my own family have faced these discussions. Whatever pain he had to go through to come to such wisdom, Ron bore the cost of his wisdom lightly.

I left New England for seven years and returned, this time to Portland, just around the time Ron's partner John had died. I read about that in the *Globe* and sent Ron a letter. He not only wrote a heartfelt response but asked me to send poems to *Hanging Loose*. This is another example of his generosity. Despite his own grief, he was making room for someone else, choosing to widen the circle. Ron stood against barriers; he opened doors, encouraged others. If I am talking more about Ron as a man than a poet, his poems did and still do the same work. His writing refuses to hide or be intimidated, it is open to all. I suspect the world is full of poets Ron has mentored, and many more people who have taken heart and found courage and companionship in his writing. The more I think about Ron, the bigger, the brighter he grows. Not gone. In so many ways he is still with us, shining.

Cornelia Venendaal

Letter from the Editor

(Typed on a half-sheet of yellow paper)

Dear Connie,
A day and a half in town. I've just been to
a Hanging Loose meeting in Catskill, then Nico and
I went from there to Ithaca, (Lavender Hill), where
friends have acres and acres of land. Now we're
zooming down to the Cape, where I'll squeeze a last
week + in Truro before coming back to my first classes
next Thursday (whoo and whooff)

But this is a business letter.

As you can see, we are returning "It Won't
Be a Broken Marriage." The other poems—"The
Carpenter and His Child,". "Must It Be? It Must
Be", and "Consider Anything, Only Don't Cry", —
I am happy to say, left my fellow (and now one
female) editors unanimously stunned, and we are
printing those poems in our 30th issue, which is
scheduled for next spring.

Well, well, well,   love,
                     Ron

*

This letter from Ron [Schreiber], his words and voice take me back to a time when we were both members of a writing workshop which met in homes on Beacon Hill. It was my first workshop and it gave me encouragement and new experience—Ron's long lines of free verse and his art of directness and integrity were a resource.

When the seven members of the workshop planned and established a non-profit cooperative press, it was "the year Adrienne Rich wrote *Diving into the Wreck*, and Roe vs. Wade made abortion a constitutional right…. It was the year the Watergate hearings began." (Anne Marie Macari, *Lit from Inside / 40 Years of Poetry* from Alice James Books)

Today I look back and think the long productive life of the press began with the definition of its purpose and way of operating—and with the name Alice James, which Miriam Goodman suggested . And with a group of people who worked well together, individuals and equals. Ron's experience and skills as an editor of *Hanging Loose* were vital in the everyday working of the press. His critical judgment, production skills—he typeset Jean Pedrick's book, *Wolf Moon*—and his expertise with distribution.

Most of all, he was fun to work with. He understood cooperation. His energy, humor and good will could make hours go by quickly. The day the press was incorporated, while we were celebrating, I will never forget, Ron, standing next to me, said, out of the blue, "The Dutch connection." Meaning, I think, the life experience that went into our two books, *The Trans-Siberian Railway* and *Moving to a New Place*. (Ron's lover Nico—Nicholas de Ruijg—was Dutch; my husband emigrated from The Hague.)

A Militant Among Us:
Ron Schreiber and the Good Gay Poets

David M. Eberly

Ron Schreiber is a poet of the collective. "I love many people," he wrote in "the tenth of November:" "Nico, Tom, Peggy, Larry, Russ, Tom, Larry, Bob, Clive, Linda, Michael, Dick, Emmet" ... "I also care a great deal about many other people I have not yet learned to love." Writing this, I was surprised to find how frequently Ron's name appeared among others.

Aaron Shurin has described the beginning of Good Gay Poets in *Deep Gossip*. "Fuck that," he thought, after being excluded from a reading at the radical Red Book Store, "I need to be with some gay poets." So Charley Shively, Ron, and I found ourselves in Aaron's Central Square living room, together with John LaPorta and Charles River. I can't remember who knew whom. Boston was a small town; all of its gay radicals could fit in one room and often did, at Sporter's. Despite its size Boston become a center of gay organizing with New York and San Francisco. Aaron considered Boston's *Fag Rag* and San Francisco's *Gay Sunshine* "the theoretical agents for the emerging gay sensibility." "Calling oneself a gay poet," Ron would later declare, "is a political statement and an affirmation of oneself as an oppressed minority."

In "on moving on," a poem dedicated to Alan Helms, his colleague and roommate with whom I would live with for a decade after he introduced us, Ron described himself as "a bedraggled militant." Among us six, Ron was the oldest and most established: a professor, an editor, a published and anthologized poet. But there was an underlying comradeship—we were all meeting one another no matter what our external circumstances, having come out as gay men and finding our voices as poets. As Amy Hoffman, a founder of the *Gay Community News*, described those of us who shared the common space of its offices on Bromfield Street, "We supported the most radical expression of the gay liberation movement. We believed in upsetting the social order and in creating alternatives to traditional gender roles, definitions of sexuality, and hierarchical structures of all kinds."

"Six of us met every Sunday for a year, the good gay poets we called ourselves," Ron wrote. If we did, it may have been more for mutual support than critique, given our poetic differences. Our influences varied widely: Duncan, Williams, Stevens, the Beats and the

Confessionals. Over the year we planned readings and publications. From our group emerged the Good Gay Poets' first title, Aaron's *Exorcism of the Straight Man Demon.*" The Good Gay Poets would go on to publish Walta Borawski, Stephanie Byrd, Sal Farinella, Maurice Kenney, Adrian Stanford and ruth weiss, among others, and controversially championed John Weiners, *Behind the State Capital: Or Cincinnati Pike*, altering the perception of his later work.

It is our poetry readings that I remember most. Often crowded, sometimes raucous, they were, always by their nature, political. Standing alone or together at the Charles Street Meeting House, college classrooms and auditoriums—Ron and I once read together at UMass Boston—bookstores and bars, we were speaking out loud what others had not heard, the truth of our gay experience. What we thought, what we felt, whom we slept with. Reading together, we became comrades.

Ron played a crucial role of editor championing gay poetry in the wider poetry world. As a founder of *Hanging Loose* and Alice James Press, he was among a select few in the gay world: Winston Leyland (Gay Sunshine Press), Larry Mitchell (Calamus Books), Paul Mariah (Manroot), and Andrew Bifrost (Mouth of the Dragon). More names. Ron encouraged me to submit poems to *Hanging Loose* and a manuscript to Alice James, which led to a life-long friendship with his colleague Cornelia Veenendaal.

Writing about *Fag Rag* in *Insider Histories of the Vietnam Era Underground Press*, Charley Shively described how "an anarchist commitment to having everyone participate in every part of the paper led to many battles between the more 'professional' and the more 'amateur' members. That same division would appear less dramatically in Good Gay Poets. Ron uncharacteristically excoriated one member of the group whom he first crossed paths with at a gay liberation meeting in his poem "speculations:" "when you're here, I have to pay attention to you / know you're waiting for a response, needing someone's approva / ... you turning our conversation into your listening post. / & I don't trust you." (Given its details, I know it is not Aaron, Charley, or me.) Aaron returned to San Francisco and Ron, committed to *Hanging Loose* and Alice James, gradually withdrew from group. Charley Shively became its dominant voice, determining who would bear the GGP imprint. Ron would not be named as one of those whom Charlie proclaimed, "helped extend gay male poetry far beyond the ordinary." But he did.

"A Place for Me":
On the Poetry of Ron Schreiber

Kevin Bertolero

> *I wonder whether*
> *there'll be another*
> *faggot in the dunes &*
> *if we'll like each other*
>   —Ron Schreiber, "re-forming the beach, Long Nook"

Several years ago, I took a workshop with poet Vievee Francis in which she had us try an exercise where we traced out our "poetic lineage." We started with ourselves at the center of the web, and connected to us, branching out, we listed the people who had taught us, either directly in a classroom or through the books they had written. We tried to list out all the people who populate the world of our poems, who have influenced our work in some way—this meant relationships with other writers, artists, friends, loose acquaintances. Branching out even further, we then tried to list the influences of our influences. This took a bit of time, and in some cases a bit of research.

I sat there for a while trying to populate my web. Schuyler and Dlugos were there along with O'Hara and the other New York School poets who had meant a lot to me in high school. I listed out the poets I had studied with in my MFA, and then whoever their teachers were at their respective MFA programs. And then, most important to me, there was a thread dedicated to Ron Schreiber and the world of his poems. I had discovered Schreiber's work entirely by chance, happening upon all six of his books sitting together at a used bookstore in Syracuse, NY while visiting family over Christmas break the winter prior. I remember first picking up *Tomorrow Will Really Be Sunday* (1984) and being struck by the bright pink and blue cover. I flipped through and read a couple poems ... and then a few more. And when I looked down and realized there were more of Schreiber's books on the shelf, I started flipping through those as well. I must have sat there for close to an hour reading his poems.

I remember wondering to myself who these had belonged to? Clearly, they must have come from the same estate, though there were no handwritten names inside the covers. I couldn't be sure, though as a poet I also couldn't help the feeling that these were a gift, that they had been waiting for me to find them. That weekend I placed the books in chronological order and started reading. And reading Schreiber's work in its entirely, book to book, tracing almost the full arc of his career, you get a sense or idea of who he might have been. For me it felt like shaking hands with an older generation of gay poets, his poems populated with friends and lovers, other writers and artists, often taking place in the same towns and cities I myself had grown up in.

I remember that Christmas break, sitting in my childhood bedroom, crying after having finished reading *John*. Though I found I was emotional for other reasons as well. Looking at the small stack of books I had just devoured, it felt as though I had discovered a lost influence, or perhaps even (poetically) a lost friend. Immediately I started researching Ron. Not much came up at first with a basic Google search—I had to dig deeper. I started looking through the databases at my university library and that's when I uncovered a broader network of poets and writers who I hadn't heard about before, whose work I was unfamiliar with. The poets and writers who—connected to Ron—would soon populate my web of influences.

In his introduction to *Orgasms of Light: The Gay Sunshine Anthology* (1977), editor Winston Leyland writes, "I coined and defined a new term, Gay Cultural Renaissance: 'a rediscovery of the Gay Cultural heritage and its expression, especially since Stonewall, through art, music, literature, film, and in many other ways'". What Leyland describes here was a loosely organized movement of gay literary culture that was taking place across the country, comprised of work from a number of gay writers who were publishing in many of the same venues: *Gay Sunshine* in San Francisco, *Mouth of the Dragon* in New York, *Fag Rag* in Boston, and *RFD* (or, Radical Faerie Digest) in Iowa. Near the center of this informal movement—alongside writers and editors like Winston Leyland who ran Gay Sunshine Press, Charley Shively who founded Good Gay Poets Press, and Andrew Bifrost—was Ron Schreiber, the co-founder of Calamus Books (with Larry Mitchell), Hanging Loose Press, and Alice James Books.

Through his own writing, we're able to make out, if not the details, then rather a loose history of this overlooked period in American publishing which followed the civil rights movement, coincided with second wave feminism (and that Bookstore Moment), and was directly tied to the gay liberation movement from Stonewall in 1969 through the height of the AIDS crisis. Schreiber's poetry is unabashedly autobiographical, and he writes in great detail about his personal relationships, which is what drew me to his work in the first place.

In his debut collection of poems, *Living Space* (1972), we see Schreiber's insistence on rooting his work in both time and space—whether geographically or internally—alongside his personal relationships as well as his political consciousness. From "Rockport poem" to "summer song" to "dreaming of the Middle West," we're shown a speaker with a sense-of-self clearly defined through history, memory, recreational drug use, and a genuine care for the people, pets, and living things around him which he interacts with every day. In "no where else," he writes,

> this place
> these
> two bodies
> one when we
> make it that way.
>
> Sufficient
> to each other.

These poems are love poems, together working toward the common goal of depicting a queer domestic life that's all encompassing for the speaker—and in this way too, for the reader.

Moving to a New Place (1974) marks a further development in Schreiber's style as his lines grow longer and we see more travel poems. The poet's world expands now from Brooklyn Heights to Big Sur, yet the domestic spaces remain as lucid as ever. In "the image of you vivid," a poem dedicated to Schreiber's lover, Nico, he writes,

> the years we've been together blur into your shifting image
> that I want to touch   even though I'd be afraid
> if I were with you   frightened of your fear
> trying to hide my own   your body is more vivid to me
> than my own body   just sitting across the room
> or crying in Larry's apartment when your mother died
> or spitting on me in our livingroom   or falling asleep
> with the television on   or flirting   laughing   dancing
> swimming in the Atlantic   wherever you're at   whoever you are

As readers, we're allowed into this personal space, welcomed and invited even. Sexual and emotional desires accompany the commonplace, and the poems feel almost like textual polaroids, snapshots of an interior life that is both shared and fulfilling. Likewise, we can see this openness reflected in both Schreiber's personal correspondence and memoirs from the period. He shows no hesitation in sharing details and personal notes, reflections on intimate relations, as well as arguments and disagreements. This only heightens the autobiographical elements I can surmise from the work itself. As an editor too, Schreiber was unabashed and honest. In a 1979 letter to poet Aaron Shurin, Schreiber writes, "I want us [*Hanging Loose*] very much to do another faggot poet ... but of course also there aren't all that many faggot poets out there that I find stunning." His poems sharply reflect this critical sensibility, but that criticism is also often self-directed when not aimed at others whom he's made enemies of.

With *False Clues* (1977), Schreiber's writing becomes less insular and more social in many ways. Nearly half of the poems in this collection are written *to* or *for* a friend—B., G., J., Steven, Tom, Randy, Mary, Keith, Wayne, Dick, Lee, Kevin—and the number of people who appear in these poems is significant as well. In his poem, "to G—" he writes,

> you come to visit,
> come to visit. we have
> not been a crash pad
> all summer for anyone,
>
> & we don't start with you.
> if you visit, come alone,
> Tom said, or with someone,
> we said, anyone but your
>
> latest lover. you've
> wanted to come each time
> with a new lover. I guess
> you don't have friends.

The poem proceeds to reveal that this is only a bit of sarcasm—"if you visit again, bring / yourself, whatever you / feel about that person / you live with all the time ... & everyone / will miss you when you're gone." We're introduced, however briefly, to this circle of friends, to Peter and Mark and Francie and Polly. We're allowed to see, if not know entirely, the closeness they feel towards one another.

The following year, Schreiber published *Against That Time* (1978) as a split collection with poet Jeffrey Schwartz—his portion of the book titled *Contending with the Dark*. Here, Schreiber's poems feel almost like B-sides to what we see in *False Clues*, with more letter poems and travel poems. In "letter to Dick," the poem starts out with condolences for the passing of Dick's stepmother, but soon devolves into personal news, and gossip. He continues,

> I wanted to tell you about the question Tom & I
> discussed last night   after I wanted to go to bed
> with him the night before & thought he was sleeping
> with Rick who wanted to go to bed with me but
>
> he wasn't & I didn't know it & Tom wanted to sleep
> with Gary whom he's in love with but who doesn't
> love him back the same way: what is the difference
> we asked   between love & obsession?

And this plays out rather humorously—he then critiques a line from a piece that Dick had sent him—until we get to the end of the poem where the tone shifts yet again to a more earnest expression of what it seems Schreiber's ethos was at time: "if we only knew   you & I   what we really wanted / & how to love every day every detail of our lives." This attention paid to the familiar routines of life, and to the relationships between himself and his friends—*this* is love. This is what the poems embody and distill. This is what he remembers.

Where we can really notice another shift in Schreiber's style is with the publication of *Tomorrow Will Really Be Sunday*. These poems become more sexual in nature and the typically more tender qualities of his earlier love poems translates here into language that is more visceral and honest about cruising and gay life in the early 1980s. In this way, they take on an almost documentary nature. In "the gay beach, Boca Raton," he writes,

> —that's where I'd go if I were a faggot,
> I thought. & then I thought,
> I *am* a faggot. & then a sun-
> glassed man in cut-offs came up
> & groped me, an obese man in
> straight long trunks walked by & leered.
>
> —I am a faggot, I thought,
> —and home again. there's always
> a place for me.

We see a true understanding and celebration of gay community—however anonymous—in poems like these. In "gay life," Schreiber depicts in verse a scene he had written about in prose in his memoir, one which had taken place years earlier while he was in grad school at Columbia University. In the poem he is cruising at the docks near Christopher Street when he witnesses a man get assaulted and thrown into the Hudson River. He and the other cruising men in the area help pull the bleeding man from the water and take him home to his partner who begs them not to bring his lover to the hospital.

> We didn't go to the police.
> We took him home to his lover,
> who said, *Don't take him to the hospital.*
> *Think of the disgrace.*
>
> (His eye was bleeding.) We took him
> to the hospital & left him there.

The poem and the memoir both function as documentary accounts of this period in queer history, which only adds to the lineage of other gay writers like John Rechy, Edmund White, and Samuel R. Delany, who have also written about the underground gay culture in New York City throughout this era.

Only five years later, Schreiber's sixth and final collection of poems was published. *John* (1989), arguably his most important work, documents the death of his partner, John MacDonald, who passed away at age 35 from complications due to AIDS. Comprised of poems titled with dates, essentially functioning as journal entries, the book documents their life together from April to November of 1986, as Ron, their friends, and John's nurses all helped care for him in the final months of his life. What these poems seem to represent, in addition to their obvious elegiac nature, is a summation or full embodiment of the kind of personal poems Schreiber had been writing for nearly two decades.

This book truly leans further into the documentary nature of the poems he had been writing, and whereas his earlier poems spoke more or less indirectly or obliquely about domesticity, these poems invite us into the home and, as readers, we remain by John's side as his health deteriorates and as his and Ron's relationship is tested. As a whole, the book is devastating to read, and one struggles to imagine how Schreiber found the courage and stamina to see the project through to its completion. The collection concludes with two obituaries for John—one written by his family and published in *The Boston Globe*, in which Schreiber, John's partner of nine years, is never mentioned. The second obituary, written by Ron and published in *Gay Community*

News, almost depicts the life of a different person entirely. What we're left with at the end of *John* is a document of a queer life—a domestic life, a political life—reflected though the experience of the poet as he grieves in real time.

Looking back on his career, Schreiber has left us with a body of work that speaks not only to his personal experiences—his friendships, his partners, his travels, his politics, his desires—but also as testament to both the public and private communities in which he was so thoroughly invested. We're shown almost an entire life in the brief span of six collections, and each of the poems therein speak with a certain humor and insightfulness that is entirely, uniquely his own. The poems speak more to me now each time I revisit them, and I'm able to see with greater clarity Schreiber's grief and yearning. And, perhaps most importantly, his love.

Bibliography

Living Space (Hanging Loose, 1972)
Moving to a New Place (Alice James Books, 1974)
False Clues (Calamus Books, 1977)
Against That Time (Alice James Books, 1978)
Tomorrow Will Really Be Sunday (Calamus Books, 1984)
John (Hanging Loose/Calamus Books, 1989)

Remembering Ron

Leslie Cagan

In the summer of 1974 I was at a picnic in Cambridge when a friend asked me if I knew anyone who might be interested in co-teaching a course called *Gay and Lesbian Literature* at the Boston campus of UMASS with Ron Schreiber. She had taught the class with Ron once or twice already but her schedule was making it impossible to do it again. I told her no one came to mind immediately but I would think about it.

It didn't take me long to consider the possibility for myself. I had no experience as a teacher, and nothing beyond a bachelor's degree which wasn't in literature. But I was reading a good deal of lesbian fiction those days, as were countless other young dykes, taking in as much as possible of this new world we were entering. I had come out as a lesbian just two years earlier and for some reason believed that if I was interested and committed to doing the work I perhaps could take this on.

My friend gave me Ron's number and we were off and running. A week later we met and he wanted to know about me and my interest in doing this class. He explained that he felt strongly that if the class would be reading lesbian literature that he was committed to having a lesbian co-teach it. Otherwise he would do just do a gay literature course and stick to male writers. I was moved by his commitment to lesbian visibility.

That fall I walked into that classroom for the first time and for the next four or five years we co-taught the "Gay and Lesbian Literature" class, usually in the spring semester. I don't recall now if Ron had asked the University to officially hire me on this very part-time basis or if he knew they would never say yes so he just skipped all of that. Instead, Ron paid me out of his own salary. If he was teaching three classes a semester, or six for the year, he would pay me for half of one class. I didn't get any benefits but I also didn't have to deal with the school administration at all.

I went into the experience thinking this would probably be a great opportunity to read a lot of terrific books. It turned out to be that and so much more. Being in a classroom with Ron was completely different than the classroom experiences I had during the years of my education.

He was brilliant. His ability to make texts written centuries before—whether it was William Shakespeare or Sappho—relevant to the current lives of the students was mind-blowing. The ways he set each piece of work we read—whether it was *Rubyfruit Jungle* by Rita Mae Brown or *A Single Man* by Christopher Isherwood—in the context of their times reflected his massive historical knowledge. He was able to guide the students, and me, through the readings in ways that helped us reach more deeply into the texts without ever making anyone feel less than fully able to do this on their own.

I was brand new at this but Ron never made me feel like I was tagging along. He encouraged me to take the lead many times and always welcomed my insights, as well as my questions and confusions. His excitement and joy in being part of a learning process was contagious.

Ron brought his full self into the room each and every time. Over the years Ron and I became very good friends. The man I knew in the classroom or at the beach on Cape Cod was the same person. By being himself, Ron gave permission for others to also be themselves. I never thought this was a conscious plan on his part, it was just who he was. Whether it was his deep intellectual abilities or is outrageous silliness, it was always authentic Ron. He never shied away from difficult topics nor dismissed questions as frivolous or stupid. He managed to combine meeting people where they were while standing firmly in his own identity and personality.

When I made the suggestion to Ron about co-teaching with him he didn't hesitate. He must have known it was a long shot that this would work out, but he was delighted to give it a try. That in turn made it immeasurably easier for me to jump right in. I had no idea how much I would learn and grow in this experience, and I certainly had no idea how important our friendship would come to be for me.

For many years, and for long after we stopped teaching together, I spent time with Ron at his house in Truro. There was a steady stream of visitors in and out of the house, including a few of my girlfriends. Ron and I pretty often talked about the differences between lesbians and gay men. My lover and I would go into Provincetown for an evening of dancing at a lesbian bar and strolling up and down the main drag watching how, as the night wore on and the straight people left, more queer folks appeared. It was pretty magical. We would get back to the house at 11 or 12, and Ron would be getting ready to leave for the later edition of gay P-Town. In the morning we would compare notes.

Through it all, Ron's commitment to his own writing was always center stage, especially his poetry. I loved reading his work, but what was truly special was hearing him read it out loud. It was never just words on a page, it was another rich dimension of Ron. He would laugh at his work when it was funny, he would sigh when it was intense. And when he giggled—that very special Ron giggle—after reading a poem or several poems it was his way of proudly saying "I wrote that and it's damned good."

Renegade

Linda Dittmar

There is a small memorial plaza near the Provincetown pier where flagstones commemorate people whose lives were tied to the place, many of them men, many gay. Searching, row by row, I could not find Ron Schreiber's though he might have been among them. Still, it's his spirit, more than a name, that I think of in this connection, dusted with Truro's ocean-side sands, one or two miles' walk from his old farmhouse. Typical for Ron, it was a ramshackle and weather-beaten clapboard house, where small dusty rooms and a large dining table welcomed friends, writers, and co-editors.

But during the time I knew him, Ron's other home was Boston. Over the years I've seen him live in Cambridge, in a gay Somerville commune, and then with John and two Siamese cats at the top floor of a triple-decker in Cambridge yet again. There was also the summer we drove cross-country with Jim Dittmar, shared a flat in Berkeley, and tripped on acid in a forest near Truckee, in the Sierra mountains. There were the years of his being uncle to my son, Jeremy, and the unstinting friendship and generosity he extended to so many, including long months of nursing and finally losing to AIDS his partner, John, and the friendship with Johnny, who cared for Ron at the end. And through it all there was always the poetry magazine, Hanging Loose, which I knew from its early loose-leaf pages arriving in envelopes to its bound volumes, now with glossy covers and fine art insets.

So many ways of being together for us: Tarot readings and poetry readings; a bottle-smashing 'fest' at a recycling plant on an icy New Year's dawn—brown glass, green, and white bottles, each crashing in their separate bins; playing a sharp poker game; Ron's chortling laughter about claiming to have worn a flesh-colored swimsuit when charged with nudity by Truro's beach police; sporting a headband and a feather in protest of a jacket-compulsory restaurant requirement; hours spent on word puzzles and more hours tricking at the Fenway, in gay baths, leafing through gay porn, and scoring drugs.... It was all of a piece, all of it "Ron," including military service, a PhD dissertation on William Carlos Williams, early affiliations with Trotskyists and the Radical Fairies, "laying bread" (sharing money) on people known and unknown, and decades teaching literature and writing at UMass Boston, three of those years–most improbably—as Department Chair.

A brilliant thinker, an inspiring teacher, a challenger of conventions, Ron thrived on the risk of re-envisioning things, the elation of surprise, and the joy of breaking with conventions. Close up, as in the case of poetry, he taught me to hear silence, the gaps and breaks that come between, in the middle, and at the end of lines, the effects of withholding, the power of what's disrupted, or left unfinished, unsaid, or latent. Globally, on a larger scale, I think especially of Ron's pioneering signature courses at the University of Massachusetts Boston. "Blake" came first, off-center but still acceptable. But then came "Visionary and Prophetic Modes in Literature," "Homosexuality in Western Literature," and "Gay and Lesbian Literature," each of them treading on forbidden ground, naming worlds that existed beyond the boundaries of our campuses as we knew them at the time.

I never saw Ron teach, but I was awed by the innovation of his course design, where he teased predictable expectations even when just teaching a required introductory course. It was possible to do so in the late '60s and early '70s, a time of educational and pedagogic innovation nationally, and especially in a newly-invented, urban and commuting university like ours. I'm not sure when "Gay and Lesbian Literature" was first offered, but with Ron hired in 1968, it had to be in the early '70s, not long after the Stonewalls riots (1969) or the APA's finally dropping homosexuality from its list of pathologies (1973). When first proposed, the words "homosexual," "gay," and "lesbian" still caused discomfort. "Visionary and Prophetic Modes," proposed at about the same time, was indulged by Ron's colleagues with bemused tolerance. After all, it included some "legitimate" authors, but can these really qualify as *bona fide* college courses? the department wondered.

Ron, unswervingly convinced of the legitimacy of his choices, got his way, helped by a mix of laid-back charm and intellectual rigor. Blake and the Tarot cards could cohabit with Aldous Huxley and the Kabbalah, he showed, and with other spiritual expressions within and beyond the literary canon. And being homosexual, or queer, or gay, ... Well, just deal with it. For a couple of years, shortly before he was elected as English Department Chair, Ron even started announcing himself a "faggot," enjoying the flinch that would follow, daring students, faculty, and staff to wrestle with the word and their discomfort. Casual though it seemed, his impropriety was deliberate. He was testing you, me, the English department, the university. Keenly attuned to reality, he knew us all too well to take facile assurances for granted.

In the normal course of things we did share some students, though by now I mostly can't recall their names. One woman whom I met years later, now a published author of dark fantasy fiction, told me how much she appreciates Ron's opening for her access to ways of knowledge that shimmer with metaphysics and magic as they reach for an elusive sublime. There were others too, but the one I knew best is Bryan Flynn, who had been my student while working on his Honors project with Ron. Bryan died a few years ago, too young. Brilliant and gay, he became a lawyer with the National Lawyers Guild. Doing Honors work with Ron on Jean Genet was rich with possibilities for each of them: fluid gender identities, a mordant critique of power, rejection of hypocrisy, defiance of smug social respectability, and a keen embrace of the outcast—the thief, the sex-worker, the murderer, and the racial "Other."

In truth, I'm now thinking, we teach and study our very being. Whatever our subject matter, it often includes in its folds parts of our self. As I imagine Ron spending months reading and discussing Genet with Bryan, I experience their renegade appreciation of Genet—his commitment to the dignity and integrity of people living at the margins of societies set on destroying them: Western, capitalist, colonialist, racist, sexist, and bourgeois. Remembering Ron' cherubic beauty—his blue eyes, his curly light hair, his lovely smile, his body so at ease—my mind turns to his ways of being in the world: the house in Truro, his sometimes raucous laughter, the challenging twinkle in his eyes as he'd chair an English Department meeting, his voice reading poetry where silences would resonate beyond comfort.

With Dignity

Mary Bonina

For about a decade, I lived around the corner from Ron's house in North Cambridge. There were frequent visits from Ron to the apartment I shared with my husband Mark Pawlak, and we, in turn often visited Ron and John at their place. "With Dignity" chronicles two of the last times I visited him—one morning in the late stages of his terminal illness, and then—where the poem "turns"—when I was called upon the night he died, to accompany his young roommate to Mt. Auburn Hospital, to view his lifeless body

With Dignity
    in memoriam Ron Schreiber

Summer humidity and silence fuse,
thicken the air: a warning to wait
until he says he needs something.

Shut the door. Open a window.
Switch the light on—or off.
Whatever he wants.

Outside children at play squeal.
The real thing he wants is:
for his life to go on.

When he gets up to go for milk and berries,
resist holding his arm. Just walk
alongside him in case he starts to fall.

And when he does take a seat at table,
Ahhhh, he breathes, then sighs
for the missing cereal, and he's up again

to the pantry shelf. And finally, pouring
breakfast into a bowl, he sits, eats little,
yet gushes, still the gourmand,

about the berries *bought
from the greengrocer on Huron
who gets them fresh from Verrill Farm.*

The phone on the table
in front of him keeps ringing
and he keeps answering calls.

How people do go on without
asking *What's Up?* Go on
about so and so and

the party, like a Lou Reed lyric,
gossiping, forgetting they know
that anything is wrong.

And

he lets them go on for a while,
listening while they keep
talking and talking and all

he says is *Oh.*
He says, *Uh*-huh.
And finally, *Thanks for Calling.*

There's an expression,
I'll let you go now.
It's not something he would
say—not *now*. That's not what

he wants:
to let anyone
go....

But he did let go,

collapsed next to his bed. *Fell into
the lotus position,* calling out,
his companion finding him like that.

At the hospital to see him one last time
I thought he could have been singing,
his mouth open, forming a long *NO,*

or

open like a bird
waiting for mother
to place a seed there.

Mairéad Byrne

Early Morning, Walking into the Costa

Having the look of having done
unspeakable things last night,
wearing the self-same tartan pajamas
those acts were done in,
partly.

Half proud,
half mortified.

Half freed,
half chained.

Not holding his hand
but somehow,

his smile
and your downcast eye

connected.

Mairéad Byrne

Ada's Hand and Murphy's Hair

Ada's left hand is a little beaked creature dancing to Ada's voice.
Sometimes one step behind. Sometimes one step ahead.
Sometimes commenting on what Ada just said.

Ada's left hand is in tune with Ada's poetry but it has a life of
    its own—
it's not just a poetry creature you know (though it is that)!
Sometimes it perks its ears. Sometimes it waits.

Ada's hair is cut straight across her forehead and across the tops of
    her ears
(not all of it, just the bit that would otherwise fall in front of her
    ears).
What Ada's right hand is doing through all this is holding the book.

Murphy's hair is pulled back in a pony tail.
Murphy's hair is loose, it falls around her shoulders.

Now the top part of Murphy's hair is pulled back
and the bottom part falls down like rain.

Now Murphy's hair is piled on top of Murphy's head
with streaks shooting down at angles all around.

Murphy's eyes and face are listening to Ada's poetry
but every time I look Murphy's hands sweep in to change
the particular arrangement of Murphy's hair.

Murphy's hands are doing something inexplicable in the air
above the very top of Murphy's head.

Now Ada's left hand is waltzing with Ada's voice
and Ada's right hand is holding Ada's book.

Mairéad Byrne

A Parting

I'm glad not to be traveling today and traveling's
my favorite thing. That and staying home.

I'm glad it's you, not me, who's hauling cases down,
that I'm the one who gets to turn and climb the quiet stair.

I'll miss you now, is what I said, and meant it
as I leant back on the bed.

But everything sounds two-dimensional since
I heard you wrong, or heard you right but misconstrued

and capped your trademark scorn with smartness of my own,
ebullient in the low-budget cruise of wine and company.

Suddenly I'm removed, shocked at the me I turn out to be:
I thought I was Keira Knightley nice (I am my greatest fan).

But am I cruel? The arrow missed its mark.
Perhaps nobody heard. *But I heard! I heard!*

It left an exit wound in me, narrow and deep:
Anyone could turn on me. I could turn on myself

and nothing I say or do feels real,
though I can play my part—

join the photo lineup when I'm called, link tight
(it's true your elbow tucked into my waist feels real).

I prop the street door open with one hand and lean to see
your taxi come and pass, continue to the corner

where it flops, humped up on the kerb,
blunting the corner.

Then somehow I lose track. I do not see you run.
Or load up. Or get in.

Nothing so dramatic as *time stops*—
time is real as lunchtime on the street.

The taxi disengages, rights itself and turns, then like
a 2D cutout jolts it way offstage.

It's there. It's there. It's not there. Then it's gone.
It spirits you away. And I am left.

The real that shot from me when I heard what I thought I heard
is no realer than this standing in the deep and narrow street.

My candid *I will miss you now* no weaker for my leglessness.
It found its mark, or not (how can we know when there is no
    response?)

The half-there sense I'm getting's still a there.
I turn, leave go the door, and go back in.

Mairéad Byrne

A Little Bit Scary

You plunge into darkness like a pool and find you can manage.
Let's face it: You are where you're not meant to be.
Darkness outside the glass is darker because of the light inside.

The ethereal mountain looks logical just like the logical mountain
    looks ethereal
sometimes when you walk down from the pub just before daylight
    fades.

Even the moon is a fingernail shaving, the one bright star alongside
brings Turkey to mind—another example of a place
with the wrong name or at least wrong
if the language is wrong.

Before you reach the small hill to the road the blue orange bus
    streaks by.
It might have stopped had you waited before the turn.
But still, best keep out of sight and keep
your foolhardiness to yourself.

You're out of the weeds and press on, approaching the town,
hesitating to kick a frog-shaped stone for fear
it's a stone-shaped frog.

And now it's bright. Breathe easy.
Before the traffic, before there is anyone else about,
it's just a different kind of scared.

Mairéad Byrne

From the Brim of La Coma de Burg

    i.m. *Caspar David Friedrich*

I

The poplars rise straight up
or do they dive
or rise as poplars should
straight up,
and is that their reflection in the lake
before any leaves come?

But there is no lake.
The valley is under the clearest water
called *air*.

And of course the water, though invisible, is there—
not like the glass pane of a lake, dividing

the clear poplars above
from the clear poplars below.

It is more the valley looks fresh-minted,
with its own thirst slaked.

II

A brush passes over the mountain,
leaving a village in its wake.

It is the village that reflects the water:
the reason it is there;

though nothing could look drier than the houses
latched into the rock.

III

The mountains fold out of one another,
lapping forest to the top.

They look threadbare toward the summit,
full of holes.

But it is snow, making lacework of the mountain:
white against the whitened sky.

IV

My eyes can't seem to translate *there* to *here*.

Veure is such an irregular verb.
Treballar may be a surer way to know.

Mairéad Byrne

Pastoral

The milkmaids have leached the color from my hair and cheek.
My milk teeth rattle in the box my mother saved.
Metallic buckets brim with all my juice and oils.

Outside a cricket bends an archway in the sedge.
The sound of every thing is gathered to a hum.
My parts are all unhinged and hanging by a thread.

I ratchet forward and the end jumps toward me.
Those up ahead drop handless off the belt in turn.
Like childbirth I'm wild to cede my place but can't.

Between two cottages I see a USAF F35A breach.
Imagined. Unimagined.
                    The sky, dominion lost,
steps back for fighter jets delivering
a world of noise.
                    Unspeakable. Uncountable.
Mercurial the sheep spill down the valley's fold.

Mairéad Byrne

Electric Toothbrush

Last night I saw my daughter's toothbrush in the bathroom standing like a wand on the white rhino vanity top. The toothbrush was much like my daughter herself. She was probably lying, with her clean teeth, in her sister's bed. The toothbrush was clean too. I looked at it and it looked back at me. Impossible to believe this small clean head was actually inside, regularly, my daughter's mouth. It was one of those things. Like the 3.5 million tons of garbage per day produced in the world. Or the armaments industry. Or Donald Trump. You know it is true. It must be true. It's even ordinary. But nonetheless unbelievable for that.

Mairéad Byrne

Gan in *The Midnight Court*

Gan mhairg gan mhoill gan bhrí gan sealbh gan saibhreas gan ceo gan ceo gan mheabhair gan éirim. gan acht gan reacht gan riail Gan sealbh gan saoirse gan féachaint gan feidhm gan spás gan siorraigh gan síolrach gan toircheas gan tórmach gan claoinbheart gan cheart gan tafann Gan gíog gan tlás gan choimse gan chiall gan chríoch gan chaomhnadh gan cumhdach céile gan clú gan cionta claoinbhirt. gan fear gan pháiste. Gan sochar gan seoid gan só gan síth Gan chodladh gan suan gan suairceas gan suaimhneas gan chéill gan tionscal gan réiteach gan smúid gan smáchal gan fáscadh gan sult gan sásamh gan éifeacht gan tuiscint gan eolas Gan radhairc gan gliocas gan cháim gan ceal gan fásail gan ghaois gan ghuais gan stuaim gan téagar. gan éifeacht Gan lán mo stoca gan céile gan éinne gan Aird gan chríoch gan bhrí gan bhláth Gan charaid gan chloinn gan choim gan chairde gan feidhm gan fáilte. gan tál gan tsíolrach. gan feidhm gan reacht gan dlí gan lacht gan laoigh gan chríoch Gan focal gan bhrí Gan charaid gan chlú gan chúl gan airgead gan chiall gan mhúnadh Gan mheidir gan mhias gan bhia gan annlann Gan faice gan bróga. gan bhó gan chaora gan cabhair gan ionladh gan annlann. gan chuilt gan chlúdadh gan luid gan phluid gan tsúsa gan áit gan choimse gan bhrí gan síol gan orlach gan chonn gan chairde gan dabhta gan chinnteacht gan ghaois gan choimse gan easpa gan charaid gan chiall gan tuairisc gan éifeacht gan feidhm gan chéill gan féith gan droinn gan leigheas gan bhrí gan éifeacht. Gan sagart gan chumadh gan síneadh gan bhrí Gan chnáimh gan chumas gan chuma gan chom Gan ghrá gan chumann gan fuinneamh gan fonn gan mhoill gan bhréig gan cháim gan éifeacht gan chochall gan chuibhreach gan foighne gan ba gan puntaibh gan teas gan clúdadh gan gaol gan cóngas Gan scíth gan spás gan lóithne gan bhua gan bhíogadh? gan subhachas. gan néall gan fuinneamh gan chiall gan bia gan mhoill gan féile. gan leigheas gan éinne gan suaitheadh gan dabhta gan soilse gan déanamh. gan bhréig gan ríomh gan riall gan trua gan tréithe gan bhrí gan éifeacht. Gan radharc gan bhrí gan éifeacht gan fear gan cuibhreach céile gan trua gan fáth gan spás gan barrghoin gan gotha gan geall suilt gan toradh gan urraim gan eisteacht. gan riail gan tál gan triall gan daonnacht gan lúthchlis. gan diúltadh gan cuibhreach céile. gan bhrí gan trua ar bith

Note: There's a lot that can be said about *gan* but at the moment I'll only say that I see *lack, want, anger/ache* crowding into the space made by absence and making a threnodic undersong to Brian Merriman's late-18th-century 1,026-line Gaelic poem *Cúirt an Mheán-Oíche* (The Midnight Court), a paradoxical work. *Gan* is the third most frequent word used in *Cúirt an Mheán-Oíche*, after *is* (the verb *to be*) and *an* (the definite article). It is used by all characters and makes a commonality between the principal adversaries of the court. It means *without* but doesn't sound like that word. It sounds more like *gone*. The astonishing frequency of this tiny potent word, which hammers down relentlessly in bursts or faltering heartbeat throughout, reminds us powerfully of the oral and performance commitments of *Cúirt an Mheán-Oíche*. In print it is a kind of stealth weapon, a web of fractures beneath the lively surface of the poem. Compounding its effacement, a slight distaste for repetition in English language poetry causes it to be winnowed into variants. If I were translating *Cúirt an Mheán-Oíche* into English (which I am), I wouldn't attempt to translate this word. By culling all the incidences of *gan* in the poem and delivering them here, with gobbets of what is lacking or absent attached to them, I foreground an overlooked element of the connective tissue of this poem.

Mairéad Byrne

Snow

after Frederick Seidel

Snow is more than what it does.
It lays our limits down.
Now you power through and blow.
Now you hang behind the dark window.

Mairéad Byrne

Snow Day, August

Let's have a snow day in August and let it go on a very long time.

Let the falling flakes dissolve every appointment.

Let the soft bank of invisible snow piling up at the door become a cold heap, solemn in the blue light, growing, not growing under the constant fall.

Let me watch, not act. Let me not have to shovel ever.

The light outside is the light inside, only the wall divides.

The snow makes everything quiet. It keeps people off the streets, like a hurricane, but is not noisy, never saying *Look at me. Listen to me.*

If you go out in snow every step is tentative. You clutch at the rails and set down your foot carefully as if it were made of solid bone. There is no grip. If you drive you could veer off, desperately even if it is slow.

In snow, if you get there, standards drop. Everyone is stunned by the bright light and turns toward the door *Oh boy you got here.* And that is enough.

Mairéad Byrne

A Synonym

A synonym for *enjoyment* is *solitude*. What's the first thing that pops into your head when you get the prompt *enjoyment? Alone*, right? Mightn't even be the word. Just the sense of being suspended like a mote, maybe in the middle of the kitchen as if the kitchen were a lake, everything grey, still, quiet. *Alone. Enjoyment. Solitude.* Nothing wrong with that. *Enjoyment* is kind of the opposite to what you might think. It's *order. Containment. Unchangedness. Perfect stillness. Slowness. Peace.* A kind of being held in time, in space, in the house, in the moment. What I'm worried about is how close to death it seems. *Stasis.* If joy is this retreat, what's to stop further retreat? Ultimate retreat? I think it's the knowledge that solitude takes daily effort. If you just stop, things fall apart. Become corrupt. Stink. My solitude is a kind of maintenance. I may be retreating further and further. Building buffers of long running TV shows to cocoon myself within. But I want to stay on the *alive* side of disintegration. I neither want things to come apart nor do I want to leave a mess. I think it's all about balance. A synonym for *solitude* is *balance*. For some people, enjoyment is an explosion, a freaking out. For me it is a time-lapse video, so slow no movement seems to be happening.

Mairéad Byrne

Office Politics

Office politics are part of work life. All the books say the same thing: Favoritism exists. Cliques exist. Suck it up. But I say there is another way: Build a cedar closet. Actually *build* is a misnomer. The closet is already built. You just line it with cedar. All you need is board, a saw, and nails. You can tangle with those mothers as long as this weekend project takes. It could be months. Cedar boards are thin as popsicle sticks: they crack and split. And *saw* can mean *hand-saw* or *circular saw* or *jigsaw* or even *saw-saw*. And *hammer* can mean *drill* or *brad nailer*. Just the names bring me out in a cold sweat. You're in a closet, building your own coffin in a sense, fighting for your life. Your face is smacked against 130 years of horsehair plaster traumatized by the patchwork technologies of three centuries. You're creeping like a lunar roving vehicle over this landscape with a studfinder and it's beeping as if the entire knobbly field is one sheet of plywood electrically charged. It's an adventure—a tough frontier kind which will eventually yield a space for clothes. What has this to do with office politics? Nothing. It's just you against entropy, building, keeping your thumbs intact.

Mairéad Byrne

New Clothes

It is time to get new clothes but I just cannot bear to buy any. I pass by windows and I see perfectly lovely clothes in perfectly lovely textures and colors and I cannot bear to stop. Even the cobbler on our street folds over my boots professionally when I visit to ask *How much to replace this zip?* He points out the hole near the sole (I think I have seen it before), and how the heel is separating from the sole, let alone the zip, and indicates it's time to give it up. These boots are done. Maybe not today. Maybe not tomorrow. But soon. Unpredictably and predictably too. I nod in agreement of course. I understand completely. I leave the store as if I am right now on my way to the shoe shop to buy new boots. But I am not. I see them in Rome. I see them in Berlin. But just as hard as it is to take a foot from an old shoe, so is it hard to put myself into a store, or give notes to someone for something I then have to own. Maybe that's it: I have come to the end of things I can bear to own. Are poems included in such things? I don't quite know. And like everything this poem is only half or a quarter true.

Mairéad Byrne

Two of Edinburgh's Baffling Poets

I mean—what—are they—
no—like—why—I—
do they—yeah—oh
I don't I don't I don't
know—do you—
oh

Mairéad Byrne

Just Dogs

I fear the dog & then I hear the dog.
I do not lift my eyes to see the dog.

When the dog butts into my line of vision
I will see the dog.

From the corner of my eye
I see the dog.

I stretch to my full height and march past the dog.
Rigid as an umbrella I march past the dog

who angles at me along each spoke
of the circumference.

I am on the road I do not walk
because of dogs.

I get past the dog & then there is another dog
& then another dog.

But it is not a living fence.
It is just dogs.

Mairéad Byrne

A Period

Only poets, the poet said
in the classroom,
calibrate
the weight of a semi-colon,
a period.

No.
The scrupulous editor
knows
the weight of a period:
12 years.

Come, let me breach the meniscus
to meet him in the punctum,
whereabouts unknown
but always
outside the sentence.

Lee Bartlett

Anhedonica [an irony of blush sonnet]

Begin by noticing you can't buy her liquors
Good Friday, then hang a left at the Sixth Station
Of the Cross as Lola's evangel-locator
Scans static for the desert's next absolution.
Speaking of her sundry stigmata, I assume
Spires metonymy for beatification.

Then (and without malice, some enoughs are enough):
You lay aside her *Index of Taboo Subjects*
With I can't propose to her any trade too rough
Given my own heresies (thinking what objects
We see have been conditioned by the early rain).
There was once, and only, an opportunity
For this very thing, she tells you now and again.
Here they were starkly as others, and contrary.

Lee Bartlett

The Flow[ers] of Romance
for Nathaniel Tarn, 1928–2024

In the oasis of your dream
Bluebirds are often what they seem
To be, nesting in the sweet cream

Articulation of her thigh,
A neon dream-pop lullaby.
Blue is an act that names a sky.

And when a startle-snap ignites
The scat of bluebirds into flight
You wonder through the slipstream light

How is it they rise (as feather
Bags cannot weigh less than thin-air)
And why (in rising through thin air)

Their glide ascent does not suggest
A something that may be of vast
Non-meaning, but don't choose to ask.

Equally, birds drop out the sky
Like failed renunciates. Why
They fall (not *how* in their flying)

And why they drop through the air
No matter, say, the weather, their

Attention is not drawn to you,
And etc., Her tattoo
Recalls the House of Blue Bamboo,

As in:
That we might then have lost
To this very same dust
The old- and new-slain.
They live with and through us,
And what remains, remains.

Lee Bartlett

"The woe that is marriage"

For instance, what light there is, the texture
Of it, provides a kind of scriptive economy.

This morning at your desk you try to
Recall the landscape before his arrival, weirdly
Unable to settle on any intention.
For a moment here or there you might
Refigure a certain text: your husband moving with
Blunt deliberation across the white room toward
You, say, but the time of it and the location are
Without weight, generic.
                                    This is not to argue, you tell
Yourself, that he offers much more than a reticence
Of disconnect, your life together after so many
Seasons reduced it seems to the occasional
Shadowed afternoon in the rushes. If there were a way
To abolish, once and all, this dislocating absence,
The space between event and cognition which
Remarks your elemental reproach, you
Might, perhaps, take it. Some years before you wrote
In your notebook: *light releases events*
And things away from the thing itself to the culture
Of the person or presence, but you have lost,
Even here, the source.

Later, at the pet-shop, you stumble upon three
Dapple-headed fish in a forgotten tank.
Their bodies are so transparent you can trace his
Squat fingers through the glass.

Lee Bartlett

The Price of Tea in China

She leans against the ersatz adobe arch just
Out of the late Durango sun, her
Black kangaroo-hide discoboots a radiant

Ambiguity. Meanwhile (or its nearly exact
Approximation), on her dime he tours
Iceland in his gold and silver star-

Dust kid-leather dancing-Indians applique
Nudie two-piece to get a wider perspective on
The error of his leis. Days pass, weeks even,

Until without any notice midway
Across Taos Gorge Bridge Lester Wayne's
Spankin-new candy-red Cooper

Mini (shiny violator rims and all) with
A snap ignites like acetylene and (save
The twins who have slept as usual well past

All hell breaking loose and are just now
Polishing off their elderberry buck-wheats
At the I-Hop) everyone in the roadshow

Is incinerated in the sky-shine crash-flash,
Then things really get wild:
There is a time and a place for that

Sort of behavior, young lady, her replacement
Daddy says but never much minding
The little things, she listens in one ear

And out the other, preferring at the moment
To concentrate on the price of tea in China.
Even at such a tender age she has, you see,

(And especially when she goes parade)
Serious drop-dead ladyway sex-hex
In spades, so that whenever any boy

Chances to reach for an errant eyelash
From her cheek he becomes for her
(And always) just another third-rate haiku.

On Tuesdays she crosses town to buy
Skirts from the St. Vincent de Paul as a
Tactic against the silences. On

Tuesdays he crosses himself, passing the time
Perfecting his diverse accents.
Analysis of hidden stress-functions

In the closed-field speech act is
For third-year candidates only.
This is not a love story.

Lee Bartlett

Approximation to Moments

To speak a cinematic
Language is always to a

Certain extent to invent
It: Sun-nights. Hindu discourse

Scats. Miss Tan (now divorced) is
Herself occult duly. And so

Shall the catechumen-spun nun
Realize a purity in which

All and divers city-sins would
Mask their mode of silk-making.

Fall haze? Blue curtain events?
Asymptomatic slang-wedge,

Shutterbug. Fake the picture.
It lasts a very longer.

Lee Bartlett

Film Theory: *La mariée à double face*

Fearball is watching Bogart. It is *The Maltese Falcon*.

Bogart is a detective in the *film-noir* fashion and his partner
Archer has just been shot. This does not please Spade, though
Bogart himself couldn't care less.

Archer has been killed in the usual mysterious
Circumstances. The police vaguely suspect Spade
Because they think he has a thing for Archer's wife, who
Is now Archer's widow because, well, he is dead.

The police do not suspect Bogart himself,
Of course, both because he is Bogart and it
Is not called for in the script. Bogart will marry
Lauren Bacall, who in an introduction to the film
Tonight, has talked about their nights together,
Fearball thinks, but he wouldn't swear to this as
He had been in the kitchen and more or less
Simply overheard her, though his assumption is
Not, of course, unreasonable.

Archer's death has something to do with a
Bird, though not an animated bird or even an
Animated moviebird but an art object.

Women change cabs.
They get slapped and like it.

As is usual in these cases, fat people with
Strange religious beliefs hire short henchman
In trench-coats named Wilma.

Lee Bartlett

Early Warning, and Late

Inside the round and roundly-spun cut-paper sun
Of Madame Woo's tattoo-blue transfiguration,
Sister Mary wraps Fr. Sam Beckett's last maps,
Licking sweat from the wound that is her contrition.

On the road to Damascus near exit St. Paul
Dust encrypts late light, a muezzin's shrill call,
Hangs in the still air, pulling the faithful to prayer.
Bin-Ali looks up and sees the first star to fall.

Tonight his best dream-logic will not help explain
Why the pilot in the white shroud taxies his plane
Only to idle outside The Café Stained Glass.
Leaving Midnight Mass, Bin Ali stands in the rain.

Here you can still trade anything for anything,
Though she has, he assumes, by now forgotten this.

Lee Bartlett

The Signs

She will take long walks
In the afternoon, often near
Water or along railroad tracks
Or to the market where she
Will forget why she has come.

Television will begin to bore
Her. Laundry will pile up.
In conversation her attention
Will drift. Just as you start to
Get suspicious, she will
Evidence a lust you are unused
To, having you in exotic places
Like the backseat of the station-wagon
And the children's bed.

This will throw you off the track.

But then one morning you will
Notice her lingering at the mirror
Wearing a bright red sweater and
Looking very fine, her fingers gently
Playing with her hair. And it
Will be too late as all the
Professionals in New Jersey will
Not bring her to her senses.

Lee Bartlett

Waiting for the Bus

Fearball's brain becomes a green jungle. He is standing alone in fatigues and the light is fading fast. The rifle he holds would indicate that he is after Big Game, but he can't remember exactly and he seems to be lost.

As he reaches for his compass, insects begin their night noises.

He lights a match to get a better look and suddenly the monkeys go crazy, swinging from tree to tree, squawking in high voices.

The glass of his compass is smashed and the needle is frozen.

Fearball stands staring until the match burns down to his flesh
And he curses, shaking his hurt fingers like a dirty rag.

Slowly thick snakes rouse themselves from under the vines.

Fearball begins to sweat, holding his rifle tight to his chest.
He wants his mama.

Do-da.

Lee Bartlett

Fearball in Bordeaux

Thursday morning, nine-thirty. Fearball is at the laundromat. It is on his schedule. He has proper change but never brings extra so that if people ask him to break a bill he doesn't have to lie when he turns them down. And he has his soap. He is organized.

Fearball likes his Thursday mornings in the laundromat. The long wash cycles give him plenty of time to dwell. The dryers are old-fashioned. He gets twelve minutes for each French dime. The purring of the machines helps him think.

But today Fearball is unhappy. There is a singer standing over one of his machines. He does not like the singers. They always do an English "Moon River" and get the lyrics very wrong. They repeat and repeat. He does not like the hummers either. They are always off-key and tapping with their fingers on the purring machines.

Thank God, Fearball thinks. At least this singer is not a hummer, thumping the machines. Fearball would go out for a walk, but someone might steal his clothes. This happened last Thursday morning to him also. He was unhappy then, and he is even more unhappy now. He sits sullenly in the corner reorganizing his schedule with a vengeance.

Lee Bartlett

[in the margin of Robert Duncan's Before the War]

Say something like:
A body of light,
The body is light.

Stood before your mirror,
Stood before your mirror, a nest
    of desire.
The form of you, a perfect
Order of the particular.
The way at that moment, for instance.
The light lofted
    (as in: a body of light),
Lifting, as if an articulation
    of white iris, before,
Stood before your mirror,
Nested there, nesting.

Dear Elizabeth: The body is light.
Dear Elizabeth: Your body is light,
    the passage to the passage.

Stood once as now,
Before your mirror, before.

Lee Bartlett

The New Century

God's grace gave us the poetry of
Wystan Hugh Auden and Seamus Heaney,
And for our blackest sins repaid us with
Osama Bin Laden and Dick Cheney.

George Evans

Lands End

Descargo 1

Lands End

I
Ocean Beach, San Francisco

Gull pivots in its final turn,
sweeps across surf and heads
offshore to white outcrops bristling
with birds, shuddering with huddled seals,
ancient havens in surf so fierce
skulls and boats crumple
on their boiling shores.

There it tucks its beak, resting
in sunset colors people travel far
and pay dearly to see before
packing totems and small
possessions to return
in all directions
to despair.

II

What have we done in the dark and light
to geography of every sort, internal and external
(to whatever degree we're able to assess) that we're afraid
to admit, the secular and holy, so bound together neither exists,
and forms of insanity bind us to days rolling on as ever, as during
any time? Have all times felt this way, or have we alone destroyed
    these things
in measures above all history, from burnt landscape to acid air, fish
and birds left swimming in muck and plastic, animals and flora
disappearing as we punch the air and dance imagined
victories, drawn to godliness in a universe sprinkled
with recycled pixels and molecules from the first
bacteria landed from space to the latest genetic
organ miracle that died no matter how
immortal we made it.

III

Yes, I'm sullen, but so is the ocean,
and wind stirred by wings, and sand,
that prone mortality just lying there
until ocean or wind reanimates it.

The worst of anything isn't
visible at first, and the sullen,
the passive—waiting, existing,
or the ocean curling, rocking,
sometimes enraged, others flat,
nonetheless the same—exists
to exist, lives to live, acting
without purpose against
concepts of purpose.

IV

Drinkers sing and mumble at the sea wall,
cars park facing the shoreline for sunset,
watching sea and surf, salt air perfumed
with cannabis, pelican Vs crossing above,
wave after wave from the south—invading
bombers, calm, unruffled by powerful wind,
shaken but unwavering formations, perfect
though not geometrically exact, none deigning
to glance down at these mortal coils (tightly
wound, explosive) because they're unreachable,
unflappable while they flap who knows where.

V

We leaned at the sea wall watching summer equinox sink in fire and foam explosions, orange and purple clouds streaking the horizon.

What is it we say or don't say that changes anything? We've learned those matters, but have not extinguished our own fires. Time will do that for us, dragging us to eternity with our faces, none of it ours to decide.

We're old now, like time travelers to a place where what we've seen and known and felt no longer is, and things we understood no longer are. Then we become suddenly young again. It's a trick we know, but not something one can teach.

It takes a lifetime and luck, sometimes bad luck, and like any understanding of anything, it's never perfect, often brief, promising but unreliable, the way being young feels, though you don't know it then. What is it about this place?

All words are tired, but explaining things revives them, as the ocean rolls from calm distance to a roaring seam where we stand drenched in color and regret and promise, part of the roar, part of the endless waves.

VI

Washed ashore: jellyfish, sea grass, seaweed,
porous bone and polished glass, the world
threshing, sorting, recycling, renewing,
the indestructible
                      fragile
                                  universe
                                                breathing
here and in the vast untouchable
regions in every direction beyond
Earth's ovoid sphere—science may come to understand,
but it will be no more than description of the indescribable,
say an exoplanet 385 light-years from Earth, or planets that rain
diamonds, or a flotsam scattered beach
at the outer edge of a city.

VII

But that vast expanse
is not like an ocean,
it is an ocean.
It's not like beauty,
it is beauty—
no beginning or end,
constantly rowing in
from the distance
where the universe
starts from scratch
each morning,
and ends
unresolved
each dusk.

VIII

For people living in their cars, the universe begins at dawn, its colors rise and fall in waves against the windshields and beach, the ocean a swirling, humdrum but violent source of gods, myths, tales, yarns, and infinity, nonetheless named Pacific. Flotsam whirls in sea drift and soap suds: rugs, cushions, Styrofoam cups, plastic lids, condoms, dead animals, all tossed from passing freighters and cars in the shadows of the Golden Gate Park windmills, north and south, sails restored but unspinning, locked down, unjousted in a classic sense, but sometimes a dreamer's object in a yet Quixotic town, beach demarked by O'Shaughnessy Seawall sprayed and scrawled its length with names, obscenities, graffito colors, artless as a truck driver's foot, whereas the ocean can only be ocean, not a mural reflected on windshields of the poor living in their cars, and art not always a scream scrawled by desperate paint and glue huffers—neither can be priced (though much is sold in art's name), nor fill an absence of attention or direction in young, struggling, exhausted hearts.

IX

Bludgeoned by the powerful and the weak,
the poor move on. Nothing can be said
about history except it makes a mark—
the mark it actually makes and the mark
we want it to make, two things impossible
to sort. The poor are pitied and abused,
reviled and paid lip service (more pairs
impossible to sort). People don't want
to become poor, but know they very easily
might, the fearful, insoluble dilemma
of income and status driven democracy:
free to live, free to die on the streets
with nothing, not even a name, let alone
a history the free or rich will remember.

Soon we'll dedicate another statue to the rich,
and the poor will sleep against it in the sun.

X

Late at night the resident homeless guy at Lakeshore Lucky
supermarket sits in a special cubbyhole until midnight closing,
a corner once used for self-administered blood pressure tests,
later for discounted near-expiration food, then vacated until he
pulled up a chair and started sitting there and they let him.
It was good for the world though his stench was eye watering.

He slouches, trying to rest, safely ignored with his smartphone
plugged where the blood pressure cuff once was, and no one cares,
which is good for the world. An old lady whispers, pushing
a lightweight cart for seniors, "He's someone's son, you know?"
We do, and he could also be a tech bro, but unwashed with matted
hair, scraggily beard, earbuds, glued to his phone, gazing at it,
knowing his time is almost up and they will make him leave,
though it is raining, very cold outside, with no tomorrows in sight.

XI

Children at the beach refuse to stop playing in soapsud surf
and chemical foam washed ashore from passing freighters
as if in a bubble bath with yellow tinged foam, laughing
at those who warn them, near a fish with a nail in its eye,
another in a jug, one with a bottle in its mouth, a high top
tennis shoe with a foot in it, and miscellaneous bones roiling
in sand smelling of salt and oil mixed with offal and excrement,
oblivious children, charmed by surprise, tasting the foam,
becoming the poison ocean, that stunning wave-ridged body,
its mercurial pockets shining, leaping life and death.

XII

The coast seems rational, its sempiternal ocean motionless but
    motion itself,
the current a double river flowing two ways, outward and towards
    its banks,
but its shores are not parallel as in the understanding of rivers—
there are tides, wind drift, currents, gyres, innumerable
miles between solid grounds, and if the ocean stops,
we die, all of us, and every living thing.

What arrives here eventually returns there,
wherever there happens to be, and to
what end or purpose we wonder
but will never know because
the beginning is the end,
which to the cynical,
and in fact,
is clichéd.

But it's not personal, it's physics. Afterlife
is not implied, but after-existence
is a given—when you get
pulverized, what's left
is you.

XIII

One early morning near the south end beach where sand is black, the color of rich soil but where nothing can grow but wind swirls and latticed flats, a crowd gathered, people living in their cars, locals, joggers, tourists, hands clasped front and back, nodding as at a funeral, commenting, wandering around, poking a pile of tombstones unearthed by storms, children exploring, dogs barking, excited by so many people, dog-dancing at the peripheries of the sharp-edged heap, innocent like the children and ignorant of solemnity, the names and dates from other eras abandoned as wrack, dumped at the edge of their city, their country, memories discarded for a landlord's fever dream, San Francisco's bane from the first day the first native Ohlone was murdered for land, or Christianized by massacre, or locked in a Mission for rebirth, birth in reverse, which is yet another story though not completely another story.

Possession of any inch of the illusive, shifting peninsula, any thimble of San Francisco earth translates to wealth from gold rush to gold rush.

In early twentieth century, cemeteries were scraped away for real estate development, repurposed for landlords, the bodies dug up and hauled south to mass graves in Colma, city of the dead, though many were left behind and still surface time to time on rainy days or during construction.

By decree, tombstones and monuments were left behind for ninety days to be freely claimed by surviving families—a boldly cruel act of charity in a city of transients, drifters, carpetbaggers, gold diggers, fly-by-night entrepreneurs, con artists, common landlords, even landlords' landlords (so-called fleas with fleas). After ninety days, unclaimed tombstones were dumped at Ocean Beach, riprap to reinforce the seawall, hold back untamable sea, or recycled as sewer linings, an act one neighbor noted suited some, especially, he said, any who accidentally dodged Hell.

XIV

The universe, vast temperament, exists outside time
though not outside motion except for measuring distances
never to be traversed by conventional means—though what is
    convention
but that which comes next, and then becomes mundane?

Outside the moon and sun, wandering planets,
shifting stars, it all appears still, brushed
by occasional objects sparking against
the atmosphere as if tools
against a grindstone.

XV

The mundane happens while superstructures and stars explode and implode, wars begin, end, begin again, end again, governments and corporations start and fold. Through it all, people walk to streetcar stops planning what to do for lunch, thinking about their kids, spouses, lovers, partners, friends, tragedies landing on everyone without warning or meaning, while always some place in the world seems to be falling apart, and sometimes it really is, yet people work, complain, overdress, underdress, celebrate, cry, laugh, marry, get educated, inoculated, make love, make bets, go to church, work, use drugs, get into debt then out, wander lonely, drink themselves into stupors, sleep standing up on the bus, revel in groups, protest en masse, pick sides, crash cars, overdose, get convicted or exonerated, impeached or not, vote or not, plan for or fear the future then sweat and suffer to reach it and sometimes do, everything happening in a swirl, a whirl, and then, on no particular day, they die, get buried, or cremated and scattered to the cosmos, or kept in a jar or vase or box on a shelf or mantle, gathering dust and pain, anniversaries—none of it predetermined, planned, forgotten, or, on a later day, remembered.

XVI
Dutch Windmill, Golden Gate Park

Though bolted in place, unmoving,
sometimes the old windmill squeaks,
rocked by sea wind, sails straining to spin,
upright against cerulean sky, that band of light
and air keeping us and everything, deserved or not, alive.

If you lie on your back in the tulip garden looking up,
its blades do spin again, as earth spins, revolving around the sun
orbiting in its ellipse, solar system in tow, through the Milky Way,
traveling itself to Andromeda—everything moving through the
    universe
at 338 to 398 kilometers per second depending on the season,
always moving, the opposite of death—everything living,
alive, and pressing close enough to earth one can feel
the spin, the constellations, all, en route to infinity.

XVII

Due west the jagged Farallon Islands sit in their eponymous gulf ringed with crashing waves and the vast blue Pacific where dolphins, whales, and great whites leap, while earth-sluggish

seals and sea lions melt into island crag and rock, indifferent to the festering but beautiful city from which the islands are barely visible, and only on clearest days, horizonal splinters

afloat, untouchable, distant like the dead one imagines unexpectedly, or memories, and out there the rookeries abound, gulls land to scavenge among colonies of petrels, murre, auklets,

cormorants, puffins, oyster catchers, guillemots, all future extinctions on rocky landscape cacophonic with them, islands crawling with mice dropped from ships and gone uncountable,

preying on eggs, pursued themselves by burrowing owls drawn by them from the mainland, to also prey on other birds; islands once protected by isolation, boiling in eco-competition,

earning the name sailors gave them, Devil's Teeth, grinding life in their jaws, spirit islands, death islands the Miwok floated their dead to wrapped in Tule reeds through choppy waves.

Undisclosed sea locations west: nuclear dumps—one radioactive aircraft carrier, and 50,000 barrels. Ci* count unknown. Golden Gate Park windmills: barely visible on clearest days.

*Ci (Curie): The amount of ionizing radiation released when an element (such as uranium) spontaneously emits energy as a result of the radioactive decay (or disintegration) of an unstable atom.

XVIII
Entangled Whale

Buoys and ropes stream from the sides
of its mouth, winding beneath flippers
and aft to wrap the tail, plastered in
flotsam-splintered nets. Dragging knots
and football field lengths of fishing line,

as it dives its tangled flukes rise, shining
collage, horizontal against the sky—hooks,
bobbers, flattened cans, cruise ship jetsam,
Styrofoam, seaweed bulb and root. Up again,
wheezing, a blow of ocean prisms from its head.

When its eyes clear foam it calms to a floating
stare, trapped, debilitated, resigned, it struggles
to dive, half does, then dives again, deeper, maw
gaping over darkness, leaving the aliens behind.

XIX
Moss Beach: South of Lands End and Ocean Beach

Wading shore brush, ice plant and pampas to open coast over crunching shell and sand, tripping over twist-tied and knotted plastic bags of trash dumped by those who treat the world as a trash can and unredeemable, beyond surf lace to moon-pocked outcrops, tide pools where waves explode blocking human screams and laughter on shore, all sounds indistinguishable, ocean roar diminishing everything inland, bastard and saint alike, spray erasing then flooding the rockwork sheathed in kelp, water filled craters sparking sunlight, waves hitting and sinking back to their source the way men and women fall back after rising to live, to get over, go on, leaving behind life and disaster, but at the tide pools only seaweed is left behind, plastered to rock and ocean flow, a steady green to catch fog light when it rises. The tide-abandoned seabed shines, wet desert surrounding the outcrops stretching for miles, and tidal mirrors left behind float on the rock shelf—complete worlds.

One with a small bright orange crab flung sideways by moving shadows, an ochre sea star, a sunflower star, and purple urchins locked in clusters near blue and green anemones, flower creatures with stinging petals forced to wait for the tide to return, or to battle there, wreathed by spiny corals, sponge, mussel knots, and fluttering kelp.

If only the human world was organized in such pristine disarray, beautiful regardless of the luck of the draw, the tide that carried them, the fate that gathered their disparate but interlocked lives in glassy pools to survive or not, forced to wait until the ocean inches back setting octopi and grunt sculpins free, forcing multitudes of turban snails and chitons to lock down or be spilled back to the depths or plucked by birds that pierce and skim the waves, dive and patrol the upright sea palms, upright in breeze or submerged, and hover above flattened seaweed ready always to rise again, unpeel their jungles back to life when their tide comes, abandoned until then, glued to rocky shore, as disconnected as humans waiting for ships, ferries, subways, buses, or those who cast for fish, forced to learn all things have their pace, even loose sand collaring shores, rippled by wind into furrowed brows only to be erased, drawn down to safety beyond the reach of storms, if only a little while.

XX   *Highway 1: North Back to Ocean Beach and Lands End*

Tussocks grip dune tops above shore, clinging to the edge of landslips, ocean washing land away below, claiming it back, erasing it.

Klepto gulls mimic bad government but are disengaged from humans and their dealings, possessing only life, feathers, hollow bones.

They too are voracious but lack the human-only doubting of the need to live, our worries real and imagined held equal, our lives a daily grinding at solid ground, wearing worlds away, erasing them.

Human Earth: oblate spheroid rife with tragedy and gossip, mourning and hilarity, emotions as uneven as its terrain, justice the same, poverty widespread as oxygen but visible everywhere, spins through space, a perpetual wobbling, cities and villages floating among stars and planets, the one perspective from which all people appear equal outside the state of death yet feel nothing of the motion and excitement transporting them.

XXI

When fog comes in, it's day. When cherry blossoms fall, it's snow.
In spring, orange poppies and yellow clover everywhere, and blooming trees.
Summer brings the smoke of distant wildfires, at times the blur is orange
and rusty skies linger for days—what once was pure now chokes us,
but there's still the Pacific sky at sunset, unlike any other.

In fall, crows, scrub jays, and hummingbirds rule—it's how we tell winter's coming.
But all year there are birds of many stripes, from hawks to parrots, wrens to eagles,
geese, ducks, swans, coots, loons, great blue and night-herons, egrets, kingfishers,
gulls, pelicans, sandpipers, cormorants, owls, kites, kestrels, vultures, California quails,
turtle doves, pigeons, wild turkeys, swallows, pheasants, a panoply of sparrows, juncos,
chickadees, mockingbirds, woodpeckers, scrub jays, and migrant flocks in fall crossing
Marin Headlands going south along the coast over Lands End—watching them is a matter
of watching life pass with longing, obvious beauty and adventure out of reach.

But the ocean curling white crowns out of the distance,
a majestic nothingness of gravity and water,
is our one true possession.

XXII
A Distant Armada

In a thin light band between fogbank and ocean,
a cloud armada floats along the sea line

at the horizon, joined by miniscule freighters
from the real world while the sun drops

through haze, rigging lights from a crabber
flicker and jewel the hard gray water.

What was it we said we'd do, where did we say
we'd go when there seemed only open vistas,

even pressed by opaque above and hovering
over depths that proved bottomless—

where did we think we'd go, drifting, sailing,
tacking, running aground, sinking, relaunching?

It's all in a distance seen from land, mid-sea,
inching across the divide to the edge, then over.

XXIII

Graying sky before sunset, distant blue hills, crab boats rocking west to the horizon shrinking into distance, flood light glitter ready for the night catch, and dog tongues flapping chase last sticks along the foamy seam of teal, darkening Pacific.

Shell hunters and couples painted sunset hues, pelicans afloat in red, the shine left by waves pulled back, vast mirror combing life and flotsam, polishing, renewing the shore, dragging disorder back to calm a moment, as beauty does. The worst has happened many times and continues to happen. Where are the codes, who tells the story, what is the story?

All this beauty passes and comes back—land of the dead and ever-living, unstartled atheists, unrepentant junkies, holy rollers, crushed cultures, scattered tribes, homeless masses, inventors extraordinaire, ruthless armies, barbed wire borders, heartless government, endless rolling hills, race wars, homegrown religions, laws and anti-laws, all to be acknowledged, absorbed by a land unstable as the ocean itself, rocking, shaking, frosted waves steadily crashing from the unknown.

Ocean movement we understand, but not why it moves, and not shaking life itself, that earthquake. And that's not land we see emerging but rising water, and no events and no barriers will stop it.

XXIV

The ocean is a noisy dream
beneath setting sun,

the city is a riot
beneath waxing moon,

the world a blue dream
enwrapped by icy space,

and all things on Earth
are targets for the stars.

George Evans

Descargo 2

San Francisco/*San Pancho*

Caballero Águila

Aztec perched
on white fire
hydrant (work
shirt, baseball
cap, tennies),
eagle warrior
—*caballero
águila*—
soldier
of the sun,
sweating,
waiting
for hourly
wage work
in sunlight
near bronze
eagle warrior
memorial statue,
dancing arms
outstretched
under overpass
freeway north
entrance, Cesar
Chavez Boulevard,
San Francisco,
San Pancho,

2024, planet Earth,
Estados Unidos,
where free people
are treated
by requirement
like trash.

                    San Francisco, Mission District

George Evans

Sleepers

The length of the esplanade, homeless real estate,
fiberglass tent poles arch, multicolored patterns
pixilating waterfront and factory landscape with
domes, a keyboard with colored keys from the air,
say from drones or UFOs sweeping back and forth
above them in vigilance according to one resident
both wry and insane, exhausted and dropping off,
no drugs, bone tired, sick of the minute to minute.

Seen from skyscrapers, an ancient mosaic
depicting encampments, armies of the poor,
lost, useless, displaced, neglected, downtrodden,
overlooked, abandoned, denied, discarded, sick,
ignored, ripped off, torn to shreds, impoverished,
short changed, harassed. "Serious pains in the asses,
who can't find their own footing like everyone else,"
officials say under their breath in board rooms and
at city hall, all landlords, wealthy politicians, or both.

George Evans

The Altar

She sleeps in the ICBC (Industrial and Commercial Bank of China) vestibule, north corner of 20th Avenue and Noriega, converting it to a *retablo* every night she's there—who drifts and roams—a bright altar facing the intersection catty-corner, one block east of once another corner bank (now brokerage) with a bullet hole in the upper right corner of its west-facing gold aluminum window frame, put there in 1974 by Patty Hearst after robbing a once-Hibernia Bank next corner down, one block west (now health clinic)—it can all be seen on Google Maps. "*Hearst—heart with a twisty S,*" she says, fencing herself in for the night with the train of suitcases and wheeled baskets she moves piece by piece, inch by inch, corner to corner, mile by mile, every day, all day, shooed as a pest door to door down to the ocean and back, exhausted, overweight yet endlessly hungry, hesitant to beg but begging, ashamed to beg but begging, and, even with her stench, beard, enormous weight, and hair plastered by years of weather, she's fearful of city shelter men "*who'd even rape gopher holes,*" preferring doorways, bus stops, trees and bushes, lulled by dreams of further, simpler worlds, "*Swept out to sea, embraced and gently rocked.*"

George Evans

Early Spring Mariachi, New Millennium

El mariachi with a smartphone headed south on Mission
near 25th walks past

DANIEL'S ♦ JEWELRY	•ANDREA•
2865 Mission St. (415) 525-0591	Perfumes • Originales

RECARGAS•FAX•ANDREA•FAX•PERFUMERIA
MONEYGRAM

       livelihood clenched by the neck
in his other fist, up on his shoulder like a load of cane,
strings gleaming, the sleeves of his work shirt rolled,
his straw field hat cocked, leather face stress-sculpted
by sweat work and worry, dark from sun labor on his way
to stroll La Taquería and sing off-key for the goose-eyed
emigrant gringos new to San Pancho in its latest Gold Rush
gorging tacos burritos quesadillas y cabeza y lengua y sangre,
teeth coagulated with food blocking articulation y clarity,
generation of the final years of 20th Century violence, start
of the next, end days for remorse compassion concern—children
of electro ether and keyboard existence paid in hyperspace gold
dust for playing video games and typing money code money,
a ransom for their youth, attention, conversation, curiosity,
amusing themselves with face y pudenda y excrement photos,
sending them off via hand held robots to the human universe,
fangs dripping, eyes Orphan-Annie-blank, white skin crawling
with tattoos of illiterate Chinese characters, cryptic religious
and tribal symbols, cartoons, and the usual tacky flash,
sweatshirt T-shirt ballcap fashion exuding permanent
adolescence, casual links to the cosmos, boxed

in by heartbreaking self-obsession willful
ignorance wikipedic half-knowledge,
onanism dopamined petextrians,
deadwalkers
all.

George Evans

Near Fourteen

13.82 billion years ago the cosmos came into being
and took that long to produce those who believe war
can improve existence, and those who believe tiny,
expensive robot phones improve existence, phones
manufactured by slaves, containing elements mined
by slaves, constructed with components fabricated
by slaves, giving people opportunities to talk about
things they cannot shut up about, things so important
they ignore where they are going and drive their cars
and trucks, bikes and airplanes into and over things
and people, sometimes crowds of them, chattering
on the same phones built by slaves, or auto-searching
for noodle shops or places to get a haircut and tattoo
while the cosmos swirls and ancient dust devils roll.

George Evans

In the Mission @ La Taquería

Holding ½ dozen shiny

    foil birthday balloons

        aloft ecstatic near three

            feet tall floating she marches

                the color-tiled sidewalk

                    of her sixth birthday party

in puffy sleeved dress tiny

    smiling Latina doll complete

        with rosy cheeks and patent

            leather shoes who may never

                be so alive again but probably

                    won't remember. Remember?

George Evans

Late Afternoon Dog Walk, Geary Boulevard, Richmond District

A distraught but determined woman fast-walked down the sidewalk
    rocking
a terrier with the same disheveled hairstyle as hers in her arms
    knotted
punkish mohawk tufts above their foreheads and the same startled
look in their eyes they barreled towards me, seeming humorous
at first, but the woman was holding the dog, a wrecked Jack
Russell, like a hand grenade or pistol, so I jumped out
of the way to watch them pass, the woman's hips
pumping up and down as if riding an invisible
bike, the little dog shivering, eyes bulging
just like the woman's but tears splashed
from hers onto its mohawk, *You son
of a bitch,* she yelled at a car, then
a truck, then a bus, then the sky,
then with a shrug looked back

to shoot one at me, indignant
at my attention, their mohawks
peroxide blonde with the curly tips
fringed pink bouncing wildly, howled,
and the Jack Terrier, also clearly needing
a drink, howled too, they tilted their heads back in
unison yowling she shouted lines from the Preamble,
We the People, then sharply changed the subject, *We are
not the People, we are tenants, consumers,* then abruptly spun
walking right into lunatic Geary traffic in the middle of the block
diagonally heading for Tippy's corner dive, waving her fist shouting
We are the Dogs, dog vibrating, howling ever more loudly, excited,
    sharp

pitched, *Unalienable rights* she yelled switching documents, arms
   held high,
squealing doggy balanced on one hand, yelping as they were sucked
   beneath a bus.

George Evans

Outer Sunset District

Headed for the edge of paved earth squealing towards the Pacific, drowning it out, street racers knife the wind and peel rubber past dive bars going upscale and not, Chinatowns, Irish enclaves, Little Saigons and Russias, Korean pockets, Italian fogetaboutits, Arab bodegas caged barred and weaponized in fog, failed renamed reopened failed again renamed and reopened restaurants by the dozen, pizzerias, taquerías, mom and pop and offspring corner stores, and homeless throngs hiding, shrinking, resting, sleeping on sidewalks, in doorways, cars, RVs, behind bushes, in and under trees, cocooned in cardboard, huddled along urinous footpaths leading to the ocean across the coast road into the ocean, rolling surf with bones and shells, their blank eyes fixed with revelation that when you're down, all the way down, finally really really down, there's no way up or in to whatever's being sold rock bottom in the Republic that day at the western end of its land.

George Evans

Hummingbird Wars

Hung against fog above avocado trees the male dives then shoots
back up with a tail snap just before slamming into earth, parabolas
traced in its wake, a courting creature with no enemies but gravity,
living for nectar and mating wars with other males, all miniscule,
weightless with sawtooth beaks, a mix of bee and alligator,
with no intentions of sticking around.

Like many men they're friendless but want trade-offs, fly, hover,
and near-mate midair, migrating to the tropics to shake off lice
and bad scenes, building shelters with found materials
and no regulations, hatching offspring outside, teaching
them to fly, hunt, mate, and leave home permanently
without remorse or regrets, training them to buzz
the earthbound humans, who complain about
everything, so loudly and uselessly lost.

George Evans

November Scene

The crab boat fleet becomes visible at dusk,
evenly spaced across the horizon looking back
at once-a-fisherman's town, haven for those
who worked without screens or robot glow
blocking Pacific teal and its rippling.

As sky darkens their floodlights blend then
disappear among glittering houses on the coast,
each imperceptibly rocking heavy with crab pots
and crews so exhausted they don't know they are
or where they are, catching second wind to go on,
deep at work, glancing up at a city they can't afford
even after record harvests, even if they wanted to
live among smart phone zombies with their heads down
babbling and marching crosswalks to their claw markets.

George Evans

Daguerreotype Portraits of Gold Rush 49ers
An Exhibit

Such sadness in the eyes of men come all the way
from hell and gone to find nothing, nada, zilch—
plows, gals, families, and churches left behind—
each one looking as if he knows he's lost the gold
rush lottery and might die at any time, soon
as he leaves the portrait studio, say, and walks out
to the wheel-ditched street or mud gully where another
Gold Rush dreamer staggers, frustrated and angry enough
about everything under the sun to kill him for a glance,
a stumble, a dare, a thing to do on a lark, and there
he'll lie, like a heap of cloth dropped from a wagon,
dreams and aspirations gone as quick as gold dust.

Desperate, disappointed, young, hungry, some
vicious looking, cutthroat, dandified, mortified,
stupefied Christians, Christians of every stripe,
Jews, Celestials, Quakers, Mormons, Buddhists,
Hellfire Preachers, Agnostics, Evangelists, Atheists
Apostates, Heathens, Unbelievers, Utter Disbelievers,
armed with pistols, knives, squirrel guns, rifles, shivs,
swords, machetes, hatchets, brass knuckles, blackjacks,
clubs, nunchucks, dynamite—so young, all that youth,
subdued horror and despair behind lachrymose eyes,
weary, raggéd, exhausted, brothers and friends, wrung,
hung out to dry, down at the heel, soles flapping, every nickel
washed down one slough or other—no matter who they were
they were no more, unsmiling no matter what, even while
playing accordions banjos, tambourines, fiddles, not one
smile. Some say it was the nature of the daguerreotype,
but it was the gold.

Most struck out and went home, trudging mountain and plain,
indentured for beans, hardtack, transport, bartered for muscle
and blood, no guarantees, nada, zilch, only to die in Civil War
where many once glitter-obsessed dreamers perished in atrocities
of free men clashing in a freedom-obsessed Republic
over the right to own other men.

George Evans

The Holidays

The houses along Lake Merced's north shore
are decorated with lights, deceptively festive
like freighters inching brutally across the dark
Pacific visible between western hills sloping
to the sea creased and brittle with earthquake
scars, histories, feet and wheels, time and wind
from slapping waves and fog—it's remarkable
all the suffering in the world can't end human
faith in religion, possessions, traditions, no
force on earth strong enough to wake us
to the pain. Along with heart, bone, skin
and desire, we are born with instinct
to remember without knowing we remember
life bears its own, and everything in its, end.

George Evans

Hippie Agonistes

> *God, when he gave me strength, to shew withal*
> *How slight the gift was, hung it in my Hair.*
>   —John Milton, *Samson Agonistes*

Slumped in a wheelchair watching *Streets of San Francisco*
reruns in a flophouse dayroom,

he doesn't get why nobody cares about that world anymore,
his land of love beads, sandals,

peace signs, and patchouli—they talk about it now and again
as if it's gone (electronically,

on handhelds), but it's right there, it is, déjà vu all over again,
proving that cliché—Vietnam,

Civil Rights (different names and labels, but still the same),
Hendrix too—*Hendrix Lives, I Say!*—

and Clapton is God—Beatles, Doors, Stones, Dylan, Richie
Havens, Gordon Lightfoot,

Grateful Dead, all still make the rounds, the dead refusing to die,
and either all are still going on

or he's tripping, stoned out of his mind, just imagining he's old,
a conundrum like Chuang Tzu's

butterfly, so maybe he'll wake up or come down, it couldn't
happen soon enough—getting

old is uncool, real or hallucinated—too many aches and drafts,
all that creaking with little more

than strands of hair down to his shoulders—not easy to survive being shorn, it saps your strength,

robs identity—even the word "hippie" has come to be an insult in the mouths of the young

(Century 21 young), raised by those who always went for money, leaving rigmarole like peace,

love, and understanding behind where it always belonged, though even they longed for such illusions.

George Evans

Coyote Music

Speeding through timed lights along Sunset Boulevard near midnight after work paying no attention to scenery, tuned to stumble drunks and cell phone addicts crossing traffic blindly mid-block, and potential speed traps, in a hurry to get home, read news from the outer world, and if not too unsettled fall asleep quickly for as long as possible before fast approaching morning shift, when something flashed past

the trees and I slowed, dismissing it as cat or dog until there again, then gone again, pacing me, melting into landscape with octopus skill in this electro technocrat city inhabitants are all diminished by (lost spark metropolis, once dreamscape now dystopic, wrung to bone by bureaucrats, employless billionaires, endless lines, hordes of typers with glowing palms), once simultaneously civil and wild, now tamed

and crowded to hysteria, and once devoid of coyotes from early times until they started crossing the red bridge southward lit by yellow bulbs, Chinese lanterns in the fog, sauntering in from dusk-blued Point Reyes, loping, pausing to glance between rails at the sun dropping silvered Pacific. Was it wistful, I wondered, thrilled to be crossing, or sense the danger in our wreckage and think of turning back? It carries all it owns and keeps moving. I had that sort of life once and sometimes miss it, but never the coyote ability to thrive on mice and air. I slowed to swing the car with headlights off and watch him turn the city back in time and ecology, but faster than the thought he disappeared, absorbed and became the darkness, camouflaged against car or tree in the wooded road dividers, also from another era, or blended into construction equipment left overnight, using skill and caution to bend the world to his shelter.

Then I too was gone, but more gone, realizing differences between us he couldn't be bothered with—that I regard him with envy, say, or regret my death before dying, a useless, laughable human skill that could make him howl while he runs with light and dark absorbing, expelling him, then breaks towards heavy foliage and disappears before even reaching it, yelps and yowls passionately for company of his kind, hunts without fear even seeing us before we see him, and simply lives to live and moves on, unwhimpering, not us, but somewhere deep inside us, in long abandoned forests or dens.

Sunset Boulevard

George Evans

Arborist

The old tree in the yard has breathed the air
of generations, absorbing sounds, observing
births and deaths in ways we humans can't,
each stranded, woven into tree ring silence.

So many dead of so many things, you'd think
we'd think this strip of light tethered to cold
universe, a far greater emptiness, was enough
and worth all stars beyond. But not yet. Now
we live and hide in words, stop talking for safety,
and have yet to say anything worth hearing.

*

The crash continues as speeding cars slam into the mass
knotted on the highway. For crash read government,
for cars read politicians. A young person asked, what
is the role of politicians, and all I could think to say was,
"To lie about lying." "And the government?" he asked.
"To lie about politicians," I said. "Who governs, who leads
then?" he asked. "Don't ask stupid questions," I said.

*

This morning it was announced the center of Earth, its core,
stopped spinning, hopefully just a pause before reversing course
they enthused on the radio in bubbly voices. This not long after
learning the moon is leaving Earth's orbit, at least moving away
@ 1½ inches per year, and has been for billions of years, something
important to know right now for some reason. Also, a winter
    asteroid
"the size of a delivery truck" (cargo unstated), after orbiting the sun,
will pass Earth in "one of the closest such encounters ever
    recorded,"
closer than some satellites, followed not long after by another one

"the size of the Eiffel Tower" spotted hurtling towards us, and
 another
on the way, in spring, twice as tall as the Empire State Building
 (more exactly,
"217.4 stacked giraffes"). For a week the image of .4 giraffes hung in
 the air.
Icebergs and governments collapsing; earthquakes and dictatorships
 on the rise;
volcanoes and guns going off; fascism and racism in a dead heat;
 and because
of the Russian war in Ukraine the Doomsday Clock was adjusted to
 90 seconds
before Armageddon. This in case you were not already scared
 enough of everything.

*

Congress is busy banning books,
but not a word about guns, plus
banning abortions, but not a peep
about hosing down the homeless
or killing skells. They're banning
TikTok while lying to constituents
is in vogue, and strain to prove
pronouns are deadlier than bullets.
They're also busy banning politicos
who can read from important panels,
along with those who know anything
about history, geography, law, foreign
languages, diplomacy, or statesmanship,
yet after several new mass shootings
including a mushroom farm massacre,
a dance hall massacre, a gas station
massacre, a farmland massacre of six
featuring a headshot 10-month-old
in the arms of his sixteen-year-old

headshot mother, plus a Kindergarten
teacher shot in class by a six year old
with a pistol, not one word about guns
in the hallowed halls, though banning
gun regulations is in the air.

*

The war we should avoid is the lover we pursue.
But omnicide besuits us.

January 2023: Low key U.S. war in Somalia
comes to light—ISIS leader and ten cohorts
smashed in a raid while living in caves.
One American troop suffered a dog bite
by an American dog that couldn't tell
one troglodyte from another.

Damnatio memoriae enfolds us.
Many things happened but did not happen.
Many things happened that did not happen.
Many things did not happen that happened.

Many who did things did not do them.
Many who did things did them wrong.
Many who did things no longer exist.
Many who did things did not exist.

*

Terra nullius no longer exists.
Everywhere has a landlord, every speck
of sidewalk, inch of gutter belongs to someone
not you, someone with a deed, no regulations,
and no understanding, tethered only
to the grave we are born with.

Olena Jennings

Language I

I left and then I would try
to find him,

shout up to the window.
I waited long enough
for him to call.
I wanted to dance again.

Finally, he called.
I canceled all my plans.

We went to the store together
already drunk.
I asked him for his watch.
He put it on my wrist, metal warm.

Then we bought steak
overwhelmed by meat, the fleshy red.

I met him in an apartment
I wanted to scream.
I felt I might die,
but there was the roommate.
I held it in.
I suffered.

I was always suffering
in different ways.
Sometimes over academic presentations,
floating out of my body.

I suffer with so much language
inside me. It builds up around the heart,

the letters pushing at muscle.
I want to scream, but there is language
stopping me, telling me
to make coherent sentences.

I count the nights in different apartments.
He takes a picture. I don't want the photo.

He left marks, seen when I was in front
giving the presentation,
though he told me they were invisible.
The touch of the words

from thick books was there,
his philosophy branded on my skin.

Olena Jennings

Language II

The language that I learned
as a child, while my father
spoke a different language,
made me feel original.

The words so colorful
that they fell away.
The colors were in place
of language. In French class

jaune
jaune
jaune
jaune

Blocks of color
instead of words.
He worked with fabric.
I waited for phone calls.

Once my crush came over
with his friends and took me out.
They made crazy moves, swinging
from the ceiling of the nightclub.

I had cocktails
that weren't worth counting
the rest of my change,
metal cold in my palm.

The color blue shot through
my legs.

He would rip them from my body
for his art.

Without the words,
without the colors,
I am a room for sale someone
steps into with a vision.

Olena Jennings

Language III

A Ukrainian Easter egg.
I wanted my lines to be perfect,
but my hands were unsteady.
When I learned to ride bikes
it was the same way.
I wanted to ride that straight line
down the alley past the garbage cans,
but I wobbled and fell.
I still have scars.
He asked me
to hold out my hands
so he could examine them.

A Ukrainian Easter egg is dyed
and explodes. I was too lazy
to blow it out. The sound
reminds me of the grand finale
of the fireworks we watched
from my grandmother's porch.
I was always afraid
of falling through the cracks
between boards. I was full
of unfounded fears.
When I showed my grandmother
the scars she too was convinced

they were the work
of the men
in my nightmares.
My hands trembled as I clasped
a necklace.
So, he reached over, his fingers
too large, too clumsy for such

small findings. Then I reached
up and his skin
was dewy.

Those men that walked
along the side of the highway
with the stray dogs
when he opened the door
to let me out
my neck heavy with the beaded
necklaces that were brighter
than the street lights, flickering
for help.

Olena Jennings

Language IV

One word doesn't
correspond
with another.
Is it a translation?

Are you leaving your body
in the words?
Is it a translation,
the *shmatok* of your heart?

You are ready with the translation,
The words are a little wet.
They were pulled from language,
language is water,

you swim through it
as if moving your arms
against the hard linoleum floor,
the taste of footsteps in your mouth.

Sometimes you are screaming
through language.
Sometimes you are trying to break through
the translation to find your own voice.

You go on to write your poems.
The words coals
in your throat. The need to suffer
for a moment, gathering their heat.

Sometimes you catch their spirits
hovering above you, flickering

like half burnt-out bulbs,
before they disappear.

Olena Jennings

Language V

as I walk beside him, a steady beating
I recite the alphabet, the longing for letters
the craving for the є and ï
surprises me
to learn the sound he has strung

around my grandfather's neck
like the beads when he worked in a factory
I imagined the floor, so unlike the polished
floors of the house, bare
so he felt his skin against concrete

the cold when he took me down
to the basement to learn
about the tools he used to create
spaces, the hammer and nails,
and the metal and wood

I learned to let my body
take the shapes of the letters
he looks down at me from the second floor
next to the painting of the asparagus
seeing my є

my body walks the rooms
of the house he has built
for you in the middle of the block,
he looks across the room at me
from the couch, seeing my ï

as I walk beside him through the streets,
the steady beating of the drumsticks
against a bucket, I am surprised

he has learned the sound of my longing,
the ɛ and ï

Olena Jennings

The Soft Sign

I make a word whisper
in my mouth
with a metallic taste
сталь.
It was whispered to me,
against a background
of alcohol,
the tools
to repair shoes.
We were on our knees,
cold cement,
as he showed me
how to replace a sole.
He cut leather
almost without looking,
his hands in command
and when we were done
my hands smelled
of steel сталь.
He had a vocation once
and then he immigrated,
worked on a farm.
It became a memory
and suddenly
it was my memory too.

Olena Jennings

Outside the House

She dipped the eggs
in a dye of onion skins.
She remembered the way
the word цибуля
blossomed in her mouth.
The onions used for dye
had been cut into the liver.
Dough was folded
over the mixture and it was baked.
I didn't learn to be domestic.
It was the opposite.
I watched layers of dust
build up on the bannisters.
My drinking glasses were so cloudy
I couldn't see through them.
I learn the opposite of domesticity.
I learned not to live in the house.
I stretched out in gardens,
on piers, and on park benches.
My body never conformed
to beds, couches,
and chairs. My hands never
held spoons.

Olena Jennings

Tracing the Lines

The poppies follow me, like I
follow myself through rooms
in the world.
The poppies in my grandmother's vase.
Now they are against the fading grass,
pale in the sunlight.

I have not lived it,
but I remember
the red crepe
fabric that has been eaten
away by the cold. Snow
in her exile.

Silk red
against icy white,
like her heart
against her father's white canvas
when she was forced
to leave him.

In her black leather shoes,
which she wore in the train car,
the chill seeping in,
without having had time to take
the suitcase filled
with all she loved.

I have not lived it,
but I remember the forced labor
the bodies against mine,
the fabric eaten away,

and my father holding out his hand.
I barely grasp it.

Olena Jennings

Derhachi

They sent her a letter with the photo once.
Her bones took the shape of their handwriting.
The letter was delivered by the friend from the DP camp.
The woman kissed me
and left a mark of spit
in the shape of a map on my cheek.

It is not the way I wanted to imagine my grandparents'
hometown,
the four sisters in the photo wounded in the bombing.
It is the closest to war
I have ever gotten.
Their black dresses, stiff against their bodies,
already a sign of mourning.

They ate beets so their lips were red,
confused with blood.
In the end, my grandmother had only the garden,
behind the brick house.
She imagined them all digging up the beets,
eating together.

The glass would have shattered when it happened,
the façade would have crumbled.
The century didn't matter,
the house was meant to be taken away
by any means.
All they had was the garden.

Olena Jennings

Reflection

They had stopped where he didn't get a tattoo,
where something else was engraved
that he brought back with him
to the sea. I step inside.

He had subscribed to a theater magazine in the Navy
and saw plays, one of them Beckett,
and another reminded him of the strawberry field
in his backyard that would represent Tacoma.

There is always water moving
around us, pushing us forward.
The bodies had been buried
without family members present.

The port call in the Philippines had become
the only place where he could phone his mother.
He was reminded of home
and the Sound.

Impossible to get away from water
sometimes he felt
he was drowning and he would tell the woman
he loved so briefly

that he was drowning
and he could not stay married to her
because his head was not above water.
I too step inside.

Olena Jennings

Famine 1933

Ingredients:

Flour
Water
Dry Yeast

Recipe:

Walk with your sister through city streets, over bodies. A boy flies by on a stork, handfuls of feathers, grasping, but no one is having babies anymore. Your mother is accused of eating, filling her stomach with bread. You make it, pouring warm water into the yeast. Laugh, the way you might laugh with discomfort at a funeral. Mix flour, water, and yeast. Knead. Your neighbors, so hungry, were rumored to have eaten a dead body. Taste. Is it your story to tell or should it have died with her?

Olena Jennings

Exile

Her father spoke up. For her,
his voice was louder
than anything else:
the sound of her mother's singing
in the kitchen, folk songs about
cranes and foxes and missed
connections.

When they came for her and her father,
the bottom of the box car
was like being dragged along the road,
the feather grass caught in her throat
until there was snow, cold
as ice cream they had eaten
in front of the museum

with the painting of Cossacks
that she remembered so vividly
she used to see it on the bare walls
of their house. When they arrived
there was work, mining the hard
earth. Their stomachs empty
like their cupped hands.

At least they were together
when letters came from home
written on paper with bitten-off
corners. They were ravenous.
It hurt to swallow when
there was nothing. They didn't
know how to dream anymore.

But when they returned, they were
whole and her mother was whole.
There were folds in her mother's skin,
swinging like paper garlands on the holidays.
The year had passed without them
and she was a miracle and they were
miracles.

Olena Jennings

Waves Whisper Loss

When she has lost
pieces of her past
and she calls to the photos
in her mother's album,
crumbling them beneath
dry fingers so they fall
like sand on her bare feet
as she walks along the beach.
Memory claws at her. It is summer.
She sits on a blanket
with the friends from
her hometown. They have
always been there and now
she can hardly remember
their names. She tries so
hard to pull the names from between
her lips on fishing line that they
become chapped. Her friends are
lost in the blackouts,
their voices muted beneath
the explosions. Finally, one,
Mykola, is out and the hook
catches in skin. She should
have protected him
in the warmth of her body,
so like the sea.

*

When their mother says their names
the wind swallows them
Maria, Halyna, Melania, Oleksandra, Fedosia
her five daughters.

First, Maria will leave,
packing her leather suitcase,
folding white underwear, a sweater
with pearl buttons and a map,

which will lead her to the city,
the building with the gargoyles
on her left and the river on her right,
a job as a secretary in a stuffy office.

Second, Halyna will leave,
for a curly-haired man
who promises her happiness
and dessert every night

a sour cherry pie
that would turn her tongue red
like warm blood coursing through
her veins, in love.

Third, Melania will leave,
scraping formulas in her notebook,
numbers recited as she walks
to the red university

named after the poet
who will also teach her
how to infuse her equations
with passion

Fourth, Oleksandra will leave,
her hair tangling
and her skin veiled in sweat
as she hikes up the mountain

in a country they only studied
in the glossy pages of a textbook,
where she would remain
through dinner, before moving.

Fifth, Fedosia will leave,
in a black dress,
mourning her mother,
no reason for her to live

alone in the house,
with the smells of her mother's
cooking pressed into the chair
where she sits for a final moment.

Olena Jennings

When She Was of Flour and Eggs

Her grandmother
kneads her stomach
The old woman thinks it is Easter bread
with golden raisins and saffron

The holiday is approaching
They circled the church
three times,
leaving footprints in wet grass

She lies on the wooden table
Her arms out
The cross is broken
She has saved

The wine and bread
in her mouth
It is the longest she has gone
without swallowing

Christ!
She cannot say
Her stomach is tender
Is rising

Her grandmother stands
over her
Hands tired
from creation

Olena Jennings

Mirror Sounds

What music?
What music?
He said through a pipe.
I didn't know how
to answer because there wasn't a hint
of music anywhere
and I thought of my grandfather's
old record, the one with the dove.

I played that record
behind the closed door.
When I danced, my body moved
into what they had left behind.
My body moved like the flowers
on my grandmother's dresser,
leaning
towards the sun.

When the old man stood
in front of the bus,
luggage spilling,
he questioned
the music,
smoke gathering
around his mouth,
just like my grandfather.

Olena Jennings

Travelogue

Their language remained,
the words making maps
in their mouths.
The maps led to the farm,
rich soil and wheat,
maps in their mouths
moved like rivers.
When I saw
The Swallow's Nest
I thought of my grandmother
looking out at the birds
and my grandfather feeding them.
They both spoke to the birds
in the language of my travels.
When I returned,
they did not acknowledge
where I had been.

Cracks and Apertures

Kirk Glaser

These poems capture moments of awareness—streams and tributaries, marshes and ponds and lakes, backwaters and eddies of observing self in relation to the seepages and floods coming from within and without. I hope their ecosystem can support life, that a confluence comes into view—maybe a river flowing, an ocean receiving them. The poems come from several decades, some already coalesced in manuscripts, others meandering into channels for this spoKe purpose.

What makes a self? was the question that kept coursing through these poems as they pooled together. Many arose from hours sitting on a cushion in a Dharma hall or on the ground under sky and trees. Some, mostly the last handful, address this more directly: poems attempting to capture meditation, the experience of observing the self quietly, for long periods (hours, days, weeks on retreat), with all the thoughts and feelings and levels of consciousness that arise and fall away while seeking a quiet, observing mind. Some weave passages of sutras and Dharma studies into them, trying from other angles to "see to see" past the fly-buzzing mind that composes this entity called self, so fleeting and fixed at once.

Many of the poems delve more into a particular self, into experiences from life as a partner and father and citizen of this strange world. Some poems are born from dreams, some are word dreams following sound to sense (maybe), or are made of sentences found and fragmented and reimagined into a new dream. Some take an odd snippet of news that sinks its hook—Francois Mitterrand's last meal, for instance, in "L'Ortolan," and imagine this in the context of Earth's assaulted ecosystems as well as the Dharma—both representing the law of nature. And while ecopoetics doesn't run through these poems as much as in other work of mine, there are still many springs and rills. Some poems speak from and through such concerns more directly, if in varying ways, such as "Wind," "Shards," "Some Days," and even "After the Years." All these poems feed into the wider flow of the Dharma-centered poems, or so I feel, or at least hope. They are events and states of being from times in life when caught in the purse-seine of emotions and fears and judgments and doubts. Caught and not able to see that anatta, no self, can free the net. And that this liberation doesn't mean "all problems solved" or "suffering gone," but understanding that the problems are not the net, the web of suffering is how one reacts to them. Tricky, as the constant ebb and flo of a life, and the limits of my practice, mean those moments of liberation are fleeting. Perhaps the (separated) pair, "Book of Nights" and "After the Years," demonstrates this best, the former being deeply caught, the latter slipping the net, a poem of healing and reflection on life that points to the final poems.

Anatta remains elusive in these poems, yet as my poetry and meditation practices continue, I find myself drawn toward understanding *no self* through words as well as meditation, if that's possible. I am curious what awareness can breathe in my poetry the closer I get to anatta. I try to silence the *I* in many of these poems, think about it directly in some, yet *no self* seems uninterested in writing poetry—the mind grasping words (at least mine, so far) is built of too many emotional, relational, and cultural formations to bring back more than mist and fog and flickers of light from that awareness. And what is this *no self*—something like where consciousness is aware that a being exists only in the relationships, thing to thing, body to idea to feeling to belief to object to experience. Tease apart the relations and emptiness remains, awareness observing the flow of life all around. Such is the state I tried to capture with "Glass-Bottom Self," a poem about a memory arising during a retreat when sitting in adhittana (*strong determination* when eyes stay closed and no movement is made for an hour). A poem that attempts to trace the wondering of why this memory, why now, trying to trace it to origins, seeing how the mind connects thing to thing along the way, how a self coalesces and crumbles moment to moment.

I hope some of the poems capture those dynamics—allusively in images and sequences, in patterns of syntax, in associative leaps where I try to capture what is observed and thought and felt by a mind attempting to observe being. Those flickering moments of awareness netted in words. Words whose meanings lie in their relationships, in the emptiness between them. Emptiness as breath, breath as word. The space between the words where poetry exists, as Octavio Paz said. Or as Leonard Cohen put it, the crack in everything where the light gets in. Poems as cracks, fissures, fractures, apertures. I hope the crevices in and between these poems scatter a bit of light, and maybe a bit of water from the spring spills through as well.

Kirk Glaser

Breakout

Asleep all night in muted light
while the prison doors creak open
and the inmates slip into the dark.

Futile to hide in the closet
under parents' clothes
breathing the dead leather of shoes

when the blood longs to escape
and the heart beckons the fugitives
to break these ribs deceived

by their firmness, their sutured order
into believing themselves fixed forever,
the true keepers of all the I conjured itself to be.

Let them come, those resolute, clear-sighted
outlaws hidden since birth, to pick
their teeth with my bones, let them

strain legs and arms, put their backs
into it, pulling the self through
the routine corridors and into open air.

Better to bubble under a hot sun and
let skin dry into parchment
than stream in these foolish hardened walls.

Kirk Glaser

Wind

clatter of leaf on concrete
train horn
    commuting air
        distant
as owl call
    across canyon

fart of superannuated
    muffler
exhaust
the voices
    climbing metal stairs
        chatter of days
without direction

spiral of wind
    seen in matter
      dead leaf
carried, dropped
    dragged on concrete
        drawn

by mind
    breath
        threading
motes of dust
    microbes
all that has been
    and will be
into lungs
    tissue
        blood

the coursing
    of air
matter
no end

Kirk Glaser

L'Ortolan
The Gourmand's Last Supper

The last delicacy he ate, a small bird
fattened in the dark, drowned in armagnac
the lacework bones breaking inside his skull
cloistered beneath an embroidered cloth
to savor the aroma of his joy
and hide the featherless head singing
between his lips from god
as it fell to the plate
and its organs burst liquored fat
into his mouth, and he tasted the bird's life
nesting among Moroccan wheat,
the salt air of tumultuous flight
the sweet lavender seeds of France
trickling down his throat the juice
that propels him into the next life
where he walks on bones and feeds the cat
looking for home, no song in his heart

Kirk Glaser

First Rise
No one knows where and when this dew-like existence will drop into the grass.
—Dogen, "Regulations for the Auxiliary Cloud Hall"

Burn the bridge that led you
to abide days like an urn stuffed with ash.

Fist *if* from the ridge where
you polished its hateful shell

balanced there by will alone,
savoring the hell you made

of other people's wrongs.
Tip your hatful of false promises,

bid it farewell, stop climbing that
slippery mad slope you call life,

the pratfalls taken among primroses
for no one but your self

satisfied mouth filled with dust,
favoring pity's astringent petals

flavoring the path as you picked
yourself up, brushed off, beat the bush

looking for others to nod, a fellow
sufferer, a breast to cry on, no matter

no one else to blame, no beast but the slights
real or feigned, imagined over and over,

a mile-high rise from here to
where you thought to be.

So next trip while you're down
on the ground, don your eyes

and notice the drop of water
at the tip of the grass blade,

one of thousands whose stay
you never bade a thanks

for holding still in its perfect sphere,
uncaring wind or sun or stray leg disturb it.

Kirk Glaser

Shards

A bottle shard
washed up in the tide

edge that cut
              a man's throat
worn to a smooth   time   kiss
of current   water   seasons   a man

a file in a coroner's office
photo in attic box

a green light
              held to the eye
sun   high overhead

Kirk Glaser

Those Days

In those orange days delaying the unbelievable
from dragging its pitcher of fish down the street
and into the ladies restroom, in the slow paste
of the exact, single dimension hanging its cloud
over the glass nose of the dog, I would remember
the little yellow bird delaying its song until the cold
would shape itself into a chunk, a plate of ice
heavy as jade, sinking the thermometer close to the bone
when it would sing a single note, exact as a whisker
crouching on the rim of the fishbowl, a sound so violet
it would round the fish into a cluster, a slender knot of fish
hanging in their bowl in the shape of a woman's waist
slowly expanding, contracting, twirling in their invisible cage
of water, the absurd motionless air of the restroom so great,
so fine, so dimensioned to fin the unbelievable into a shape
pink and black and in those fine days ready to kill.

—*Remix of lines from "Hopskotch," Julio Cortázar*

Kirk Glaser

Book of Nights

Say you wake up lost in a decade
of life mangled in lover's blood and lies
you told yourself,
the only choice left to sit
staring at the self in its delicate burning
the silence eating away
at loss until nothing is left.

Say you wake up whispering the name
of the woman beside you
and the syllables make no sense, no matter
what order you say them,
so you try your own name and find
the tongue won't let go of your teeth.

You tell yourself it's over, trying it on.
The fit is bad, the sheer fabric
of nothing eats at the skin
on your shoulders where your daughter rode,
the sleeves make your fingers impossible to reach,
and when you pull the cloth across your chest
the lungs collapse in the folds,
no breath to be found.

You prefer the same old coat
with its holes grown big as galaxies emptied of stars.
This can be patched, you say to yourself,
or the holes hemmed into pockets
to catch the dust, to make new light.
But can you hold the needle
between nubs of bone, what remains of your fingers?
Is there thread enough left

to pull from your gut
to make the sutures required?

It doesn't matter, you tell yourself,
rummaging in pockets
for the knuckle bone you misplaced,
for that scrap of paper where you wrote a name
a phrase, sure of its meaning
wrapped around the stone of a fruit
whose roots you thought to fill your pockets,
whose branches would lace themselves in sky
to shade the two of you, whose leaves
would always speak both your names.

Kirk Glaser

Father / Time

ragged sheet-
   metal
   profile

of a man   edges
   eaten
      by time

      a hole
corrodes   outward
   from the chest

   where blood
     chews
   iron into self

the heart   beating
    to burn
    through

Kirk Glaser

Full Moon in Late Holocene Sky

reading Cavafy
    his ceaseless circling
    around longing
for what was and what never was

around the fear that today will be like yesterday
and yesterday just like tomorrow—
    a month of the same gray city
    inhabited here or elsewhere
no matter what ship or difficult road taken
to reach it
    the same high wall or closed window

or worse
        an open one
with its own tyranny of time and the possible

        solstice moon climbs   never rising
        as it scales granite and trees

        stepping up the ridge
        as if weighted down

        on its southernmost orbit of the year

        a light bisected by tree trunk
        bent oval by limbs

as if longing were ever an answer
for anything
    other than lament

as if he could hammer it with words
into a key
to unlock a gate past the fear
    that the same things will happen
    again and then happen again
piling boredom upon boulder of boredom
to the peak of Mount Monotony
    that has no peak, only an always rounder
    higher mound to clamber over

        the moon's arc
        is the mountain's arc

        drifting up   tangled in conifer
        as if unsteady   balloon

        blown toward the peak

        snagged by the spear
        of one last tree

as if longing and lament were real
and not merely what the mind conjures
out of human heaviness
inattentive to the ever-changing light
    inside each cell

as if the chandelier in the small empty room
burning with its sensual fever
    will go out
if not blown line after line
poem after poem

into flame of a day or a moment
   throughout a twenty-third year
possessed by the breath of an ancient
Greco-Syrian magician

        at last the moon   a globe
        to an eye
           hovering

        as if deciding
        to roll down the valley

        or launch   into sky

        as   of course
        it does

Kirk Glaser

Give Way

Trees give way to streets:
What kind of idea are you?

Who can say a word
does not have substance.

City makes a world
disappear, another come

in multitudes—bricks
and knives, glass

and guns and bread
flowers beside fruit,

borne by a few words:
ship, truck, want.

Kirk Glaser

Under Currents

When the body dies
does memory flicker out
like light   when the filament
breaks in a worn bulb

And suffering   does it cease
at life's close   or surge
like a current snapping
frayed strands   those who remain
holding the ends

What is suffering   but memory
caught in the spinning blades
a life that flickers
through hallways   rooms
                          Or is seized by what inhabits
to the last breath
                 the house   darkness that eats light
when it sputters out
        to feed a desperate flame

Kirk Glaser

Cremation

After fire and dust
    what is a life?
Memory and nothing,
    the past an urn on a shelf—
all compelled to walk the path
    through the cold ash forest,
sloughing the triumphs
    and ruins of a few years.

Against what we inherit
    is it enough to hold
our child, touch lips,
    dig hands into earth,
set them to work
    for pure sake of serving
moment upon moment?

Is it enough to sow
    into the slagheap
of the past and smother
    what reaches for us—
a seed, pyriscent,
    waiting in dry bone powder
for fire to crack the urn-shell,
    twist roots into the house
foundation, sprout fingers
    of a seared hand.

Enough to sate
    what eats at this world
flowering rust and ash?

Kirk Glaser

The Waiting Coil

The dirt yard at the end of the afternoon
breaks its light against the cinderblock house
shaded by mango and papaya, weed trees
under which kids play, chickens peck at crushed fruit.
We enter, hot and dry from the bus ride
to the outskirts of the city. In the narrow room
with its thin mattress on an iron cot,
the contortion of a boy forms in the dilating pupil,
knobs and bones, spine twisted and arched as if still
recoiling from what hit him before birth, neck and head
turned in opposition, straining to face what's next.
Frozen, he's half risen, he holds his hands
in his hands, fingers gripping.

The women—mother, aunts, neighbors maybe—
part and stand back while you and the other
therapists from *el otro lado* touch the body.
I see hope and magic in their eyes, as if in a hot
afternoon after siesta you can find the thread
to pull on this boy, unravel the twelve or thirteen
years of palsied growth, the daily feeding
and washing by female hands, the turning
of his hardened form relentless
except for cell building upon cell
like the grape vines growing against
the eaves of the house, pushing and pushing
until they have nearly destroyed themselves
in coils. A maze of dry muscle tensed
to baffle puberty. And then the intelligent eyes look
at me, the man in the room, appraising worth.

Kirk Glaser

Beyond the Temples
Palenque, Chiapas, Mexico

Hunched on the forest floor
in a clearing along the path
we eat our lunch, while under us
rhizomes multiply faster than
blood cells in our veins,
the soil pulsing as eggs break into larvae
and pupae writhe to become legs and wings,

and between our legs lizards crackle
from rotted logs dripping fungal fire.
Overhead vine leaves climb cell upon cell
to swallow trees, giants who erupt with red
and yellow and green
toucans and parrots, our ears filling

with their song and the hum flutter buzz
of insect wings and bird wings,
the rustle and drop and muffled cries
of creature on creature mating, hunting.

When a group of women and children appear
around the path's bend
climbing from their village,
the mothers' and grandmothers' brilliant geometries
embroidered on fields of black and white,
the forest's thousand greens patterned
in the molecular maps of tree leaf, root, mycelium,
of jaguar eye and monkey tooth
they carry through generations
on their shoulders and chests.

The children run up to us.
"¡Plumas!" they cry, hands outstretched.
"¿Tienen las plumas?"
Feathers sprout from my skull until
I look at my hand holding a stick pen
hovering over an open journal,
like some bone honed from a plastic bird
or the jade rods streaming from the ear lobes
of Pakal the Great's death mask.

I hand it to a boy and "¡Plumas!"
the others yell louder, crowding us.
"Nada mas," I say, lifting hands open
to the canopy. You give them yours
and still the cry for *mas plumas*,
knowing more must fledge
from these two alien beings.

Until the women call the children away
and continue uphill to the city
with bundles of babies and neatly folded cloth
and produce for market gathered on their backs,
leaning into the path, faces still,
eyes set with fatigue or wariness
or annoyance or whatever it might mean
to them, our sitting here in their forest
with our backpacks and lunches.

We watch them disappear, and I try to make
sense of the wild rush inside me the same
as the night I sat awake in prayer on Inyo Desert hilltop
and a kit fox circled me, sniffing closer and closer
until its nose brushed mine and I flinched
and it ran into its dark familiar night.

Kirk Glaser

Some days

to sit counting grains of sand,
piling them high to hide in their shadow

from the sweeping light and wind
of a thousand thousand years.

Other days to breathe skies filled with smoke,
forests billowing in and out of lungs,

and struggle still to find metta, an ember
of love in a cauldron of fear, send it

to the keepers of the land, the storytellers
who wade through blood and oil

to gather the words, the myths, the scattered
seeds and plant them, defiant, again and again.

Kirk Glaser

Glass-Bottom Self
—While sitting *adhittana* at Dhamma Mahavana

In a boat on a river, a boy can't get past legs,
the adults and big kids who huddle
around the glass bottom feeding their eyes
on the colorful fish, a world floating below,
their laughter and look-a-theres that he wants.

His grandmother takes his hand
and leads him to the stern,
pulls a tissue from her shiny black purse,
tears bits to let him drop over the side,
their white sails scudding away in the boat's wake
under canopy of greens, bits of cloud
like the big ones billowing in blue above.

> I could say "I," but that boy
> is not *the present, only an elusive reality*
> *moving from an unreal future*
> *to an unreal past.*

All those legs he could not push past,
bones in boxes now, ashes on shelves or scattered
over water, a mountainside by those who held dearly
a flow of consciousness flickering in form.

Grandmother, mother, father, all the Ever-
glades plowed, paved, turned to tract homes,
suffering salt intrusion from rising seas.

A flotilla of paper strips caught in a neural net,
dissolved in no time,
a thought that arises, drifts across the mind
to disappear again.

There is no thought, only thinking.

Paper, once tree, pulped from a southern forest,
old growth or second growth,
now measured rows of renewable forest product.

> *A complete description of a thing requires,*
> *besides its analysis, a statement*
> *of its relations to other things.*

There is no boy, only boying
up in memory,
> *a subterranean flow of being*
> *originating in past action,*
> *surfacing unexpectedly*
> *by the influence of circumstances*
> *favorable or obstructive.*

My brother's still alive, would he remember this?
Or would his simple big-kid joy gazing through the glass bottom
make it forgettable?

If I say *he* of *me*, what am I missing
about the nature of the mind mining this memory,
this sankhara uprooted from store consciousness.

> *Just as neither the same nor another is reborn,*
> *no identity exists moment to moment,*
> *yet to dissolve is not to disappear.*
> *Thoughts and feelings combine each moment,*
> *others conditioned to appear under favorable*
> *circumstances later. Thus the life stream perseveres.*

Bits of white paper on green water growing smaller
and smaller in a child's mind's eye, disappearing
in the distance, until no more are dropped to follow.

Notes
Adhittana (Pali): strong determination
Sankhara (Pali): psychic formations that shape identity
Store Consciousness: all the memories/feelings/reactions of a life stored within oneself–roughly the "unconscious"

Passages in italics (most paraphrased) from *Abhidhamma Studies: Buddhist Explorations of Consciousness and Time*, Fifth Edition, Venerable Nyanaponika Thera, Boston: Wisdom Publications, 2010 (First edition 1949).

Kirk Glaser

Mud Pond by the Dharma Hall
Summer Solstice

The clouds that spilled themselves
over the banks all winter filled the pond,
living out their nature to be not cloud.

There is no purpose in suffering
yet it has its reasons for arising.
The mama bullfrog floats head up, eyes open,

in the brown June waters, done casting
her sheets of jelly specked with ellipses
become commas become tadpoles.

They dart into the murk when I sit
on the bank and grow still. The surface
of things, while in the space between each breath

every particle in my body arises and disappears
more times than there are stars in the galaxy.
Soon one tadpole, then another, drifts up

like a thought from a cloudy mind,
their fat oblong heads tilting skyward,
tiny legs dangling from the base of translucent tails.

Some touch lips to the surface
and sip on air, gills gone.
In another month the pond will be mud.

How many have become a dragonfly's wing,
scale of a snake, a feather on the turkey hen
who each afternoon sips and pecks at pond's edge?

The nature of suffering in the order
of conditioned things becoming each other
differs from the ill being created by complex minds

devising LLCs to hide landlords across state lines,
behind laws where the savviest lawyers
can't sniff them out. Half a month's wages

from the single mother with two children, three jobs,
for the two rooms whose ceiling sags with mold,
or the vet on disabilities who can't hold a job

because of a severed hand stuck behind his eye,
the bloody holes of faces visiting each night
while rats scramble behind his ears.

The tadpoles' tiny mouths send ripples
spreading the breadth of their home
to disappear at water's edge. A few,

metamorphosis complete, may find their way
to the big pond before this one inches itself
into clay and air. Will memory pull them

back if clouds fill the hole another winter
in their becoming not cloud? This little pond,
its surface reflecting a single oak and sky,

image of peace for a mind considering
how calm creates a basin for muddy memory,
for desire and fear to seep in, fill with suffering

that storms the body, thundering for response,
desperate not to surrender its home. But if no reaction
comes, turns to mist, nothing to cling to.

My butt begins to hurt, flesh on rock apparent reality not yet escaped. I stand. Tadpoles scatter. A flycatcher drops to take a bath.

Kirk Glaser

Physics of Stillness

Stare at the mountain until it arrives
at sense door of eyes no more
a dream of clear skies in my

time doesn't tick anymore, not much
anyway in a digital age, a hum as it curves
over gravity, trapped like us

by large bodies, history
I pray my daughter to escape
not make, then why did I ever imagine

to outwait the cicada screaming
invisible on the manzanita
before I move to scratch

my bites, bobbing my head
to hunt its form like a poorly designed bird
sitting in the dirt, only the tick

of madrone skin splitting in the heat
sheets of it falling on my head
I want the music so

I and it, cicada, might connect
identity desire scanning the body
for silence, the physical hum of atoms

in the cells tissues skin where
is it really zero at the bone
or zeros and ones or ATGC

and so on distracted by information
the mountain heaves again
in particles of sunlight sharing

this experience should have
at least taught me my notions
of external progress a trap

of my time in its laws
that bend bodies to grave
misbegotten will in the name of

the name of, what was it
motionless clinging to the branch
the smooth skin

the breath that saves me,
that makes love and time
and good luck of location

and others' suffering
through progress for me to be
father to a daughter open

Kirk Glaser

After the Years

My hand at rest
on your hip
as we drift to sleep

hand that raised iron
to sky dropping
all day unaware

of itself as it talked
to rock cracked and opened
into veins the soft

flesh pulse under your skin
proximal to these bones
humming articulate sensation

until after the first fall
and rise through sleep
when we turn into

ourselves for the night never
alone with you now
after we came so close

in the distal reaches of
day after day forgetting
the who, the why, the want

I hunkered down
in the blunt radius
of walls grooved for silence

while you tore at the face
tracing veins
looking for a way out

when really it was in
to turn and the I
needed to crack

both of us compelled
to suffer the red
flow molten to meet

here under the surf
breaking against cliffs
a mile away

rolling through sleep
up into the opening of
you beneath my hand

Kirk Glaser

Irritant in the Solution

Falling asleep   the slip past
another day walled
in fire's husk
a question floats
why believe   a life any more
than a shining pebble
    batted about the sea?

A pearl   ill-formed   luminous
knocks against tidal cliffs
of the brain's vault
pale glow   in night ocean
drifting behind eyes

It batters against
smooth walls   clamped shut
the inner surface
of the self   rough shell
    locked to rougher shoals.

Let go and drift
    through dream   time
tap against   another life
dare to crack
open and swell   flesh
to taste   salt-sweet
flesh   pearls spilling
from adjacent beds
into the current
no choice   but trust and love
no joy
but to share all that time
will carry away

The pearl that endures
flesh and shell   born of irritant
made into shining
seed carried   life to life
the chance
to be perfected again

When the land   breathes fire
ocean tides tug
    the pearl
homeward

Patrick Sylvain

Tracy K. Smith

Patrick Sylvain's poems teem with time: memory and history mark distances across which these poem's stretch, gathering up moments past and people now gone, into dialogue with the present. Nothing is lost; nothing and no one is ever fully surrendered. Poetry becomes a site where histories both collective and private can be regathered, remembered, revisited and tended from an intimate distance. The distance of a whisper or an embrace.

Indeed, much of the investment across these wide-ranging poems has to do with creating the terms for an intimate engagement with the past. Why? Because we continue to live with the past. It shapes us. We continue to bathe in its wake. When Sylvain writes, in "Your Songs," his seven-line elegy to Haitian singer-songwriter Manno Charlemagne, "you croon to the stars a soothing song / that begs the gods to end people's misery," I am reminded that every poem may be an act of (or a prayer for) intercession. Often, I get the feeling that it is we—the poet and readers together—who are being urged to intercede on our own or others' behalf.

Language—which brings us into the presence of people and places so vulnerable we ache to protect them—is at once a refuge from the forms of inattention and disregard in which we too often operate, and the element in which we might articulate alternatives to our ongoing history of loss. "Poets, sing your burden: the page can bear / any load," Sylvain writes in "Holy Words," an *ars poetica* whose speaker "reject[s] collusion with silence." In these poems, words bear witness to unspeakable brutality and acts of harrowing resistance. Words attest to the losses we "survive with stammering tongues." And in Sylvain's poetics of activism, words do their work across the realms of conscience, conscious awareness, and imagination. The result is a body of poems equipped to fuel our vocabulary for possibility, for intervention, and also chastening us for the moments when words, and people, fail. I'm thinking, in particular, of "A Night of Injustice," Sylvain's poems of poignant empathy for Abner Louima, the Haitian American victim of wanton police brutality in 1991, and the image of "A unit / of stars streak[ing] by, wailing."

Sylvain's poems invite a gathering. He calls out in solidarity to fellow poets, like Seamus Heaney and Yusef Komunyakaa, and also to the unnamed subjects of photos by Manuel Alvarez Bravo. "The Feel of Earth" articulates a deep yearning for home: "I to go outside and find chickadees" and "droplets on dark green blades of grass." From his current life, the poem's speaker longs back toward Haiti, the place ardently alive even in the conscience of poems rooted in the United States—poems like "A Night of Injustice" and "Boston Capitol Steps, 1987." Yet here, the poem does not seek the register of collective history; it wants a visceral return to the sensory world of the speaker's childhood home. It is a wish to move across space, yes, but also—and perhaps more so—to be at home across a range of realms.

As the social conscience in Sylvain's most searing poems reminds us, death and loss are inevitabilities brought ever nearer by the human drives for power, and power over others. Unjust policing. The tyranny of colonialism. War. Even the visual gaze by which another's body can be framed and momentarily claimed. Life—human life—is too often about *taking*. Perhaps this is why Sylvain's brief lyric "Granular Descent" determines to contemplate simple contentment and joy in life on the earth: "We should…lick each other's lips, / fill our lungs with shared breath." Yet like so many of Sylvain's poems, the plenitude here remains aware of the inevitable counterpoint of mortality. Perhaps this is why the poem is launched with the conditional statement "We should"—as if the greedy delicious joy of love in a garden, and beloveds who "fill [their] lungs with shared breath" must inevitably be tempered by the inescapable awareness that we descend from and return to "the birthing earth." Quietly poignant, the poem affirms the blessing of love while also asking us to imagine the distance between the here-and-now we humans make, and the Eden that should be.

These are the poems of a poet awake to the world, and willing to sing of what may yet be.

Patrick Sylvain

Invocation

If you could sit underneath a cotton-silk wood
and grill a snapper to the bones, you would.

If you could summon God to help you swat flies
from the parched, begging mouths, you would.

If you could chase dandelions with a brush
and paint the reposing sun, you would.

If you could smooth out dreams of refugees
against the tides of slicking tycoons, you would.

But, the imagination flaps and falls.
Leaving incessant waves slapping rocks.

An uplifting voice breaks out: "Yes, you can do it."
You close your eyes and glide.

Only, the blue skies turned into burnt lilies,
the mockingbirds become deafening sirens.

You string your prayers, like kites, and fly them
to the stratosphere, vacant. Shock, you remove your shoes,

and descend into the waiting room of believers
enduring a cacophony of wishes and dictates.

Then, you spot a French dictator whose scissor-like hands
you avoid shaking. Your eyes scan the room-filled with flesh-traders

flipping verses, you try to remember history as you watch
flippant redeemers pastorate with the Conquistadors' swords.

You close your eyes trying to switch channels, frantic.
But the flame of the burning monk forces you to pray.

Patrick Sylvain

The Magic of Rhythm
for YK, RP, ME,

I will study you,
Angiograph your arteries
Of imagination like talking drums.
Drum-talking my syllables to
The apex of cortices, until ears bleed
Their stubbornness to foreign rhythms—
Since there are no calabash trees in Amherst,
And you—never saw a moor—
Not even the sea, then you will misread
My temperamental waves that gush
Agonies like moaning whales.

You, rhythmic master, you make sparrows
Dance on naked branches. You, canvas
Painter, heighten the blues of blue jays
And the reds of cardinals. In the pale
Light of gloomy nights, you induce clarity.
I will study by rote the murmur of your breathing
As I unpack the cadence of a tailored sorcerer.
In this land of Bishop, Dickinson, and Frost
I will not be a *scarecrow in a shawl.*

I was not baptized by a bishop,
And no deacons ushered in my pulse.
My tropical land is absent of frost.
Green leaves are nutrients for hawk moths.
And in the foliage of synonyms,
I want to be a new leaf, potent, consumable.
I've learned, the rhythm of this land
Does not echo in calabash gourds,
But glides on harp strings—hybrid lines, I am.
My rhythm, like the *kora*, will be a new breath,

A fusion of hearts and lungs until the body no longer
Sustains the flaming fluids of external arteries.
Then, like a *Jali*, I will walk into the sunlight
Far away from decrepit ghosts, pluck my strings
In ostinato riffs, and dance my genealogy.

Patrick Sylvain

Cantor of the Irish Spring
in memory of Seamus Heaney 1939–2013

With keen, incisive sight, you witnessed limbs
Torn from their roots as elements countered
The Crown, and the pecking orders of crows.
You crossed yourself, knowing the long, searing
Sufferings of the Celts—robbed, split over crossed-bars,
Boundary lines, imported crucifixes; however small—
Soldiering a splintered identity,
A way of cupping, cuffing the land.

Your mind 'was its own bull-pen'.
Your tongue ploughed the land,
Tilting and harvesting unified syllables,
A state, a mind, a state of mind, a multi-vocal
Irishness that silences spiteful nozzles, muddles through
Your incessant drinking from the brain's rain, a reign.

You entered a chorus of departed poets,
Their tongues permanently lit for recitals
To the gods. Lucid images and lingering sounds
Planted permanent pews inside us. Language remains
A host for our inexhaustible communion. We praised
Your rhythm of rain through a canopy of poignant syllables.

No starched flag, nor barbwire
governed your tongue. You wintered out
the old snows that cracked fertile land,
And with your plough-like pen, you dug for verdant
Earth as you squared your lines into ameliorative spaces
Of the *field of force*. Commodious poet,
Herculean earthman who libated with raindrops,
And comforted Ireland with your tending plough.

Poetry was your religion; you became
A liniment of a poet—constant and astute.
You became a touchable and luminous garden spirit.
You entered history unswaying, unwavering
Leaving us a language of fresh mint.

Patrick Sylvain

Boston Capitol Steps, 1987
in memory of Antoine Thurel

Somewhere in this ancient town, you stepped
From a bath smelling of coconuts and limes.
Your 56-year-old body—the age my father was
In the fall of 1986—earthly black and smooth,
Concealing the pain from numerous Boston winters.
Over the years, you smugly stepped onto Beacon.

Preoccupied with work and an eventual return
To your troubled land, you were troubled by the states
And its beacon—an eagle that refuses to share
Earth's bounties. You decided to be the sun
On the footsteps of the Capitol where Charles
Sumner's 1871 Haitian Medal of Freedom hung.

You too desired freedom, a permanent summer
Filled with azaleas, hibiscus, bread, and shoe-wearing
Children running with flamboyant, paper-thin kites,
Unburdened by the desires of Southern planters and hog
Farmers. Buffered by colonnades and cigar-smoking barons,
Dragging history. Tanks crushing fruit-stalls. Burning dreams.

When your knees touched concrete shortly before
Seven in the morning, your fingers were determined
Not to roll rosary beads, but to unscrew the can and
Perfume the air with the essence of industry. Ignited,
Flames flared 20 feet as commuters implored for mercy.
Your burnt body engraved the crumpled granite steps.

Patrick Sylvain

A Night of Injustice
for Abner Louima

In the pre-dawn of humid August heat,
lovers and strangers danced slowly
on an unbuffed wooden floor. Bodies
tightly held, defying light in the dim room.
Hands embraced backs, buttocks,
passion inducing grooves.
Perhaps someone got jealous, grabbed,
or slapped somebody else's lover.
A brawl broke out, no guns, just swinging fists.

The music stopped, panic-filled screams
boomeranged. A hand dialed 911.
Puffing officers in dark blue,
stormed through Rendezvous Night Club,
where Haitian immigrants gathered
to dance under Phantom's honey-thick
tropical rhythm. Black backs met
discriminating billy clubs frantically swinging.

More officers rushed out of wailing cars,
brandishing Nines and shotguns. Brooklyn's
Flatbush Avenue became intoxicated
by the frenzied footsteps of the city's
Gestapos with rhinoceros-like strength.
Even the saints stopped marching to gather
their unshed tears in prayer. A unit
of stars streaked by, wailing.

When Abner Louima, a thin, dark-skinned
security guard, tried to reason, his ribs were greeted
with breath-stopping jabs. Handcuffed, head-locked,
canopies of black migrant bodies, canned.

Blood-stained, had Abner known the reputation
of badged uniforms, he would have avoided Officer
Volpe the way he sidestepped Duvalier's bogeymen—
dream predators, ecstased by others' torment.

Behind the prison wall of a Brooklyn precinct,
Volpe concocted a sadistic game of Sodomy.
Inebriated by frenzied rhythms of kicks and
punches, freedom waited with an axe.
They danced around his limp molested body,
Abner's dignity flushed in a polyrhythm of groans.
His life hung on a thread of luck, threads,
hundreds of yards to stitch him back to life.
The world stared as justice was lost for words.

Patrick Sylvain

Existing

In the cardinal points of belonging,
royal robes draped over the Atlantic,
archipelagoes became aristocratic underpants.
Slovenly calicos for field hands
laboring arduously in the tropics.

In the cardinal points of belonging,
tongues waxed to reflect the dictum of dominion.
French, a lingua franca of guilt.
Buffed tongues alienated from
the playground of kinship, over-enunciating.

In the cardinal points of belonging,
skins French fried in plantations' skillets.
Millions seasoned, sizzled until nouns drowned
in cauldrons. Molasses coated descendants' tongues,
too heavy to accentuate the unforgiving "U".

We are naked in the cardinal points of belonging,
conquest is a violent intimacy.
Fragmented beings praised at the Eiffel Tower,
forgetting the grammars of overcast humiliation,
the syllabi of plantations, drowning nations.

In the cardinal points of belonging,
machetes and swords swung against
the dictum of dominion, but the scarlet of royal
robes only bled anger. Garroting autonomy,
millions survive with stammering tongues.

Patrick Sylvain

A Curtain of Grief
for Alee

Gold may be eternal, pure, and flexible,
yet not a stubborn, loathsome heart.
The lamp of youth will dimly itself
to the battling wind as unmet desires
and loneliness seep into weary arteries.

Hopes decay beneath winter's harsh realities:
an empty bed, neglected skin, and a solo purse
struggling to meet marital obligations.
How long would a bridge endure
under a seismic and mournful wind?

A curtain of grief veils your cornea,
forgetting that bridges are built for crossing.
It's not a sin to self-exile when your vowed
monarch brings stone-crushing dreams.
Freedom is a noble word.

Despite chisels and the care given,
some stones resist sculpting. Your art
can still be crafted, but not with that medium.
Flaky yet stubborn. Seize your tools
and follow the alleviating light across the bridge.

Patrick Sylvain

Different Sphere

Tonight, memories are like an army
Of wasps in my head, droning the past
With fragmented wings. I crave sleep.

I want to transpose you into a different
Tense, a present, an ought, a being here.
I want to free your shadow from the "there."

The timeless there. The other world, there.
Your world is too immense for me, time
Never ceases to end. A sleepless realm.

I crave dreaming of pelicans, of egrets
Perched on cows' backs, of children
Cartwheeling into the warm Caribbean

Sea. See, my mind is restless.
A rushing wind brings you with folded
arms, looking over me as if I were a ledger,

measuring my modest progress.
When I merrily look up, you smile.
Your face fades into my own mirror.

Patrick Sylvain

Dancing Ghost

It's 1969, you awaken in a small village near Saigon.
Sounds of jazz crawling through the cracks of dawn,
A trombone's wail embracing your skin.

There is a bed for two made of packed straw,
Where dreams dance with whiskey and smoke.
Your body exudes a hymn of weariness.

Outside, there's a river of rain,
Each drop plays its own rhythm
As if conducting a symphony of your longing.

You feel like a small man, already wasted at 21,
Lost in a maze not of your own making,
Yet the music whispers promises of redemption.

Your memories of home drowned in bottles,
But Coltrane's saxophone lingers on your tongue,
A bittersweet melody of nights gone by.

A young Vietnamese woman in purple underwear,
Her eyes, two constellations of empathy,
Watch over you, makes you feel human.

In her gaze, the moon gleams like a dancing ghost.
A flicker of grace that reaches your soul,
She embraces the beauty in your brokenness.

She offers a hand, a lifeline to salvation,
And in her touch—the slow tapping notes of her fingers—
You see your dormant trumpet demanding your song.

Patrick Sylvain

Daydream in Sepia

It is 1931 in Mexico City, behind the Cathedral,
in the heart of a tenement where Manuel Álvarez Bravo
captures you, a dreaming teenage girl who leans
on wrought iron railings as if lost in a deep sepia dream.

Beige or yellow grubby dress, thick black stockings
tightly hug your dancer-like legs, your right foot
barely resting on the bottom railing. Your shapely
curves, touched by mid-day sun, are hiding secrets.

Regardless of my epoch, and where I'm writing this poem,
your time is still 1931, and you're still young. Álvarez Bravo
saw a stunning, pensive being, as I see you though his camera's
eyes. You hold the softness of your face: symmetric, unrouged.

Your torso tilts out, as if timidly yearning
for a better future, or for a desired merchandise.
Head bowed with a world-weary grace. Eyes downward,
left hand cupping your cheek in contemplation.

Thick braids frame your face like a curtain,
like two dark coiling cobras inspecting
the courtyard below where a treacherous boy
is perhaps playing soccer or kicking it with another girl.

Behind you, bathed in soft sunlight, lace nets
gently flutter, a French window opens to other dreams.
Invisible contemplations intertwine there,
like gleaming threads in a vibrant moonbeam.

The railings are not bars to your prison, but a steadfast
reminder of your boundaries where hopes are confined.
Yet in you, as I bring you close, a daydream is stirring,
as your hungry eyes ponder the world and its marvels.

Patrick Sylvain

Guardians of Sleep
based on Manuel Álvarez Bravo's 1938 photograph,
Good Reputation Lies Sleeping

1
Out there, in the nourishing sunlight,
that bathes your body, deepening
the brown of your yellowish skin
like a slightly ripened corn. *El Sol,*
that your ancestors worshipped and built
pyramids to, traces the contours of your firm
and youthful body. The world's learned gazes
have an existential and aesthetic debate
over Manuel Álvarez Bravo's composition of you:
bandaged thighs, smooth lower belly pristine
in partial white wrappings. Your "good reputation"
is mocked by your exposed breasts and sex.

2
As you lie there on top of a hand-woven
multicolored mat, I wonder if you really care
about surrealism or how André Breton
will talk about the meaning of your hanged
man-like repose: eyes closed, right leg folded,
left arm behind your head, and left leg outstretched.
Four Mexican *abrojos*—spiny cactus, avocado-sized,
stand guard like erect spikes poised for protection.

3
I wonder if André Breton would inquire
about your name and where you're from!?
Would you simply be known as the girl
who lies sleeping? Would you become another
Maria with a "good reputation?" No, a pristine
one. One whose body earned global adoration

like the other sanctified Marias who brought
grown and powerful men to their knees, praying.

4
You're probably dead by now, but the photograph
of you is immortal, youthful, timelessly guarded
by the four erect spikes *abrojos* that vowed
to lethally pierce any realist, structuralist,
Dadaist, or surrealist who might try to experiment
on you the way some of their ancestors, perhaps,
violated the sacred reputations of young *Aztecas*.
Let them dare touch you—your protected milk
thistles will teach them an anaphylaxis kind-of-love,
persistent and deep, each spine an allergic memory.
They will call you a *bruja*, a witch for warding off evil.

5
Out there, in the nourishing sunlight,
that bathes your body, your bandaged ankles
hold a story woven in the dance of Anna Sokolow's feet,
bound and bruised in demanding rehearsals.
Your supple and yet muscular body is not a surrealist
project. Surrealism, here, takes root in arid soil,
mocking its European birthright. Manuel Álvarez Bravo
displays you in a landscape where dreams sprout
from cactus and sand, where the sun's relentless gaze
reveals the harshness and beauty of life, of light,
of darkness where purity and vulnerability coexist.
With eyes closed, wrapped in contradictions, perhaps
you are dreaming of meeting André Breton, this curious
French writer and philosopher who might see your body
as a landscape of desire. But, you'll gently offer him
an *abrojos*' thorn of your supple truth. Unbandaged.

Patrick Sylvain

The Feel of Earth

We're already a few days into winter,
yet the weather lingers, mid-fall, low 50s.
So far, the days are gentle on my skin.

In this early morning of silence, I sit with
my strongly brewed dark-roasted coffee. There is
a drip from the sink, and the refrigerator's recurrent
low whir hums like a distant crop plane.

The windows are closed. A soft morning sunlight
filters through the naked cherry blossom tree.
I want to go outside to find chickadees.

My coffee still warms my hands; no crowing
roosters in these parts of the world. I long
for the scent of warm earth, damp with dew—
Self-contained droplets on dark green blades of grass.

I miss my childhood home. I miss the hawking
chants of banana and avocado vendors announcing
the morning along with pigeons' and doves' cooing.

Here I am, in my adult home, where my last son
was born, feeling like a stranger. I cherish this place,
I cherish my life, but it isn't where I was born.
This patch of earth feels cold and absent of roosters.

Patrick Sylvain

Holy Words

Words return to us when the mind
finds peace, no longer restless, no longer
seeking to find a lost or displaced key.

Words don't perish; they pause.
Humans may fade, but memories blossom
among the living. Fluttering. I crave
to be showered in words, to float within them.

I yearn to persist like fresh springs
beneath bamboos, where wild grass
perfumes the air. I am intoxicated,

watching egrets gracefully glide. I yearn
for wings to soar above this earthly realm,
unlike Lazarus, who emerged from the dead.

I ponder, can one be struck by stray words,
fall lifeless on the spot? There's a gang
of syntax on the prowl. I am loaded.
I reject collusion with silence.

I am not a holy zombie. I want to ascend,
to fly, to rise into the pages of history,
to converse with necro-masters who turned nations
into zombies. I desire to nurture words.

Feed them to the dead so they may possess
language when they finally rise.
I do not desire phantom mouths for them.
Phantom belongs to the opera.

Poets, sing your burdens; the page can bear
any load. There is no gravity. There are graves.
Graves hold departed poets, but their words are not
piled in forsaken cemeteries. I long to ascend.

Patrick Sylvain

Granular Descent

We should drink Shiraz
beneath our garden's spruce,
lick each other's lips,
fill our lungs with shared breath,
remain drunk until
we descend in fine granular form
into the birthing earth.

Desant Granilè

Nou ta dwe bwè Shiraz
Nan jaden nou anba pye episeyas,
niche bouch lòt,
ranpli poumon nou ak souf pataje,
rete bwè jiskaske
nou desann nan fòm granilè mens
nan tè natal nou.

Patrick Sylvain

Your Songs
for Manno Charlemagne (1948–2017)

You have said that you've grown tired of snow,
the crunching sound beneath your boots, and
still, you were shocked by the coldness of the state.

Your true being belongs in the tropics,
where waves sing with each tilt of the moon,
and you croon to the stars a soothing song
that begs the gods to end people's misery.

Chante Ou Yo
pour Manno Charlemagne (1948–2017)

Ou te di ke ou te fatige ak lanèj,
son k'ap krèpkrèp anba bòt ou, anplis
ou te toujou choke ak fwadisman leta a.

Esans nanm ou kache nan zòn twopikal,
kote vag lanmè chante ak chak panche lalin,
epi ou chante pou zetwal yon chante kalma
ki sipliye lwa yo pou mete fen ak mizè pèp la.

Michael Franco

Songs of the Harper
from A Book of Measure V *iii*

i
Every detail begins

    to tremble

The death of a Tree

the daily cup cracked in a short fall
to a wooden floor
coffee spilled in reaching for it

The Older cat picking up
a cold   sneezes from sleep
and circling once
keeps his place there
on his antique chair
from where great
forests and vast
flocks of birds and a random squirrel are pursued
in dreamy stealth

But xpectation is not delivery and sound is but host to a certain yearning
that returns on its own Season—an off rime in
 a line of continuing enchantments (I sing Oh I still sing still
call you—should I say beckon and welcome the intrusion of
the archaic—where
As if leads and jostles with hints of what could or should it
cling to had it the strength had it the will of an arriving curve)
and I do still
I do as I once
first did and still in quiet

from all that was all that it is or that remains
  take Heart and sit now remembering the absolute
of its invitation to just stand up and wander down or up to
where ever it is or was I thought you were and join you there
 in Song in or out of tune and time
       the continual of any rime
  is a season   is the whole of any reason
to return or remain.
And I return   I remain
here   where I am your follower
your companion
your friend
your son and daughter in the Work at work
that so sweetly so unrelentingly
 surrounds us

In returning each step steps each echo echoes
beneath a growing weight that accompanies or awaits
the continuous line of arrival we are

the mysterious

clings to us so close
intimately it would seem that
it can not in this plain sight be seen

and so then in its
  obscurity   clearly
like magick or memory guides
the now from far or near silence
as it steps again or again steps
to return to where it thought it was
but now with a gentle stumble is.

The far can not recall the near and the near
can fall back and back again into only
the now.
The boundary I once thought to cross remains

over there
where it all along was

Michael Franco

Songs of the Harper ii
[Small Song]
for Tri & Joth and Vesper Maya

so many so often look to the far shore
of all the over theres always seeing or attempting to see
all the possible that lingers just out of sight
across the sea of today tomorrow and the next
though the always fog
beyond reach beyond beyond
calling   it seems calling us out toward
   some day
 in an endless series
of when
so that the news of today
clear and ridding the sound of leaves answering wind
that turns and fetches through all the 4 directions–
goes without notice
arrives without a look up
or around
and is suddenly   it seems
 there
in your arms
turning in a twist turn wiggle toward what
you just can't Know but turning just the same
to reach up or out in an amazement of just being amazed
Let this
carry the now three of you then
even as you cling tight to each other you are
all moving
flowing   in Now
   are   a small creek or river which it is doesn't matter
but movement is your constant
 your
Evening Star

Michael Franco

Songs of the Harper iii

constant
 and Source and meandering river that carries me
back to my self reflected in reflecting.
 all surface and knowing
  clouded and general and yet even
that too rippled from off-stage or
 leaf fall alighting in mute announcement
of Here.

I float on
in thought
s felled and true to a wind that spins
the compass needle again
to come home
I ride on random cling to the same and repeat.

Michael Franco

Songs of the Harper iv
[Small Song for Susana and Cornelia]

Plainsong and angel chorus and a light
angled and moving to full
across the wood floor of my kitchen
city chicken roosters nearby and a new neighbor fox
perks & sits head cocked
to listen
backing trucks beep
and flutter dove wings
to mild alarm
gust of wind moving now south to north west
with the thought of back quick forgotten
in its rush
thrush or sparrow
patient wait
to flit and alight
soft   soft
on a wire
calling the old song
as all things do now
call
the old songs to sing
again anew

*

we   are   abroad in the light
that catches up with us from behind

Michael Franco

Small Song
for Teresa Salgueiro

The day
my son was born
  I was
for the first time
handed a compass

 True North
is
an always Direction
even
 as the needle spins

*

sufficiently sufficient is perhaps enough

*

By the quick leaves falling brought
the seemingly firm concrete to a rest of sorts
feet shuffling to equal freedom
from future's looming presence by the by
transfigured beyond mute or withheld utterance
music performs performance of or swirls in landing
rests and marked silence blossoming there
ahead of everything riding a cut in the air's former warmth
that attempts again and again again caress
that fumbles all acquisition with portents
that clear and wind their way
towards true
 fall

Michael Franco

Songs of the Harper v

With the skill of the archer   each
harp string sings
   Release   By the Harper's hand released
reaching to pluck from silence
    the sound it seeks
   it searches for in that   Place that is always reaching
to touch the tumble of Song's quick
step away
as if the Heart had let go its beat
into the air
only to follow it
up up and there to where itself
in silence

again

rests

Michael Franco

Songs of the Harper vi

As in Music
all the in-between comes to matter

in silence

anticipation resting from   what is to come
the moment
that
 in pausing calls what just happened
to task.
  there   task thy maids and exercise the loom Homer says

and I would
    bring the end to the middle & let it twine and twist
its way toward
what   seems

one

looming alone

before harmony's embrace
slips in to remind that the Harper
is not   alone

the Harp was there
before
calling to the hesitant hand
to take it up and
join in

the lone voice too often
remarks its loneness as
a loon in constant
taking flight
calls the Air to come
 and take it up

OR   take me there in clarity transfixed and resolute
in wanting to see
that grace resides on the everywhere shores
that surround me
   instruct me
in Being
even as they announce the continual of tides
that ebb and flow as tides do ebb and flow and I
am somewhere that is nowhere
that is sure in foot or purpose
but I have danced along clumsy and awkward in
my joy of wet feet
and sandy knees
and pure and clean not knowing swung 'round
on the long xtended fingers of so
wanting to

Michael Franco

Songs of the Harper vii

For now   I Pull for the far shore
   and linger   as I do

a hesitation that slips time
   —tries to store it away
despite what I know
of the oar dip the trail of individual drops of water
the surface swirl
 behind
all
disappearing in the wake of where I am
I Pull   for the far shore
the slip of water against my oar
my music my sound track
and more and more my Guide
who schools me daily in the
  overthere
as I attempt a meander
to ignore the current
that in elegant silence
propels me from below

The water is quick and still and this instructs me
The air is hot and cut deep with cold and
this   instructs me
Each oar dip negotiates a circumference that does not linger
in the images it spins
and this too
articulate   mute   designed
begins direction
calls the rhythm
tells me "look There where you are you were
and are again and will be"

and that
*it is all
moving liquid and absolute
in its bright and gathering fetch
across such stillness

I Pull for the far shore
what else
am I to do in this
 terror of delights

*

Rain in the dark and a far light from a window divided
by wind and branch
and this thought

———
dearly bright the labyrinth turns
at a penny-each clip
of time decorated events
and startling snow accumulating absence
which each   command their
own again another turn
into the expected un
expected closure that
opens   breath taking airs that lyric vistas
toward now bare oak branches
that twine into
snow bearing evergreen
to locate and
release and again
for good measure   still
   beneath stars and
the cinch of boot on small coarse-white

and you can follow this
to where you are
turning
 to every season

before you

the 4 directions are

 held
in the one compass
   you hold

Michael Franco

Songs of the Harper viii

Just as a matter turned
to dance on Spring's
dark branch bobbing
with bird weight,   pending
leaf swell on still north wind
  fetching   thought
forward and back folded
upon a self in constant
movement layered in
layering formed and
left to precarious perch
far too high for old
comfort's waiting
ways to anchor   a
   way home
to begin

Michael Franco

Songs of the Harper ix
[The Harper Pauses at the River's Edge]

Everywhere and all enlightened in
what ends slips slowly slips then
falls if only but never far or far
enough for beyond but lingering just
   there   just   within
without
recalls   all
the careless moments that
refine remorse   collect into a period
now complete in its sentence of
   never
ending in the near

bright   purpose
of a firmly

plucked string

*

    Called

is without command

a release

to follow   alone

the concert Mistress   stands &

calls the Key

Sends to the approaching

Air an intention

that answers her in repeating
     in tone searching
   for what She herself released–

   Calls   that recall

in breath and resonant string

    search

    just beyond reaching

held & let go and held

    again   in common

All   before the Playing

    now

begin

*

random and various

   an   answering

  tone

in reluctant custody

sashays in the would-be

   airs   itself

in ribbon twist intention

     Whitman-like & as

       There

  as air

departing to an everywhere

  & all at once
     silent

in name only

A small bird in a
large tree

looks down

I quietly walk beneath it.

The dirt path compacted

A stray weed

blooms

Orders

   so you start

    perhaps trip

   it is after
all a Journey
so you start
and a relief of sorts
comes up on what had been
an originally flat
but lately crowded and contoured map
and the various figures
on it become late or tenuous or vibrant
vessels carrying
    now

Everything
forward and
beyond that
needless Place called
Boundary which is
but isn't and this

   vessel
whom I am now watching pass
will carry this world that
    I know

all its habit and assumption
quirks and dramas

far into a future   where

Everything that I am
will not
and yet will

reside

*

The Border is sealed
and yet I will escape

but will not now or then know

This isn't what the Border Guard told you
but it is indeed what he meant
at least what she meant to tell you
that you from brightness
forgot to hear
or tell us too

that the Word who was your companion
sent you back
but you forgot
forgot to return or
to tell us but
called to us you did
to see
in the bright morning or was it to hear in the Song
that fear   the true
un meddlesome one
that carries us
in rime's arrival
forward or returning

is a warm and continuous companion

whose song sings true

before it takes flight

the night   a morning
brings first light

A few and seamless sustaining
paths beneath the strong lines
and recessed shadows of Empire
sailing above me

How many arrivals until a life
rains down from itself
onto a dry day

rising   (does it
   it is   after all
unseen so it may   be
that it takes
from the air what
would   be flight   to
escape on a rain
as a message   a scent   sent
to us to take in take up
   allow   absorb

spreading cell to cell

  in blossoming announcement
of any day in August
any the august day

  defining a flow
from still memory
     a   hot and humid
still

of Virginia   tidewater   1960

to just now   also past

chasing

*

 The secrets are

not spoken of

by anyone   deserving

to speak them

    Silence   articulates

   its Self   with sound's
surrounding   landscape

itself silent   without

bird call   sun rise
color flick of cardinal
just   over there

   rat!
scurrying in old dry leaves

to reach his nest–

smoke twists of
air rising from
studio wood stove

climbs an M

   mountainous   against
the mounting
soundings—

which the Mountains
   (stretched North to South & out across the
Landscape from Time's
articulate alphabet)

and the 4 directions

  draw from

  in deep late day

    breaths that bring certain and specific clarity

    which all said secrets see through

or pass through on their way

back   to silence

Michael Franco

Songs of the Harper x

But it is an Ocean and from it all the mermaids singing are
our children and their music too which they Sing they Sing
those songs that
are our hours that float in time's remorseless current
back to our ever stopped ears that Listen still in stillness waiting
on the shore of our murmuring former Selves that glisten
in a dew and spray collected that awaits
a day a tide a full sun rounding and chasing the fog
back into its attempts at night

with calls that leave us tempt us relieve us
in our recall

we   Hear   you there in The Far

welcome you Home

our songs

   now so sweetly
   as you set out on your own

return

Tuesday 26th december 2023
430pm
& again for Fran. for hers of the25th

The claim is always
 Golden & Beyond

knowing what is
generally so accessible   to Know

& at that   a would-be illumination
but only and no more   than a
position scurrying to a pose that
in looking
 down
acquires a height

just to look back from

  along the way and

     beyond

light skip toward forever
begins to seem a return
of some kind of familiar

     a new   old place

   that greets
an aroma stretched to filling

the air   the senses
and so a life echoing

in thought   returning
or scampering merrily
beyond

collecting

*

The measure is long
nights and
quick days

*

So then Everything Sings?

   or at least seems to

Ice crackling off roof

 low bending branch
of hemlock 's thump of snow onto snow

   cat chirp from his
observation window

   birds outside
like wise in a random
chatter clattering
at full feeder

   huge isolate Cardinal
signal chirps alerts
from same hemlock

    Water from heat sing-whirls around perimeter of
house
younger cat stretches
and trills from folds of a down comforter

Winter   Aria
 that moves as mercury
as I think

the mumbling lines from a stone's plunge into still pond
coming to mind

a grand   pin point

circumference of everything

   Everything   everywhere

*

The Commerce of an early rising
before even the cat's attendance
to this spring sun

a line of light across the floor
admitted entrance
through a conspiracy of window
hemlock and the outside
into this house is
 a morning compass
come True to seasoned North
in residence at
the end of a shoe
or the stretched arch of a waiting cat

Yet   what Poem
          is not erasure
what form functions
but to enclose every
word a sudden
barrier   to a flood
of being flowing out of recall

      recalls   Play
as when children we would build

dams and diversions
against a projected flow
arriving
in our releasing of it

*

residence to a notorious
branding of sympathies

    reticent to launch
or return   In faith

I search for sight's sound
in small places
of brilliance
   not   mine
   nor mind
but light none-the-less

illumined   itself

and consumed in bright
longing   that

  there –just there
will sketch in the recalcitrant
 dust just as here
in my house
a geologic architecture as good
as any–   that carefully
   unnoticed
in marks   makes silent

accumulation

Time's   movement

   which
       (as always when
        we aren't looking
settles

into
a Poetry
collecting

around us

The Harper reaching
for the new string to string

is the intention

A broken string sings
but quietly

resounds its thought in clear difference

listening
in its wrapt coil to what has and will

have resonance

*

freshly transfigured
& encamped to ward

the Luminous
earth is a river

as the river is an Earth
that flows on
and through in the illusion
of beginning to end which
neither offers nor illustrates
in its never returning return
of ever changing coordinates
that reside in perpetual
skimdance across its surface–
that
in its very refusal of form
delights in its guidance
instructs impermanence the
knowledge of which
is only a rumor

is
Love

*

all then and now

the water that flows

all the earth it carries carried

    all the swirling along
moving
toward morning
and every night it flows
and as it does an earth
of mud a river of mud
laying mute
beneath all that deep clear water
flows

above where
mud
runs thick

and settles

RECORSO

Well—that was then and this this is now and now is mercury and light and fire and my dear cat curled to my right before the wood stove december outside in full sun and near everything now teetering on the edge of something else but animate near all things now are and delightfully and disturbingly so. We come loose like water starting slow before a flow certain and specific wells in place to carry everything up and away. Today is yesterday as yesterday's today is laced with accumulations of debris and silt that settles to await what follows behind. Building what Now that can be claimed or made to hesitate before it too lets go magnificently joyful lets go.

    Curious then how Time serves us calls us allures all thought with a jostle or sure wind—a direction here or there turning and returning to remind confront or caress All of it an old Song or a new tune caught up and carried into the path of Habit's clear crystalline comforts.

Colors: Intersecting Paths

Hoyt Rogers

To accompany my contribution to this issue, *spoKe* has requested a preface of three or four pages. Though I don't often write about my own work, I'll take this is as an opportunity to surprise myself, by detecting some unsuspected, internal gears. These poems are among the first in an ongoing verse-cycle, Colors, which already comprises fifty segments. They posit the existence of an intersectional, non-binary, feminist, multiethnic, environmentalist, Hispanic-Caribbean artist who composes ekphrastic poems about her/his/their own artworks, and then "paints" over them with digital hues. In that version, they appear with contrasting text and background colors, which can be altered ad libitum, or revert—as here, at the editor's behest—to black and white. To some degree, the verse sequence runs parallel to a gallery of prose poems shaped like rectangular paintings; these "word-scapes," under the title *Canvases*, were recently published as an online chapbook by Mudlark. They can be viewed at https://mudlark.domains.unf.edu/chaps/mudlark78/rogers-cover.html

In that instance, the editor chose to reproduce the variegated shades; accordingly, the polychrome potential of *Colors* can be sampled in the twenty-four panels of *Canvases*.

The similarities between the two series go beyond the superficial aspect—though as David Hockney reminds us, "in a picture, surface is also depth." The underlying themes mimic each other as well, beginning precisely with the play between surface and depth, conveyed by such painterly tricks as blurring, perspective, odd juxtapositions, partial figures, and reflections of the unseen. The final poem in the prose series (in its black and white variant) combines a number of these elements:

> Why collect more experience? Linear, sequential: a raging thirst, a hunger never satisfied. Images, you pullulate through every pore: overflowing, inexhaustible. You stream from bursts of radiance, millions of miles from here. You walk us to the horizon of all events, the gates of singularity, where the spectrum begins again. When you lust for me, I'm an envelope, and your letter says: Whose? Through painting, surfaces bloom

in unattainable desire—as a halo, an effulgence that pierces every appearance. Branches, a trellis, a porch, a mote of dust grant us this paradox: the unseen blue, reflected by a window, merges with the pane itself. As we pause, what we overlooked adopts another name—or none at all. The familiar stage-set, in our watchfulness, has already flowered. Standing at the door, I'm opened by what I open, seen by what I see. The future, turning back on itself, dazzles me. Reds, blues, yellows. Colors, mirrors, blanks. Absences, I am you.

The larger point-size is needed here to maintain the rectangular contours. Readers of André du Bouchet, whom I have translated at length, will recognize a fleeting homage to his ekphrastic oeuvre. Both the verse-cycle and the prose poems are connected to passages in my forthcoming novel, *Midnight at Sea*, the second volume of *The Caribbean Trilogy* (the first, *Sailing to Noon*, has already been issued by Spuyten Duyvil Press). One of the main characters in *Midnight at Sea* is a painter named Virgilio, who lucubrates in visual blocks; sometimes he executes his conceptions, but often they're merely suspended in his mind, like the canvas cited above. In addition to his own artworks, he evokes plates from the *Taíno Codex*, an indigenous manuscript from the early sixteenth century. In that apocryphal tome, one of the last Native Americans of a Caribbean island has created a codex like the Aztec and Inca exemplars, with pictorial panes scattered throughout the text. This is how Virgilio depicts one set of illustrations, about the arrival of the Spanish conquerors:

> I was only a child when the Caribs
> raided our village, killing all the men.
> They came from the Other Great Earth,
> a land to the south we left long ago.
> One of them took my mother as a wife.
> The marauders stole all they wanted
> and settled among us, fattened
> by our yucca, iguanas, and fish.
> Here I stand, in this blue-colored pane
> of our only book, our painted tomb.
> I'm keeping watch at the top
> of a cliff along our coast.
> I scan the horizon: I see

that something far stranger
will happen to us now.

       Below me to the right a mirage has appeared,
     the most outlandish of all the cohoba pipe-dreams.
     Not slender dugouts, but wide, square houses
     tugged by clouds, puffing with labored breath
     across the waves. I tremble from head to toe:
       these must be the airships of the gods.
     As in our ancient tales, they have returned
       to conquer the world, to wrest it back
        from the feeble hands of mankind.
         Are they good spirits, or bad?
   Their vessels creep forward, ungainly as manatees.
   These are not travelers from the Other Great Earth,
     but aliens, whose powers we can't conceive.

    In the next panel I quake even more—I lose
    my foothold, almost tipping over the ledge.
     I blast a warning with my conch,
      though I've already guessed
      that this time, there's no reprieve.
 These are not our Carib cousins, lashed by murderous rage;
     these are harbingers of our final doom,
     for all of us who wash in Atabey's streams.
   Lunging along the central pane, as shadowy as night,
   I race down the path to the bottom of the cliff.
   I reach the village just as the ships are drawing near,
     their bobbing heads of cloth saying yes
this is the place, yes we will crush you, yes we will enslave you,
   yes we will hound you till the hour of your death.

Again, I have converted the multicolored original into black and white. In all genres—whether narrative, prose poetry, or verse—I am exploring how an artwork can generate an ekphrastic "word-scape," only to pivot back to the optical plane once again. In *Canvases*, the pictorial rectangles almost detach themselves from the character named Virgilio, though his sensibility still informs them. In *Colors*, the verses are much more centered and compact, as if to hone the cryptic lines into a blade. They mean to show various ways of slicing through experience, permitting each cut to expose a fresh cross-section of the real. Besides the non-binary gender of the speaker(s), a motif unto itself, throughout the cycle there are recurring gestures towards stagecraft, the

Taino, the tropics, Caravaggio and other artists, ecological degradation, painting techniques, plants and animals, everyday life in the barrio, European vignettes, family "values," the nature of memory, and above all, the seduction of the image. Only a picture has the capacity to draw us in, to expand our vision, to freeze the music of time, to remove us from ourselves—and in the process, to turn us into ghosts.

Among the leitmotifs above, theater heads the list. Despite Romantic appeals to "sincerity," all writing is basically an act, as Shakespeare proves in sonnet after sonnet, play after play. In his intimate diaries, Baudelaire sums up art in a single word: "prostitution"; enticing illusions signify more than sentimental realism. In our time, what we might call "literary cosplay"—donning other identities for narrative or poetic ends—has become a highly fraught pursuit, given our justified distrust of "appropriation." In my novels, as in my poems, I have channeled dozens of disparate voices, cultivating an inner dissonance. On a questionnaire not long ago, I was asked for my gender, my ethnicity, my age; but I left the spaces blank. I grew up in a multivalent world, and I thrive on ambiguity—like most of us today. As to the sex assigned at birth, the response might be a mistake or a caprice, for all we know; as to genetics, there are too many factors to count; as to chronology, some body parts age faster than others. In the realm of the imagination, there might be endless answers to the simplest questions, responses that wobble with each passing mood.

In the all-important matter of "appropriation," we have to interrogate who is appropriating whom, and to what ends. The hall of mirrors can be exceedingly complex; it can verge on a self-denying labyrinth. This comes home to us in *Appropriate* (intended as both adjective and verb), a brilliant play by an African-American about a family of déclassé whites in the American South, squabbling over the legacy of a country estate. The playwright, Branden Jacobs-Jenkins, deliberately disregards the speech patterns and behavior "appropriate" to his subjects; he "appropriates" his personae into a historical nightmare, where all their words and acts are fundamentally "inappropriate"—from their origins in the slave economy to the climactic collapse of the "big house." Pointedly, he omits the black supernumeraries who routinely adorn such a drama, in the guise of a stoic or recalcitrant "staff." The corrosive spirit of Lars von Trier's *Manderlay* looms magisterially over this raging, tragicomic, foul-mouthed agon, a microcosm of these United States.

In spinning my tales and poems, I hew to a more understated strategy, though it also tends toward subversion. I steadily consult

Hispanic-Caribbean, European, and American friends, to gauge whether the dialects, attitudes, and reactions of my characters are credible, at least. Besides the ins and outs of idioms and regional identity, I also map the byways of gender; here too, I often send my manuscripts to representatives of various bents. Goethe maintained that a male author has to be partly female to write about women—and presumably, vice-versa. In his book on Genet, Sartre dissects sexuality as a parabola of possibilities, where each person lands somewhere along the arc. But what if the spectrum shifts from moment to moment, iridescent rather than fixed? And what if this applies to language and ethnicity, too? These are topics I often debate with my current interlocutors: the aforementioned Virgilio, and the ever-present Artemisia. In undertaking *The Caribbean Trilogy*, and its offshoots like *Canvases* and *Colors*, I have been "possessed" not only by the painter, but also by a meta-fictional persona: a Sicilian travel journalist and devotee of meditation retreats. Artemisia's notes, which she and I discuss in long inner dialogues, are the foundation of everything else.

Like the inhabitants of Canuba, our composite Caribbean enclave, Artemisia was raised on an island known for its folkways and quirks of speech. Because of education, employment, and sheer rebelliousness, she left her native Sicily early on. Over the decades, she has adapted to many languages and cultures around the globe. Her universalism persuades her that any foreigner can grasp her birthplace as she does: from the inside. Utopia, dystopia, or both at once, she gladly gifts it to others—all the more freely, since for her it subsists in an unredeemable past. With equal honesty, she faces the dilemma from the other side, as a resident of Canuba. How can Caribbeans like Virgilio incarnate a place they've disowned? How can they save their Atlantis from the tourist tsunami? How can they reclaim "their" island, when even their memories are mostly myths? Of the many uprooted souls I have encountered over the years, Artemisia alone has sailed beyond the "untold want" of a permanent home, greeting each successive harbor as her Ithaca. But by incurring so many displacements, by enduring the pains of so many rebirths, she has only made her nostalgia more acute: it has become a yearning for nowhere. This is what John Crowe Ransom calls "a cry of absence, absence in the heart."

In the end, Artemisia is the (relatively) female side and Virgilio the (relatively) male side of a dyad. Whether expressed as travel or art, their journey through the rush of images culminates in the creative void, perversely understood as a vacant stage that rings with presence. As I've listened to their urgent, questing voices, I've wondered whether such concepts as the "other" and "othering" might be amplified. In any given group, aren't outlying members the "others" in relation to the nucleus? And doesn't that core sometimes implode, so that the excluded become the included? Both Artemisia and Virgilio have revolted against the patriarchy, the family, and the Church. Polysexual nonconformists, they are "othered" within their own societies. Their "mother tongues" have devolved into a delta of interlacing idioms. Could this be "the way we live now," culturally as well as linguistically? More than a two-lane street, tolerance may be a multi-vectored thoroughfare. We often forget that to the "other," we are the "other," too. Temperamentally, the warring forces within our own personalities "other" all the rest. We will never know each other fully. But do we even know ourselves?

I seem to have strayed far afield from the topic of colors. No, I would contend: quite the opposite. Returning to Goethe, it has often been observed that his *Farbenlehre* (or *Theory of Colors*, though Lehre implies a "teaching") is more a treatise on the psychology of hues than a challenge to Newtonian optics. In one of his final works, *Bermerkungen über die Farben* (Remarks on Colors), Wittgenstein analyzes the self-contradictions that proliferate in the very words we use to designate the shades of the spectrum, and which extend even to "colorless" terms like black and white. Similarly, biology tells us that there is no such thing as a single ethnic lineage: we all derive from a convergence of myriad strains, no matter how our secondary features, such as skin-color, may have turned out. Thanks to constant mingling through immigration and exchange, our cultural strands are as intertwined as our genes. If divergent narratives can coexist, and prose poems can be refracted into verse, perhaps "otherness," "appropriation," and "intersectionality" can be energized through a fusion of clashing ontologies. Such an experiment, so problematic in our daily life, can only be conducted—uniting a sequence of words, a collage of colors, a span of pages, a gallery of canvases—in the cyclotron of art.

Hoyt Rogers

Canvas

Why collect more experience?
From now on, the canvas is blank.
World, you look through me;
both of us are lucid, translucid.
For everything, there is a style.
My skin unpeels, like yours:
this is the pneumatic style.
Still, we both give pleasure.
How can I deserve you?
World, I see through you.
How can you desert me?
I hold all this in mind.

Hoyt Rogers

Maker

Colors: a question of mood.
In barrios, the guys get upset.
Hey Factora, hey screwball.
You're a crazy pendeja.
Don't you talk to my wife.
Don't put ideas in her head.
I just laugh: Felicidades.
Congratulations, friends.
Factora is my nickname:
the maker, the hacedora.
Our memories already lie.
The future waits to act.
A wave rises and falls.
For now, this is the crest.
Tree, shadow, scattered leaves.
Yes, someday, maybe, no.
The even wind of images.
Indigo darkens to black.

Hoyt Rogers

Words

You believe my fantasy:
for you, I draw a bogus plant.
You flower from the root;
your stamens are strong as bones.
"The Queen of the comedians."
All right, I'll watch your show.
Afraid I won't laugh? That's rich:
I'm not your usual customer.
Paint-spotted clothes, frizzy hair.
I own a diary I never keep.
I hate the be-alls, the end-alls.
Let's paint the air with air.
You and I are happier than words.

Hoyt Rogers

Whales

Today, I'm an insurgence,
a wolf that howls on ice.
Rabbit-blood flecks the snow;
it shimmers, white and serene.
Suddenly, our tea goes tropical:
water jives for the jungle cat.
Bubbles mouth round syllables.
Pronouns assume different views,
but we, I, you strongly connect.
Our cabin looks out on huge rocks;
they loll on the sea like humpbacks.
I walk on the shores you've walked.
We roll underwater with the whales.
We surface, resurface, and sound.
Our nights are one and the same.

Hoyt Rogers

Banderoles

Banderoles, I live by you.
Black, brown, green, blue.
Tell me what you want:
measure out my patterns, my hues.
Thanks to you, I have no choice.
Tigers with orange stripes
will set the towns ablaze.
White air corrodes to gray.
Azure curdles to algae blooms;
to sargasso corpses, stacked on sand.
"The end of the world as we know it."
No one ever asks: Do we know it?

Hoyt Rogers

Postcard

Sunlight on a lakeside wall…
children work in this brothel.
Some might call it a "family."
Farmed out, forced to submit,
their rights explicitly minor.
"Parents" crush them like vises.
No wonder they follow the piper;
off they shuffle, locked into vaults.
All I'm painting is a postcard.
Early wine that spills on the floor:
pressed out, raving like blood.

Hoyt Rogers

Map

No burden from the overload …
"It will all sort out in the end."
Some have trouble with that maxim:
think they're dolphins, bone china,
a cloud by day and a fire by night.
Pumpkins, there ain't no grammar.
Your orders are: lose command.
You're a wind-rose, indeterminate.
Lie back, like a map of the world,
nibbled by termites and mice:
a living map of imperfection.

Dome

Colors: a helmet, a mosaic.
Why not? "A stained-glass dome."
Gardens are canvases, schools.
Casual, joking, "whatever,"
"lo que sea," "gimme a break,"
like us chicos at the Colegio,
under the jacaranda trees. But
the ocean rolls outside our door.
Moonlight rains on our heads:
our platinum path to emptiness.
The media streams won't help us.
Distance splinters our bones.
Time tilts against us. Just as we
will be forgotten, let's forget.

Hoyt Rogers

Mirror

"Grey matters" are stubborn:
we count on life less than art.
Welcome to heaven and hell.
At daybreak, colors ferment;
vireos drown each other out—
till silenced by a downpour.
I panic when shapes dissolve.
No, first I want to seize them.
Terrified, I look inside the mirror.
Space is flat, until I'm saved:
perspective cleverly deepens;
the image performs its trick.

Hoyt Rogers

Unseeable

The skyscape, is it remote?
Blue clouds obscure the moon;
stars spin, a spokeless wheel.
We're seeing the unseeable.
The landscape, is it near?
A flamboyant tree, a brackish pond…
Orange blooms, stamens like yolks:
they reflect in the blackness below.
A breeze stirs the twigs;
they dance with the wind:
one step forward, one step back.
The leaves, the flowers fall.
I paint only the trunk.
Arrested, etched, redeemed.

Hoyt Rogers

Shaman

A shaman now, I build my fire.
Streaks of yellow bar my breasts;
I wear the bohique's feather-cloak.
I'm the woman who sees far off.
I smoke the cohoba: Areito, begin!
I plunge with a red-tailed hawk;
we mate on a mountain range of clouds.
I change, change, and change again.
I voyage through jaguars, swimming tapirs—
through boas, through dreaming sloths.
I return to the Other Great Earth.

Hoyt Rogers

Photographs

Will you come to me soon?
Dead lovers bind me to the air;
our voices wander down broken streets.
Like mists, we head for dusky fields:
shadows, always summoning,
though not always to an end…
Spirals of enclosure, disclosure;
photographs of vanished skin:
faces, begging for a future.
This is not a time we want to lose.
Hands reach up from the waves.
Find a raft to receive them—
a hallowed, secret place.

Hoyt Rogers

Children

Children love colors.
The robin's breast is red.
The blue rabbit comes unsewn.
The grey soldier has one leg.
The swans want purple shirts.
The snow-bear sleeps in jail.
Diving, I inspect corals from the past.
Their hues have turned to bone;
knuckles and wrists litter the shore.
In the long run, there's no reprieve.
What I'm losing, I'd better give up.
I swim above dying grasses;
their fingers brush my chest.

Hoyt Rogers

Nebulae

In Venice, I recall our phantom fish;
our canals, limpid till we muddied them.
Day is falling flat, upending the lagoon.
A violet haze resets the clouds.
Lamps click on, an afterglow:
stage-lights for our memories.
This theatre gave us birth.
Our boats glide on, to other ports.
Stone facades shiver like fictions—
no longer hang us out to dry.
Our pelts tatter into constellations:
Virgo, Orion, who remembers?
Nebulae ... lavender, rose, powder blue,
dimming, soon unseen.

Hoyt Rogers

Pages

Pages mumble through the night:
children's books I reread in my dreams.
Primary colors, corners torn.
A blue crane, a green tree.
A red hat, a yellow mare.
Other horses sidle to the creek:
roan, piebald, sorrel, dun,
surprised to be remembered.
They glance at me with mild,
bloodshot eyes, before they drink.
A wildfire flays my limbs.
Branches curl in the wind.
Umber leaves swirl upward,
half dryness, half smoke.
Runaway time hurtles by:
its pistons bellow and spark;
its cinders greet mine in mid-air.

Ron Padgett

September Song

It is indeed strange that music appeared behind these words in the
    autumn of 1959,
as if the igloo and the Eskimo had suddenly appeared at the same
    moment in history,
and there were magazines
that told you how to write a poem or a story
and then "place" it in other magazines and be paid for it.
In the envelope was a dollar bill from ... *Scimitar and Song?*
It was really there.
The leaves fell like the tail ends of two-by-fours cut off by a hand
    saw.
It makes a music that is both Satie and at the same time bigger,
like igloo and Eskimo
but with no wooden clunks.
But now the day—or what we *call* the day—has begun,
that is, again, that is, in 1959, and I fall into it.

PROSE

The Alchemist of Language and Ideas: On Several of Herman Melville's Novels and Travel Writings

Peter Valente

In Herman Melville's novels, *Pierre or The Ambiguities* and *The Confidence Man*, as in several of his tales as well is in his journal, he is concerned with diverse subjects such as the nature of the artist, the idea of the spiritual against the idea of materialism, and sexuality, and in his travels, he displays his insight into various non-Western cultures, and shows that his view of the world was essentially democratic. Through an examination of some of Melville's lesser popular novels I aim to show that they are in many ways more interesting and relevant to our present times than *Moby Dick*, as great as that novel is. This consideration of Melville's work took place during a period of several months when I read these works carefully and took many notes.

Melville's *Pierre or The Ambiguities* is a moral tale of the artist who would choose to pursue the spiritual path and the perilous journey he must make in doing so. Pierre's failure to reach the heights of spiritual knowledge and thus realize the full potential of his novel, is the major theme in the book. The source of the problem, according to Melville, is in the Christian idea of self-sacrifice:

> That in things terrestrial (horological) a man must not be governed by idea celestial (chronometrical), that certain minor self-renunciations in this life his own mere instinct for his own every-day general well-being will teach him to make, but he must by no means make a complete unconditional sacrifice of himself in behalf of any other being, or any other cause, or any conceit." This is because, "Our God is a jealous God. He wills not that any man should permanently possess the least shadow of His own self-sufficient attributes.

Pierre is the kind of artist who misunderstands the difference between the terrestrial and the celestial, and thus feels he must renounce humanity in order to achieve the heights of spiritual knowledge. It is the Faustian trap. Thomas Mann's *Doctor Faustus* also deals with the similar theme of the artist at war with the world, and more recently Pierre Guyotat's *Coma* also deals with this Catholic problem: Pierre [in Melville's novel] is wrong in thinking that he can feed the spirit by starving the body. He locks himself in a cold room, refuses to eat on a regular basis, obsesses over his unfinished novel (which gets rejected by a horrified publisher!) that deals with ideas he is too young to understand. It is about the artist who attempts to reach beyond the limits of human knowledge, to cross the abyss in order to find out what is on the other side. In doing so, the artist, like Lucifer, falls to earth, punished for attempting to access the knowledge of God.

Like, Hamlet, Pierre is confronted with an impossible choice, but in acting out, he does not fully understand the consequences. Melville quotes Hamlet in the novel: "The time is out of joint; Oh cursed spite, / That ever I was born to set it right." In setting things right, he destroys the two women, Lucy and Isabel, who are in his orbit, gets disowned by his family, and commits a murder. And yet, it is exactly this curious bent of Pierre's mind, the result of an unstable temperament, and his not fully understanding nature of the mystical ideas he is obsessed about, that causes him to be unable to embody his ideas in ethical action; the problem is not the spiritual ideas but Pierre's approach to achieving such knowledge : "Know this that while many a consumptive dietarian has but produced the merest literary flatulencies to the world, convivial authors have alike given utterance to the sublimest wisdom, and created the least gross and most ethereal forms." Furthermore, it is crucial that Pierre fails to realize the nature of speculative knowledge in his search: "it is only the miraculous vanity of man which ever persuades him, that even for the most richly gifted mind, there ever arrives an earthly period, where it can truly say to itself, I have come to the Ultimate of Human Speculative Knowledge, hereafter, at his present point I will abide. Sudden onsets of new truth will assail him, and overturn him as the Tartars did China, for there is no China Wall that man can build in his soul, which shall permanently stay the irruptions of those barbarous hordes which Truth ever nourishes in the loins of her frozen, yet teeming North, so that the Empire of Human Knowledge can never be lasting in any one dynasty, since Truth still gives new Emperors to the earth." Spiritual time is different from Terrestrial time. For Melville, when the soul descends in order to inhabit the body, it is imprisoned by the body, and no longer has full access to the celestial regions. But Pierre, because of the confusion of his mind, and because he is too young to understand the nature of mysticism, attempts to sacrifice his body in order to gain knowledge of God and to realize his potential as a novelist. In this respect, Lucy is an interesting character in the novel. Her experience of spiritual knowledge seems to not involve, as it does with Pierre, a rejection of the past, but an acceptance of the future. I often thought while reading the novel, that Lucy is an example of self-sacrifice that does not involve the renunciation of love and humanity.

Pierre is Melville's spiritual autobiography; in it, he satirizes the gothic novel, plays with narrative styles, and his language veers at times from sentimentality to philosophical speculation. Melville uses different narrative strategies. In this way, the novel is heterodox, "impure." Or rather, what critics like calling a "flawed" novel. But for all that, I think it is a novel of great power in tracing the anomaly of Pierre's mind, and the pitfalls of the spiritual journey for an artist. Bloom famously said about Pierre, "What was left of Melville's early audience was killed off by the dreadful Pierre, a year after *Moby-Dick*, and despite various modern salvage attempts, Pierre certainly is unreadable, in the old-fashioned sense of that now critically abused word. You just cannot get through it, unless you badly want and need to do so." I think instead that *Pierre* is one of Melville's masterpieces. It is a more forward-looking book than *Moby Dick*, great as that novel is, and it anticipates the complexities of postmodern fiction.

Another one of Melville's philosophical novels is *The Confidence-Man*. It is a diabolical book that produces more questions than it answers. Is the Confidence man an agent of the devil or God? Is he a single person, a trickster, who wears many masks, or numerous individuals playing the same confidence game? The ambiguities proliferate as the novel progresses. Can we believe in the goodness of man and have love for the world as a manifestation of God's plan? Or as the confidence man (the herb doctor) puts it, quoting 1 Thessalonians 5:21: "There is no mortal work, no cure of mine, / nor art's effect, but done by power divine." When discussing the nature of evil with his victim, the doctor assures him that "from evil comes good." So, in this case, as in many others, the confidence man employs the language of a Christian tempered by skepticism to con the victim. He is like a good Christian, or perhaps, a devil, because skepticism is not compatible with faith.

But to have confidence in your fellow man, to be charitable without a threat to the very nature of friendship, implies a kind of hope or faith. When explaining the nature of the herbs the doctor hopes to sell to his victim, he says that they cannot be known; he is similar to John Truman, another confidence-man, who, when explaining to his victim the kind of stocks he is about to sell him, he says they cannot be accurately explained, suggesting the complexities of the stock market are obscure to the common man. If we read confidence as faith or hope, then what they are really talking about is the nature of God. The herb doctor says: "Hope is proportioned to confidence. How much confidence you give me, so much hope do I give you." He speaks as a Catholic priest would. But what has become, asks Melville, of this faith in the materialist, post- industrial world? Has it degenerated into to a kind of business deal. And furthermore, can spirituality exist when it confronts the specter of materialism in a transactional world. Is love possible in capitalism? Or is it a hoax, a con.

For the cosmopolitan, a confidence-man and a Catholic, "Life is a pic-nic *en costume*; one must take a part, assume a character, stand ready in a sensible way to play the fool. To come in plain clothes, with a long face, as a wiseacre, only makes one a discomfort to himself, and a blot upon the scene." In one sense this echoes a theme in the book: taking a part, wearing a mask, willing to play the fool, willing to play the game. But in another sense, for the cosmopolitan, this requires a certain belief in the goodness of man. In the conversation about drunkenness and sobriety, in terms of the nature of truth, the misanthrope says that "since the too-sober view is doubtless, nearer true than the too-drunken; I, who rate truth, though cold water, above untruth, though Tokay, will stick to my earthen jug." This is the kind of good advice Pierre should have taken. The cosmopolitan ironically responds: "I see; you go in for the lofty." Satan remembers his fall from grace.

The truth of God is too obscure for the misanthrope, too "cold" in its remoteness from human warmth. But the cosmopolitan feels that misanthropy is born from the same root as disbelief of religion. Is what the cosmopolitan believes absolutely true? On the tombstone of China Aster, there is written about him that he exhibited, to his detriment "an ardently bright view of life, / to the exclusion / of / that counsel which comes by heeding / the opposite view." That is, he was too naïve, believing in the goodness of his fellow man, which led to his downfall. Perhaps he should have had a more sober view of human affairs, retained a certain skepticism, or listened to his friends, Old Plain Talk and Prudence. Egbert (Thoreau), a disciple of the writings of Charlie Winsome (Emerson), told the story about China Aster, and how his life was ruined by accepting a loan from a friend. For Egbert, man does not have a fixed self; he is like an actor on the stage who plays many parts, as Shakespeare so famously suggested. The Cosmopolitan wants to force Egbert to choose between confidence and suspicion. He cannot believe that trust is contingent on any other factors. But

Egbert refuses. The Catholic man sees in this a contradiction. But there is no contradiction if one believes, as Egbert does, that man has many different guises he wears in his relation to world; there is no fixed self. Egbert can say that man "was no poor drifting weed of the universe," that there was a kind of Divine Providence that watched over him, and also insist that man is changeable, with no fixed sense of himself but rather a participant in the masquerade. This is Melville's critique of Emerson and Thoreau.

Olson, in *Call me Ishmael*, writes on Melville's thought after The Confidence-Man, quoting the French poet, Maurice de Guérin: "There is more power and beauty in the well-kept secret of one's self and one's thoughts than in any display of a whole heaven that one may have inside one." For Melville, the notion that Christian actions are not possible in a worldly context, recurs in his novels. Olson goes on to say that Melville agreed with the statement of the French poet. In *The Confidence-Man*, the first confidence man that appears is mute. For Olson, this mute is Christ: Melville believed that one could not understand that which is incorruptible and invisible in terms of what is subject to decay and visible. The novel is a meditation on the difference between appearance and reality, trust and suspicion, what can be known and what cannot, spirituality in its relation to materialism. Melville had a profound need to belief; he struggled to accept a world without meaning. Hawthorne understood this when he wrote:

> Melville, as he always does, began to reason of Providence and futurity, and of everything that lies beyond human ken, and informed me that he had 'pretty much made up his mind to be annihilated'; but still he does not seem to rest in that anticipation, and, I think, will never rest until he gets hold of a definite belief. It is strange how he persists – and has persisted ever since I knew him, and probably long before – in wandering to and fro over these deserts, as dismal and monotonous as the sandhills amid which we were sitting. He can neither believe, nor be comfortable in his unbelief; and he is too honest and courageous not to try to do one or the other. If he were a religious man, he would be one of the most truly religious and reverential; he has a very high and noble nature and is better worth immortality than most of us.

The Confidence-Man ends with the Cosmopolitan leading the old man, subject of his con, away, while "the waning light expired." The last sentence in the novel is: "Something further may follow of this Masquerade." Melville ends the novel with an image of darkness. All the conversations between confidence man and victim have concluded and the stage is dark. We, as readers, realize we too have been conned; no questions we may have had have been answered. We are no closer to belief. The ambiguities have proliferated, erasing any sure sense we had of the world. We have become skeptical. Is love possible in capitalism?

As in *Pierre* and *The Confidence Man*, Melville's stories and novellas continue his themes about the nature of spiritually and materialism, and the idea of the solitary worker's despair in the age of capitalism, and in his final work, "Billy Budd, Sailor," he confronts the theme of sexuality. In "The Bell-Tower," Bannadonna desires to build a kind of magical bell tower, in which the various hours are represented by sculpted human figures. In this way, he seeks to usurp the power of the "Creator" and fashion a world on his own terms. In doing so, Bannadonna's harnesses mechanical power and Reason which have become gods in an industrial society: "With him, common sense was theurgy; machinery, miracle; Prometheus, the heroic name for machinist; man, the true God." In this way, he is different from both Pierre, consumed by his thoughts about religion and metaphysics and Ahab, whose monomania, like Pierre, drives him to reject humanity in his pursuit of Moby Dick. Melville's critique of an industrial world is also apparent in the story "The Tartarus of Maids," where he envisions a paper mill as a kind of hell in which girls have to work long hours for meagre pay. This is not the world depicted in *The Paradise of Bachelors*, where a man, after a fine dinner with friends can retire to bed, light a cigar, and read *The Decameron*. Contrasting the two, shows that Melville was aware of the problem of women's rights. Describing the world of the factory, Melville writes, "Not a syllable was heard but the low, steady, overruling hum of the iron animals. The human voice was banished from the spot. Machinery – that vaunted slave of humanity – here stood menially served by human beings, who served mutely and cringingly as the slave serves the Sultan. The girls did not so much seem accessory wheels to the general machinery as mere cogs to the wheels." The office space has replaced the factory but otherwise not much has changed!

In these stories, Melville also continues his critique of the Western, "civilized" man. The idea was made explicit in the scene in *Pierre* where he is seen working feverishly on his novel, his mind crammed with half-baked metaphysical notions, and having not eaten for days; for Melville, what is the use of Civilization, he writes, if it leads to figures like Pierre. Montaigne showed that all the philosophies about man and God have simply led to great confusion and no answers [in the *Apology for Raymond Sebond*]. In "Benito Cereno," Delano, for all his "good conscience" and general sense of himself as "good," is also capable of ugly racial stereotypes when he speaks of the docility of the slaves as an admirable quality that contributes to their "chatty" and "half-gamesome" terms, finally comparing "the negroes ... to Newfoundland dogs." In other words, bound only by their body's limits, they are incapable of abstract thoughts. Anthony Braxton has spoken about this racist attitude in connection with "swing," as if dancing to swing was the whole story of the music. Braxton's music is, instead, abstract, intellectual and thought-provoking. Think of the distance between swing and free improvisation. In "Benito Cereno," the slaves revolt. In the introduction to the stories, Peter Coviello notes that Thomas Jefferson, in 1776, voiced the opinion that that it is the duty and right of free peoples to commit revolutionary acts in the name of their freedom from oppression. One also recalls the regal nature of the harpooners Queequeg, Tashtego, and Daggoo, forced to submit to the whites, who are weaker, conflicted, anxiety-driven, greedy, and in the case of Ahab, monomaniacal.

The above tales, and their concern with racism and class, recalls a sketch from "The Encanntadas, or Enchanted Isles." In the sketch, Melville writes of a kind of free community on one of the deserted islands where "the insurgents had confederated themselves into a democracy neither Grecian, Roman, nor American. Nay, it was no democracy at all, but a permanent Riotacracy, which gloried in having no law but lawlessness." Here, outcasts, runaways, deserters from ships, and the poor would be accepted. In this kind of utopia, the Western ideas would be rejected as well as the law. It is a space where the Other can freely exist. It is an interesting passage in Melville that is not fully developed. Perhaps such a world was on Melville's mind when he wrote of fairy-land, that mystical and spiritual place that exists largely in one's mind in his late tale, "The Piazza": "How to get to fairy-land, by what road I did not know" but "to reach fairy-land, it must be voyaged to, and with faith." I'm reminded here of Captain Mission, an 18th-century pirate in Burroughs' *Cities of the Red Night* who was the leader of a kind of community of outcasts, whose articles stated: "all decisions with regard to the colony to be submitted to vote by the colonists; the abolition of slavery for any reason including debt; the abolition of the death penalty; and freedom to follow any religious beliefs or practices without sanction or molestation."

In "Bartelby the Scrivener," Bartelby rejects first the task of reviewing his work, and then eventually he refuses to do any work at all. This industrial world has made him, like the girls in The Tartarus of Maids, simply a cog in a machine, subservient to the master. The narrator slowly comes to realize, after fighting with his conscience, that he has an affection for Bartebly. Bartebly provoked this feeling in him by his own rejection of work (materialism) and silence. This is how some visionaries come to a realization of God, through negation and silence. But just as Claggart in "Billy Budd, Sailor" could have loved Billy but for "fate and ban," Bartelby can only communicate his feelings silently. There is a kind of mesmerism that is enacted on the narrator by Bartelby. Love cannot be expressed. In another sense, the story is about Melville's rejection of the conventional novel; he will create something unique and not the same as other novelists: "I have given up copying." Finally, the story shows what sadly happens to someone who does not play the game: poverty and death.

"Billy Budd, Sailor" is the masterpiece in this collection of tales. Gone is the biblical eloquence of *Moby Dick*; instead, the language is elliptical, infinitely subtle, with a rhythm that is slower paced and less propulsive. In this way, it shares more in common with the complex language of Pierre than anything previous in Melville's work. The tale is a complex story involving the fall of innocence: "Billy's agony, mainly proceeding from a generous young heart's virgin experience of the diabolical incarnate and effective in some men." He is a kind of Christ figure, dressed in white at his execution, his face, "an expression which was as a crucifixion to behold." It is about love that in being silenced turns to hate. "Billy Budd, Sailor" being the last of Melville's works, suggests that he was heading a new direction.

I'd like to close this essay with a discussion of the first of Herman Melville's three journals (1849–1850) which describes his trip to England and the Continent. This was essentially a business trip, where his primary objective was to see if he could secure a publisher for *White Jacket* in the UK since Harper and Row were going to publish it in America (Richard Bentley, the prestigious publisher, who had published *Mardi*, even at a considerable loss, and who had faith in Melville's work, would eventually publish *White Jacket*). In this journal we meet George Adler, a German metaphysical philosopher, who had created an English-German dictionary, whom Melville met on the Southhampton on his way to England. Melville spent much time with him after they arrived in England, and later in Paris, going to bars, museums, and travelling through the poverty-stricken streets, dangerous for the presence of thieves and other criminals; Melville also spent many hours in cafes and at dinners discussing German metaphysics, alone with Adler, and in the company of friends. About Adler's views on God, Melville writes: "His philosophy is Colredegian: he accepts the Scriptures as divine, & yet leaves himself free to inquire into Nature. He does not take it, that the Bible is absolutely infallible, & that anything opposed to it in Science must be wrong. He believes that there are things out of God and independent of him, – things that would have existed were there no God: – such as that two & two make four; for it is not that God so decrees mathematically, but that in the very nature of things, the fact is thus." I wonder what Melville would have thought of this way of thinking. I imagine he would have a problem with the vaguely materialist views of Adler and yet they were very close during this period.

On November 7th, 1849, Melville attended a farce called *A Practical Man* in London. The notes describe the subject of the farce: "Its object is to develop the peculiarities of a restless individual…whose brain is swelling with the biggest schemes, but is totally destitute of the decision requisite to carry them into execution.…" We do not know the extent to which Melville consulted the journals when he was writing his novels, and yet this description sounds vaguely like a plot from *Pierre*. Melville attended many dinners while in England. Some, that were casual and attended by his bachelor friends, remind us of the subject of his story, "The Paradise of Bachelors." Occasionally, the dinners to which he attended seem too formal which caused him to write in the journal: "Oh Conventionalism, what a ninny, thou art, to be sure." In his travels he also purchased many books. He notes that he procured an "old copy of Sir Thomas Browne" and a "nice edition of Boswell's *Johnson*."

The second journal (1856–57) was written during his trips to the Near East and the Continent. He travels to Istanbul, Egypt, Jerusalem, and Italy. While the first journal was largely notational, in this second journal we have some of Melville's extended descriptions of what he sees. Wandering the vast suburbs of Galatea, he remarks about the "faded splendor" of what he sees, the feeling of melancholy and the "tragic air of these streets." He views an Armenian funeral and a woman, leaning over the grave who says: "'Why don't you speak to me? My God! – Is it I! – Ah, speak – but one word! – All deaf – So much for consolation.' This woman & her cries haunt me horribly." Whether the words were Melville's own improvisation or not, or whether or Melville could have heard the woman, seems irrelevant; these words could have been Melville's own, as he struggled, like Pierre, with the growing absence of God in an increasingly materialistic world. In Cairo he remarks: "Flies on the eyes at noon. Nature feeding on man. Contiguity of desert & verdure, splendor & squalor, gloom & gayety; numerous blind me going about led. Children ophalmick. Too much light & no defense against it." When visiting the pyramids in Egypt, he writes that a "feeling of awe & terror came over me." And, furthermore, he conjectures that "it was in these pyramids that was conceived the idea of Jehovah … Moses learned in all the lore of the Egyptians." The pyramids are "something vast, indefinite, incomprehensible, and awful." And for Melville, the desert "is more fearful to look at than the ocean." Finally, he meditates on Art and its relation to nature:

> They must needs have been terrible inventors, those Egyptian wise men. And one seems to see that as out of the crude forms of the natural earth they could evoke by art the transcendent mass & symmetry & unity of the pyramid so out of the rude elements of the insignificant thoughts that are in all men, they could rear the transcendent conception of a God. But for no holy purpose was the pyramid founded.

In witnessing the vast, lifeless, deserts abounding in Jerusalem, he ponders that skeptical thoughts could be produced when attempting to envision the presence of Christ in such a vast wasteland. But he writes, "Heartily wish Niebur & Strauss to the dogs. The deuce take their penetration & acumen. They have robbed us of the bloom. If they have undeceived any one – no thanks to them. Pity that ecclesiastical countries [he is in Jerusalem] so little attractive by nature." In this passage, Melville is attacking Barthold Niebuhur (1776–1831) and Friedrich Strauss (1808–74), who in their writings, "dissected myth and tradition to determine their core of ordinary fact" and furthermore, criticized the Bible, arguing "that except for skeletal biographical facts, the Christ of the Four Gospels was the wishful product of messianic experience." Melville is critical of the scientific, positivist approach to religion. The increasing materialism that emerged after the industrial revolution, led to these increasingly critical views of Christianity based on science. George Adler's metaphysics were, in part, subject to these kinds of views. But one of the most interesting passages in this journal exhibits the democratic way in which Melville viewed Europe in relation to Asia while he was traveling on the Bosphorus in a steamer:

At 8 1/2 A.M took a steamer up the Bosphorus to Buyukdereh. – Magnificent! The whole scene one pomp of art & Nature. Europe & Asia here show their best. A challenge of contrasts, where by the successively alternate sweeps of the shores both sides seem to retire from every new proffer of beauty, again in some grand prudery to advance with a bolder bid, and thereupon again & again retiring, neither willing to retreat from the contest of beauty.

While in Naples, Melville travelled to Lake Avernus, the fabled entrance to the underworld in Virgil's *Aeneid*. He descends to the caves that were next to the lake and observes: "What in God's name were such places made for, & why? Surely man is a strange animal. Diving into the bowels of the earth rather than building up towards the sky. How clear an indication that he sought darkness rather than light." Throughout this journal Melville draws contrasts between light and darkness, gloom and splendor, verdure and the wasteland of the desert, life and death.

The final journal (1860) was written on a journey from Boston to San Francisco. The main event that occurs on this trip was the death of young man, "a good honest fellow (to judge from his face & demeanor during the passage)" who fell from the main topsail yard onto the deck. This leads Melville to meditate on the nature of death and how man copes with the loss of a loved one. He thinks of the boy's mother and her pain when she hears of her son's death. But Melville will finally realize, as is the nature of the human, that the day after this tragedy, he will go on as usual, as if nothing happened. And Melville too, "will read & think, & walk & eat & talk, as if nothing happened – as if I did not know that death is indeed the King of Terrors." It is a terror, "not to the dying or the dead, but to the mourner – the mother. – Not so easily will his fate be washed out of her heart, as his blood from the deck." In this way, Melville concludes his last journal.

The journals of Melville are largely without any literary value, unlike those of Hawthorne or Emerson. They are mostly a collection of notes on what he sees, where he goes, and with whom he meets, with little or no psychological elaboration. But the value of these journals are in creating a documentary portrait of Melville. They are also a source of information that sheds light on his novels or stories as I have suggested above. I mentioned *Pierre*, but the long discussions with George Adler could have informed the metaphysics of *Moby Dick*. Of all the journals, I think the things he wrote while travelling in the Near East were the most compelling. It is a testament to Melville's democratic view of that world, that there is no orientalism in these writings.

I'd like to close this essay with a note on *Moby Dick* from my journal, since it is Melville's most popular novel and I think, the last line can applied to all of Melville's work: "*Moby Dick* is a wild, unhinged, complex, inexhaustible work of satanic brilliance. The novel is stretched to the breaking point, until it spills over into the real (the chapters on whaling, the lists of quotes, etc.) It was as though Melville wanted the reader to walk through the fire in order to reach passages of overwhelming beauty, depth, and humanity. This is what it means, as Melville wrote to Hawthorne, for a reader to be "baptized not in the name of the Father, but in the name of the devil." It is indeed a "wicked book," a monster of complexity. There is an incredible variety of contradictory impulses in the novel that Melville synthesizes into a kind of paradoxical harmony. It is an extremely rare kind of author that could perform such alchemy!" Indeed, Melville is a brilliant alchemist of language and ideas and reading his novels and journals was an enlightening experience.

Chapter Thirteen: The Bin

Jennifer Bartlett

When you go into the mental hospital, the first thing they do is take away your stuff. They label it with tags like at the airport, but only with your first name, not your last. They put it in a closet and tell you that you can have it later. They want you to give them all your medications and any illegal substances. Next, they take away your phone, and they tell you that you can have it in the morning. After you exit the waiting area, the doors are locked. This is when I panicked, and I realized what I had done. I was allowed to make *one more phone call*, and I called my parents. Neither my husband nor son knew where I was. The nurses offered me and Ativan, which I took, and I ate ice cream.

In *Blue Nights*, Joan Didion writes of her fragility, "We are moving into another summer. I find myself increasingly focused on this issue of frailty. I fear falling on the street. I imagine bicycle messengers knocking me to the ground. The approach of a child on a motorized scooter causes me to freeze midsection, play dead. I no longer go for breakfast to Three Guys on Madison Avenue: what if I were to fall on the way?" When I lived in New York City, I made my office at the New York Society Library, a membership library that many writers join for the free working space. It was six blocks from Joan Didion's apartment; the apartment she shared with her husband Gregory Dunne, who died suddenly of a heart attack at the kitchen table while she was making a salad for dinner. After reading her memoirs, I could pinpoint her building, and I would make a note of it each time I passed it; either to others or myself. Through her writing, I could feel Didion's fragility. I knew it; the dangers of falling and the dangers of going mad.

In Gloucester, I slept under three windows in a four-poster bed. I always kept the middle window shade open so I could see the comings and goings of the sky and the nearby trees. In Gloucester, I lived alone, but I was not alone. I lived above a man named Dean who was kind to me and took out my trash, and below a girl named Meg who was a nanny. I lived beside a couple, Susan and Sharon, owners of the large house. Despite having people around, I felt alone and was terrified, even though the *entire ocean* was out there to help me. My father told me that the angels were watching. Were the angels my two landladies next door?

I found my apartment in Gloucester, Massachusetts, on the website Trulia while sitting in bed in Northern Iceland on an island called Hrisey. I was at an artist residency, Gamli Skoli, with my friends L. and William and a Bulgarian woman [none of us could pronounce her name, and we called her Bibi] who lived in Paris.

At the time, moving to Gloucester seemed like a solution to the problem that I lived nowhere. My teaching job at SUNY Oswego ended, and the library at the university did not interview me. When Liza told me she was returning to Iceland, to a remote island near the Arctic Circle, I jumped at the chance. When I left the United States, I intended not to come back. I was busy working on my extended stay visa papers. Finding a printer in rural Iceland is no small feat.

Linda told me I could print my visa application in the "public library" in the school, attended by the island's 15 children ages 3–16. I once asked my friend Johann about how the school was structured between these fifteen children, but his explanation was unclear. The bottom line was the few working age people on the island did all the jobs, and usually three or four of them. So I wasn't surprised to find the grumpy lady and her incredibly sullen daughter who ran the grocery store (which was also a bank, post office, and ice-cream shop) working at the library, which was only open on Tuesdays. I waited until Tuesday and walked up to the little school. It was like the one in Laugarvatn, but smaller.

In Hrisey, the school just closed for the summer, and the librarian and her daughters were the only people in the building. I asked if the library was open because I needed to print something. She said, "It's only open on Tuesdays." I said, "Today is Tuesday." She sighed. "What do you need?"

In June, there were only two apartments for rent listed, and both were "winter rentals." The second one was bigger, and its décor was more interesting, but the landladies who owned the smaller apartment answered my message. We did a video call, and they walked me through the apartment, which was a block from Good Harbor Beach. They had no issues with my disabilities: a retired occupational therapist and a retired speech pathologist. There were a few stairs to get into the building, and I never could anticipate how people would respond to my disability. Ironically, the apartment was where my friends from New York City spent two weeks every summer. I thought that coming to Gloucester would be a good new start. I had an interview for a teaching job at Berkeley Academy of Music, which it turned out I did not get. But I was still teaching online at BMCC. I always loved the beach, David was there, and Grace. Tara and John were nearby. For years, David attempted to "sell" me on Gloucester; it was something we shared. He would often send me old videos of the fishermen or news of people he loved. After my visit in 2022, he wrote me a letter that said, "It was wonderful to have you in Gloucester this weekend. We could love that little world together." I thought he wasn't mad at me anymore about our fight over Grace. This was the second time in a year that I signed a lease sight unseen, long distance. I thought this could be a home.

The patient reports that she has never been to detox before. She states that she is drinking 2 glasses of wine and sometimes up to a whole bottle every morning for the past month. Prior to the past month she reports that she has been drinking—one to two glasses of wine a night—but what is bothering her now is that she is drinking in the morning. She states that she does drink to help with her anxiety—she is diagnosed with GAD per her report. She has a h/o of being prescribed Ativan which was then stopped, and she was started on Klonopin. She is concerned with long term use of benzodiazepines. She also reports use of CBD and THC that have not been effective for her with her anxiety. She reports periods of time where she has not had a drink—during her pregnancy with her son, "days here and there." She states that she has never had any withdrawal issues when she has stopped and not drank. Denies seizures, DT's. She denies tobacco and nicotine use or any other substance usage.

When I first arrived at the small house by the sea, I was excited. I had the feeling of a new place, of new possibility. My room was sparce, bright. Old 1950s furniture and a huge four-poster bed. It was still warm outside, and it was safe to sleep with the door and windows open. Tara came to visit, and I noticed the day that we ate in the Chinese restaurant in Rockport I had no anxiety. Tara and I both loved the beach, and we spent hours on it, sitting and reading our books.

Once summer ended, and I could no longer go to the beach, it became difficult to relax and feel safe in the apartment. I forgot how cold winter in Massachusetts could be. I didn't have a schedule or a job. I was teaching online one morning a week, and a few afternoons, but it was difficult to stay inside alone. I was doing a terrible job with my students, barely "phoning it in."

My therapist told me that he needed to end our sessions. I never met him in person. When the pandemic came, he moved upstate from New York City, and we always had our sessions online. Covid was over; and technically, it was not legal for him to practice in outside of New York State. He stayed with me as I traveled from Brooklyn to Iceland, to New Mexico, to California, to Oswego, to Iceland, to New Mexico, to California, to Gloucester and now it was time to stop. He intended on ending our sessions in October.

As a consequence, I spent much of my time looking for a new therapist. My landladies reminded me that this was a hopeless proposition. I started volunteering at the Gloucester Writers Center, which gave me a place to go. There were three different roads to get from my apartment to the Writers Center, and I always took the long route along the ocean past the shutter hotels and the Gloucester Stage Company. As I drove this road, I would look into the ocean and imagine Iceland across the ocean. From the outside of the Writers Center, I could see the Virgin Mary wrapped in her blue cloak, cradling a schooner in one arm. Once, she had brought me such peace. I could not find that peace again. Harold and I met with a therapist about the possibility of a writing program for women with trauma; one of our many plans that did not work out. On September 25, I emailed her about hiring her. She wrote that she was full, and that there was a shortage, but she took my information, and she said put it on the list-serv she knew of. She never wrote back. I emailed a woman named Barbara on Harold's recommendation. She did not email back. I called a couple whom Grace suggested, they did not call back. I went on *Psychology Today* and contacted a woman named Christine who was not taking clients. The only person who answered me was the bad therapist. We made as appointment. The day before the appointment, I could not remember who the appointment was with. I called Christine but she texted back that I had the wrong person. Then I found the appointment.

The patient said her chief complaint was "They [stet] put me in McLean's because I was having a drinking issue, but I haven't had a drink in over a month and don't have cravings anymore. I had a very bad psychiatrist who tried to get me off Klonopin too quickly, so I started to drink to deal with anxiety and help me get to sleep. I'm just having a very hard time. I've always been very anxious. I'm going through a very bad divorce. I haven't lived alone in 22 years. I have a lot of support from friends, but I'm in a state of grief. It's getting a tiny bit better, but I'm restless and sleep all day. I'm scared and alone. I want to get on with my life but feel stuck.

On September 21, I emailed my friend in New York City who wanted to know if we were having the "same lovely autumn weather." I wrote to him that it was sunny and warm. During this time, my husband was searching for a divorce mediator; he was procrastinating and being elusive. It was at this point that David mostly stopped talking to me. I felt abandoned. I was running out of Klonopin and went to see a new general practitioner. She gave me a prescription for ten pills to last until I could find a new therapist. The night, I drove to the Church, Our Lady of the Good Voyage, and tried to get inside to speak to the priest. It was night and the doors were locked. I drove home and sat in the car looking at the stars. I was afraid to go into emptiness.

In the mental hospital, they take you in a locked elevator into a foyer that looks like a fancy private school principal's office. It's ironic that you are there of your own volition, but locked in. I was in the drug and alcohol recovery center, Proctor One. This is where you get your meds. This is the kitchen; meals are at x, y and z, snacks are always available. This is the meeting and tv room. This is the office. This is your room. By myself, one twin bed. The room was huge and the exact same green as the Great Green Room in Brooklyn. The windows were locked, and there was heavy grating on it. I asked the night nurse to open the grating so that I could look outside into the leafless trees. The attendant asked if I had anyone that I did not want to visit. I said no. I told her she could share medical information with my mother. I probably signed something.

The bad therapist had in a small house in the woods in Rockport. When we met, she told me she had lived there for 40 years. On the phone, before our first visit, she told me she would not work in January because she was taking a "writing sabbatical," and she would have sessions online during the winter, what she called the dark months. *Red flags.* Her house was cozy; she had a woodburning stove and blankets.

Our first meeting was to assess my medication and drinking. I could tell she was trying to be kind, but she was critical. When she asked me what I did during the day, I told her that I drove around a lot, she made a face. *You drive around a lot.* I met with her exactly three times. I tried to explain my history as precisely as possible; about the losses I suffered, Mel and Timothy, my sister Emma, my divorce, and my complicated feelings about my son. I described to her my difficulties of dealing with anxiety and how I came to take ketamine. Once, a finch landed outside her window; it was easier to look at the birds than her. My story was complicated, and she sometimes forgot stuff I said or didn't understand. She didn't actually "take my Klonopin away"; she halved the dose, something I wanted and agreed to. David's insistence that I "get off" benzos was relentless, and I had my own internal pressure. But reducing the medication even this slight amount was too much for me. I began sending her texts asking for help. She was slow to respond. On our last meeting, she told me that I needed more care than she could give me. She told me that I needed to go into the hospital. She said, "Let's try to find one together," she said, picking up her computer.

When you enter the hospital, you can't go to bed right away because the nurses are changing their shifts, and you must wait for your medication. It is still like it is in old movies. The nurses are in a small room with a door which opens on the top half. They dole out the medicine in little white cups. They ask if you would like Gatorade or water. I always chose water because I didn't care. I wasn't in the habit of taking pills with liquid. The nurse told me that you should always drink water or parts of the pills will get stuck in your throat. Before bed, they give you everything back except your laptop, your phone (which you will get back in the morning), and your knitting needles. Then, you go to bed.

I considered taking ketamine for a long time. I found a company online that prescribed it called Joyous. The website promised to release me from my depression and anxiety. First, I met with an online counselor. He did a fifteen-minute assessment and mailed the drug. It came in a square rectangular plastic flat container. It had 40 square flat tablets that were like flat sugar cubes. They were kind of waxy. It was like science fiction therapy, really.

The ketamine gave me a blissful, floaty feeling. I didn't have any hallucinations, or feel very high, just relaxed. I took it before bed for a couple of months, but I was still having uncontrollable anxiety. And I was taking all the other drugs as well, and drinking, with the cat. When I remember the time in Oswego, I do not remember it as lonely, although there were profound times of isolation and loneliness. I primarily recall feeling nervous. Sometimes, I would get up six or seven times at night vomiting or pooping. The only thing the ketamine did was help what my therapist called *impulse control* which meant that I was less likely to call my husband and yell at him.

The bad therapist told me to keep track of the amount of medication that I was taking and my alcohol consumption. On October 7th I noted: 40 mg of Buspar, .5 mg of Klonopin, one glass of wine, one Tylenol PM, two pills of 5mg of melatonin, one 40mg tablet of Celexa, a tablet of Benadryl, and one tablet of Gabapentin. I probably lied about the wine. I was also [periodically] still taking the ketamine. The bad therapist told me to steep chamomile tea for 10 minutes each night before bed; a profoundly hilarious solution for crushing insomnia. Grace gave me some elixir with THC for sleep. This did not help. CT told me that magnesium helped her relax, so I bought a huge container, and drank it with water or tea. This also did not help. I was trying to knock myself out to handle the pain of the mornings. I was tuning into alcoholic anonymous meetings on Zoom a couple times a day, but these only made me more miserable. The moment I work up, I would call Harold at the Writers Center. He would always have things for me to do, and we met in the late afternoons, but at five, when the sun would begin to go down, and I had to go home alone, I was full of despair. I asked David if I could come spend the nights some time in Cambridge in his basement with the idea that we could spend more time together, and I would be able to do some things in town. He said no.

Without Klonopin, I became an insomniac, alone each morning and each night in the little apartment next to the big house near the sea. I was spent nights drinking wine and watching *Sex in the City*. I came up with the idea that I could drink in the morning to get back to sleep. The drinking, although shy of a month, seemed endless. I was drunk as I drove the car along the oceanside. Drunk on the phone. Drunk at the doctor's office. My new primary-care physician refused to help me. I was called in for an appointment to discuss my cholesterol level. I told her how much I had been drinking, and I asked her to write me a prescription for Klonopin. She would not. She told me that it was the establishment's practice not to write prescriptions if I had a therapist. I told her that the bad therapist had stopped seeing me. She still refused. I asked if it was a law; she said, no, it was just policy. She asked me when my last drink was. I told her 8 a.m.; it was 2 p.m. She said, "*so you drove here drunk.*" I said that I thought the alcohol had probably worn off. She told me that the drinking was probably the result of my high cholesterol, and she sent me home. I tried to call David; he did not answer the phone.

I was out of wine. It was nine in the morning. I got in my car to drive to the health food store to buy wine and groceries. The store was called Common Crow, and I had liked it when I first came to Gloucester. They had good grilled cheese sandwiches. I drove down our short street, and there was an accident. On the way there, garbage truck was stalled on the narrow one-way street that bordered the ocean and footbridge. The police and tow truck were there; I waited but nothing happened. I decided to back up our street and go the other way. A woman with her dog in the car had pulled up behind me. I thought she left because the truck wasn't going anywhere, but she did not, and I backed into her. I was very stressed out by the situation, but she seemed calm, and we exchanged information. I went to the store, came home, ate, drank a glass of wine, and went back to bed. Later, my husband texted to ask if I had been in an accident.

Manifold Honey: The Phoenix Art of Delmore Schwartz

Michael Londra

The Collected Poems of Delmore Schwartz, edited by Ben Mazer (Farrar Strauss Giroux, 2024), 720 pp, $50.00

Only poetry refutes death. Every poem is a shield of Achilles opposing the impenetrable darkness surrounding us. No twentieth century writer better incarnated this ethical duty of the poet to resist the void of mortality on our behalf more than Delmore Schwartz (1913–1966). That's because no literary reputation in the last hundred years has been as misshapen by the opinions of critics and contemporaries, and, like the phoenix, survived. The image of the phoenix was inspirational for Schwartz, found in his verse from the very beginning ("The phoenix with eight hundred thousand memories," for instance, from "Father and Son," included in his first published hardcover) but emerging most prominently in the maligned and dismissed later poetry. This deep spiritual kinship for an emblem of resistance and renewal makes all the sense in the world, given the infamously large number of personal and professional catastrophes he grappled with, always threatening to distort and overshadow his poems. Moribund clichés abound, recycled ad nauseam, perpetuated by folk who have read little of the poetry yet voyeuristically luxuriate in the "Crazy Delmore" mythology, allowing the vicarious obscene thrill of titillating gossip to rewire basic literary evaluation, belittling and disparaging Schwartz's noteworthy experiments with style and form, innovations later repurposed—earning significant acclaim—by distinguished practitioners Robert Lowell, John Berryman, and Saul Bellow; while also in turn serving as a shadowy, subterranean godfather to luminaries like Tony Kushner, Ben Lerner, Claudia Rankine, and Gary Shteyngart, among others. For all the notoriety Delmore Schwartz endured while alive, a serious evaluation of his complete career until now has been impossible.

Enter Ben Mazer, the editor Delmore Schwartz always deserved but never got, and the bracing corrective of FSG's brand new *The Collected Poems of Delmore Schwartz*. This is a book which should take its place beside other publishing interventions like Malcolm Cowley's *The Portable Faulkner* (Viking, 1946) and Edmund Wilson's *The Last*

Tycoon, An Unfinished Novel, together with *The Great Gatsby,* and *Selected Short Stories* (Scribner, 1941). Though prose and not poesy, each of these legendary omnibus works rescued and recuperated Faulkner and Fitzgerald for a public that had discarded them. In fact, Cowley boosted William Faulkner to the Nobel Prize; Wilson's advocacy enshrined *The Great Gatsby* among the most revered examples of classic American literature in the canon. Mazer's contribution of Schwartz's *Collected* has half a chance to make the same kind of history. It appears at a cultural moment when a new generation of fresh unbiased critical eyes exists, unconcerned and undistracted by, for example, the spicy scuttlebutt of Bellow's exculpatory *Humbodlt's Gift* (1975) that brainwashed an earlier, more gullible readership. The full breadth of Schwartz's labors in these pages allows the poet to finally get his due and be judged solely on merit and not like a Kardashian.

Born two years before Delmore Schwartz's death, Mazer did not grow up influenced by the stereotype of Bad Boy Delmore, finding Schwartz's poems on his own, and being independently touched by them. Trained in textual scholarship and literary editing at Boston University under Christopher Ricks and Archie Burnett, as well as studying poetry with Seamus Heaney at Harvard, Mazer has in his locker the necessary experience and technique, along with the requisite passion for seriously good verse, to helm the complicated levers of a mammoth and comprehensive undertaking described by Mazer himself in his afterword as comprising four long and arduous years. Doggedly seeking out every syllable Delmore Schwartz committed to print, Mazer launched himself into the Yale archives, unearthing scores of unpublished manuscripts, Himalayas of lost and unknown poems, painstakingly, meticulously producing a worthy and unsurpassable end product. Attention must be paid. Mazer's table of contents reconstructs Schwartz's oeuvre in a series of tableaux, a detailed set of Holbein-like portraits over time, unflinchingly depicting the life and art of a literary phoenix.

Starting with *In Dreams Begin Responsibilities* (1938), the virtuoso hybrid text propelling Delmore Schwartz into the literary stratosphere, making him the most famous poet in America under thirty, we find an ambitious uninhibited prodigy brashly announcing himself with a masterly rendering of diverse forms: the verse play *Coriolanus and His Mother,* drawing au courant parallels between Shakespeare's tragically headstrong Roman general Coriolanus and the narcissistically metastasizing ego of the modern poet; and thirty-five exquisitely contoured songs, brilliant examples of tightly controlled verse, modelled on T.S. Eliot, and boasting some of Schwartz's most memorable lyrical formulae. "Will you perhaps consent to be / My many branched, small and dearest tree" ("Will you consent to be"). "The radiant soda of the seashore" ("Far Rockaway"). "Dropping his penny, he learned out all loss, / The irretrievable cent of fate" ("A Young Child and His Pregnant Mother"). Outstanding among the plentitude, the first two lines of an untitled sonnet: "The heavy bear who goes with me / A manifold honey to smear his face." Without doubt, Delmore Schwartz is American poetry's Heavy Bear, smearing the faces of readers (and, certainly, his own) with lyrics of manifold honey, reminiscent of Kafka's Odradek, a lusting manifestation of pure poetic *jouissance*.

Next up is Delmore Schwartz's version of Rimbaud's *A Season in Hell* (1939). When it first appeared, this was the only full translation available in English. Rimbaud was not then the perennially hot property he currently is among classic rock fans and acolytes pursuing the adolescent discipline of practiced hedonism. Schwartz put Rimbaud on the map in America. His letters show teenage Delmore away at college in Wisconsin to study with Louis Zukofsky being visited by the ghost of Rimbaud, imploring Delmore to accept the challenge of bringing him over stateside. Ripped apart by hypocritical, supercilious and jealous critics, Schwartz's criminally misunderstood and underappreciated Rimbaud began a sequence of troubles that culminated in the ultimate fall from grace epitomized by Schwartz's heart attack in a Times Square flophouse that claimed his life in lonely squalor. Roger Shattuck praised and W.H. Auden taught Schwartz's Rimbaud. There are many who still want to discount its lively virtues, but in this Collected we see the vibrant, rambunctious, zesty, bouncing, shimmering thrust and cut of burning life that Rimbaud unquestionably cultivated.

Genesis: Part One (1943) and its unpublished sequel, *Genesis: Part Two*, written at the time of World War Two, coalesce at the heart of this *Collected*. Detailing a bildungsroman in verse, Schwartz tells an autobiographical immigrant story, that of his grandparents, parents, and himself, mixing the poetic styles of the Bible with free verse, more than a decade before Allen Ginsberg's *Howl* (1956), and done with a completely different purpose and intent than Whitman's signature long Biblical line. John Berryman's inspiration for *Dream Songs* (1969), the confessional turn of Lowell's *Life Studies* (1959) and even Saul Bellow's conception of his fiction as "higher biography," Schwartz's innovative *Genesis* broke with the orthodoxy of T.S. Eliot's prevailing ideology—

impersonal writing. Merging Joyce's *Portrait of the Artist as a Young Man* with a Noo Yawk accent, Schwartz splashes the tumult of Manhattan and Brooklyn into a primordially pungent pageant that quickens the pulse with generous amounts of idiomatic language, high-minded philosophical rumination, and sharp psychological insight. Schwartz's alter ego is Hershey Green, an apposite last name, given how New York is cast as a new Eden ("Me next to sleep, all that is left of Eden;" "longing for Eden;" "second / Only to Eden"), a Shakespearean Arden, what Northrop Frye called the Green World, and Milton referred to as a "lantskip" in *Paradise Lost*, a place of wild green forests where you can indulge in creativity and imagination. Akin to Shakespeare's Rosalind, Schwartz's "way is to conjure;" along with Rosalind's paramour Orlando, who puts up a poem on every tree in Arden; Schwartz in *Genesis* transforms the everyday drab universe of dead dull objects into a magical kingdom of poetry. His heightened poetic language is a holy instrument capable of instantiating complex spiritual transformations within us. We only need to open our hearts: "Long Island like a liner sits;" "Logos, man's inner being going out;" "The audience is everywhere like stars;" "I see this marriage hanging from a ledge;" "half-truths like broken dishes;" "He sees the snow which is not snow but light;" "we come like comic strips;" "the romantic cannot forget;" "exiled to the living room;" "the ego makes the world glass;" "You lie in the coffin of your character."

    Schwartz swaggered through life like a native New Yorker, striding over the threshold of concert halls, museums, and Ivy League seminar rooms exactly the same way he did into the Polo Grounds to watch Willie Mays hit homers or the Union Square Automat for Viennese coffee and tapioca pudding. In *Genesis*, we encounter Delmore Schwartz glorying in cool city mode. Perhaps this aspect is what disturbed critics at the time of its publication. New Yorkers carry erudition on their shoulders differently than people from other cities. Certainly Saul Bellow needed to hightail it back to Chicago, far from New York and the looming presence of Delmore Schwarz to realize his dreams. Some have claimed New York is the capital of "the wrong kind of ambition," whatever that might mean. In *Genesis*, we get the splendor of sincerity and irony in the same lyrical gesture. There is not a drop of cynicism in Delmore Schwartz. Just like another quintessential New Yorker, his protégé Lou Reed, who studied with him at Syracuse University, there is a sense in *Genesis* of Schwartz's adherence to the moral obligation toward and sacred belief in the genius of love, a marveling at the beauty of the world, and an appetite for the colloquial, a passion for the piquancy of the vernacular. Many derided Schwartz's book-length poem out of distaste for the sheer display of ego. Even online, humblebragging trolls will hypocritically yuck it up, ridiculing Schwartz's vanity and conceited self-importance, as if these accusers weren't even more egregious culprits. At least Delmore Schwartz built something eternal out of his egotism.

Genesis definitely gets better as Schwartz progresses. The second volume is filled with sublime imagery and incident, but it was abandoned. If Schwartz had instead begun in medias res, not belabored the minutia of his grandparents' fates at page one of his epic—a weird obsession with backstory which continues to plague good writers: the notion that we need oodles of what happened before to sympathize with a character's identity or dilemmas—and just got right into the muck and flow of the action, maybe there would have been a different outcome for *Genesis*. But the negative reviews in quick succession of *A Season in Hell* and *Genesis: Part One* eviscerated his confidence, leading to a personality crisis that culminated in a return to the stately, less hyper, but no less lyrical *Vaudeville for a Princess* (1950): "truth is ridiculous;" "The scapeghost of your gentle jokes;" "blind as snow;" "Phoenix affection rises again and again" (like the phallus?); "The radio is poet laureate;" "I am a student of the kinds of light;" "boyhood's silver screen;" "The mind to me a North Pole is."

Vaudeville is dedicated to his second wife Elizabeth, with a nod to England's then-princess-soon-to-be Queen Elizabeth, implying that his poems are meant for royalty, whether that's Schwartz's domestic castle or Buckingham Palace. This concept solders a persona that he refined and enriched in his poems from around this time until his death, namely, his identification with the Shakespearean fool. Henry VIII's court jester, Will Somer, is the archetypal model for this poetic paradigm, the only voice Henry allowed to utter the unvarnished truth. Reinforcing this notion, Schwartz confessed this characteristic of his *weltanschauung* in a letter to Mark Van Doren.

Mazer wisely has omitted the prose pieces from *Vaudeville*, pioneering Lenny Bruce-like or Henny Youngman-esque comedic one-liner riffs on divorce, the role of coffee during the Enlightenment, existentialism, Hamlet, driving. Harkening back to the audience-addressed entr'actes of *Coriolanus and His Mother*, Mazer avers correctly that the focus in the *Collected* should be on the poems only. Black pages separate each grouped section, recalling the blackened page of mourning in *Tristram Shandy*, but also echoing how the theatrical curtain comes down marking each part of a play or burlesque show. Schwartz is gesturing toward the poet as a kind of Lear's fool, a performer on the page. Schwartz was this fool for his friends, the New York Intellectuals, and his publisher James Laughlin. This jester motif comes full circle in *Summer Knowledge* (I propose *Summer* in the title is a pun on Will Somer's name) and the uncollected and unpublished sections at the end. The phoenix idea ("the phoenix inhabits the fruit") is stamped throughout: "Phoenix Year," "Phoenix Choir," "Phoenix Lyrics." Twinning the evocative premise of indestructible phoenix poetry with the unkillable phoenix jester poet, the late poems leap out as the equal of *In Dreams Begin Responsibilities*, and surpass them in joy, adventure, profundity, freedom, penetration, eloquence, fluency, perception, and complexity. From "Cambridge, Spring 1937:"

> for now the sunlight
> Thrashes its wet shellac on brickwork and gutter,
> White splinters streak midmorning and doorstep
> Winter passes as the lighted streetcar
> Moves at midnight, one scene of the past,
> Droll and unreal, stiff, stilted and hooded.

Summer Knowledge originally screamed out for a decent editor to cull the shorter poetic fragments, replacing them with the posthumously published and heretofore unpublished sharper pieces that Mazer included near the end: "The Sad Druggist," "Immortality," "Made More Vivid by Renoir," "The Maxims of Sisyphus," "The Saxophone." Crowning the final pages of the *Collected* is the remarkable "The First Night of Fall and Falling Rain," which knuckleballs Wallace Stevens and Keats into the same unique Delmorean fantasia, polished philosophical aesthetic contemplation merged with the achingly blissful innocent exultation of a child made ecstatic by the rain:

> How suddenly all consciousness leaped in spontaneous gladness;
> Knowing without thinking how the falling rain (outside, all over
> In slow sustained consistent vibration all over outside
> Tapping window, streaking roof, running down runnel and drain
> Waking a sense, once more, of all that lived outside of us,
> Beyond emotion, for beyond the swollen distorted shadows and lights
> Of the toy town and the vanity fair of waking consciousness!

The Collected Poems of Delmore Schwartz, edited by Ben Mazer, is the perfect retort to the haters. Schwartz had plenty of them, and a lot of admirers too. Lou Reed kept the flame blazing for his phoenix bard mentor. Now we have the definitive statement of Delmore Schwartz's phoenix iteration. Here, we the next generation of poetry disciples can be seared and sing with Schwartz, apropos of a phoenix, just like he put it himself in these lines—the bird of fire still lives, refuting implacable darkness and death; onward—

> Time is the fire in which we learn
> Time is the fire in which we burn.

"A Mad Night": Talking to Michael McLure about The Six Gallery

Lee Bartlett

"It was a great night, a historic night in more ways than one," Jack Kerouac wrote in *The Dharma Bums*. "Japhy Ryder and some other poets (he also wrote poetry and translated Chinese and Japanese poetry into English) were scheduled to give a poetry reading at the Gallery Six in town. They were all meeting in the bar and getting high. But as they stood and sat around I saw that he was the only one who didn't look like a poet, though poet he was indeed. The other poets were either horn-rimmed intellectual hepcats with wild black hair like Alvah Goldbook, or delicate pale handsome poets like Ike O'Shay (in a suit), or out-of-this-world gentle-looking Renaissance Italians like Francis DaPavia (who looks like a young priest), or bow-tied wild-haired old anarchist fuds like Rheinhold Cacoethes, or big fat bespectacled quiet booboos like Warren Coughlin. I followed the whole gang of howling poets to the reading at Gallery Six that night, which was among other important things the night of the birth of the San Francisco Poetry Renaissance. Everyone was there. It was a mad night."

The building on Fillmore Street near Union housing The Six gallery was originally an auto-repair shop. In 1953, poet Robert Duncan, his lover and collaborator the painter/collagist Jess Collins and Harry Jacobus took over the lease and opened the King Ubu there, where such younger action painters as Julius Wasserman and Deborah Remington had their first shows, and more established artists like Elmer Bischoff and David Park exhibited both abstract and figurative work. The King Ubu remained active for about eighteen months, but eventually both personal and financial considerations forced its closing.

Within a few months, however, the gallery re-opened as an artists' co-operative, The Six. Three of the original "Six," Jack Spicer, Wally Hedrick and David Simpson, had been in Pasadena; of the others, Hayward King had come to San Francisco from Little Rock, Arkansas, John Allen Ryan from New York City, and Deborah Remington from Haddonfield, New Jersey. Spicer had been a close friend of Duncan's since 1946, when the two had met as students at UC–Berkeley, brought together by a mutual interest in the medieval historiography of German scholar Ernst Kantorowicz (who was on the Berkeley faculty) and the poetry of Stephan George.

Painter/assemblagist Hedrick had attended the California School of Fine Arts, along with painters Remington, Simpson, and King.

During this period, cafes in the area—the Co-Existence Bagel Shop, The Anxious Asp, Miss Smith's Tea Room—were flourishing as more and more artists, poets, and musicians seemed to be arriving from places like New York and Los Angeles. Many of these hangouts—Vesuvio's, the Jazz Cellar, the Coffee Gallery—made a practice of offering space to artists for showing their work. One of the most popular of these was the Place, run by two painters who had come to San Francisco from Black Mountain College in North Carolina, Leo Krikorian and Knute Stiles. Spicer was a regular there.

As Michael McClure told me in early 1991, during one of his visits to my home in Placitas, New Mexico, "The Place was on upper Grand Avenue, a small storefront kind of bar. Oddly, there was a flight of stairs up the back to a little balcony with a railing around it, so twenty or twenty-five people could sit downstairs and probably that many again upstairs. In those days upper Grand was basically Italian, and all up and down the street were places that made pasta, Italian meat markets, clothing stories run by people with Italian names, Italian-American jewelry shops, a couple art galleries run by the artists themselves pretty much showing their own paintings, several bars with names like Tivoli Gardens, a gay bar or two, even in those days. We're talking now about 1954–55. Interesting enough, The Place was run by a man named Leo. He had an Armenian last name, and wore small, very thick spectacles. His bartender was Knute Stiles. Leo was also an artist, so not only was this an artists' bar, but the proprietor was an artist and the chief barman, Knute, a painter. If Knute wasn't one of the original members of The Six Gallery, he was closely connected with them and showed work there. So The Place was there first, the The Six Gallery later, but I'm beginning to understand just very recently that the two were kind of reflections of each other.

"The first show I saw of San Francisco art that really moved me a lot was by Jay De Feo at The Place, small guashes—alchemical dogs in blue and red, showing slashes and pieces of brush strokes, on almost uncared for but perfect paper. I remember also a show was done there called *Secret Gardens*, Robert Lavigne's paintings, and if I remember correctly Allen Ginsberg did a poem for each one of those paintings. The whole painterly scene of that post-Korean G.I. Bill school—people who were students of Clyfford Still's while he was at the California School of Fine Arts—would gather. Jack Spicer was one of the original Six of The Six Gallery, and The Place was also his hangout. People put obscene graffiti about Jack in the john there, so that every time you went into The Place you'd go in to see what the latest obscene graffiti about Jack was; of course, Jack would go in to enjoy it also, and come out smiling. It certainly was never erased. John Allen Ryan, a poet and a painter who was also one of the original Six, was the other barman at The Place, along with Knute.

"The Six gallery was named after the original six founders. One of them was a black painter named Hayward King. Wally Hedrick was one of them, and Jack Spicer. It was originally formed to show the works of painters and as a place to read poetry. I think each of them kicked in twenty dollars to rent the gallery. Spicer gave a reading there. I believe Robert Duncan read poetry at one of the openings. The gallery preceding the Six Gallery had been the King Ubu Gallery, which had been started by Harry Jacobus, Duncan, and Jess Collins, Robert's friend. The Six was, in a sense, a co-operative reopening of the Ubu Gallery, with many of the same people showing.

"The reading that was introduced by Kenneth Rexroth, and was given by Ginsberg, Snyder, Whalen, Lamantia, and me occurred on October 13, 1955. Earlier in that year [January] there had been a performance/reading of *Faust Foutu*, Robert's [Duncan] play at The Six gallery. I had one of the roles in that, along with Duncan, Spicer, Jess, and poet Helen Adams. It was some weeks or months after that that I ran into Wally Hedrick on the street. He said, 'The things you did with Robert were real fine. Could you put together a poetry reading?' I said sure. In the meantime, at a party to celebrate the first reading of the San Francisco Poetry Center, which was by W.H. Auden, at the home of Professor Ruth Witt-Diamont, who was the head of the Poetry Center, I ran into an intense, bespectacled young man from New York who I felt a great deal in common with. That was Allen Ginsberg. We began meeting occasionally, and he told me about this mad young genius named Jack Kerouac. He showed me his letters from Jack, and he showed me [Kerouac's] *Mexico City Blues*, which I liked a lot.

"So I agreed to arrange a poetry event for Wally Hedrick at the Six, to follow up Duncan's *Faust Foutu*, to carry on the poetry thing. Spicer was in Boston at the time, so they needed poetry there, I guess. I ran into Allen on the street, asked him what he was doing, and told him that I had to put on a reading. I told him that I was working real hard and had a baby on the way, that I didn't have a lot of time for it. Allen said he'd do it if I wanted him to, and I said certainly. Shortly after that, Allen met Gary [Snyder], and Phil [Whalen], and he invited them too. So it would be Allen, myself, and Phillip Lamantia."

Allen Ginsberg had arrived in San Francisco some months earlier, leaving New York primarily in hopes of reviving an on-again off-again love affair with Neal Cassady, who was living south of the City in San Jose with his wife Carolyn and their children. Along with his good friend Kerouac, he had dropped out of Columbia University to become a writer, and as early as 1952 had corresponded with Kenneth Rexroth at the suggestion of William Carlos Williams. Now in San Francisco working as a market researcher to support his poetry, Ginsberg introduced himself to Rexroth, and soon struck up friendships with Duncan and poet Kenneth Patchen (who was living at the time on Telegraph Hill). By the time of his arrival, Ginsberg had gathered together a manuscript of early poems, which would eventually be published as *Empty Mirror*, but Rexroth was not particularly impressed with the work. As he later commented in *American Poetry in the Twentieth Century*, "In 1956 and '57 Allen Ginsberg, Gregory Corso, and Jack Kerouac showed in San Francisco. Up until that time Ginsberg had been a rather conventional, witty poet influenced by his New Jersey Landsman William Carlos Williams, and taught his letters at Columbia by Mark Van Doren, Lionel Trilling, and Jacques Barzun. He was very much a catechumen of the highly select Trotskyite-Southern Agrarian Establishment, and destined by his elders to step into the thinning ranks of their youth brigade alongside Norman Podhoretz and Susan Sontag and others of like ilk and kidney. He inhaled the libertarian atmosphere of San Franciso and exploded."

Thirty years later, Ginsberg recalled the creation of his most famous poem (and possibly the most well-known single American poem of this century), fueled as it was by San Francisco's "liberating atmosphere: "I was alone. I had the leisure of unemployment compensation for six months ahead, had concluded a longish period of psychotherapeutic consultation, enjoyed occasional visits from Neal Cassady ... and maintained energetic correspondence with Jack Kerouac in Long Island and William Burroughs in Tangier. I had recently dreamt of the late Joan Burroughs, a sympathetic encounter with her spirit. She inquired the living fate of our friends. I wrote the dream as a poem ("Dream Record, June 8, 1955"), about which in a few days Kenneth Rexroth, an elder in this literary city, wrote me he thought was stilted and somewhat academic. A week later, I sat idly at my desk by the first-floor window facing Montgomery Street's slope to gay Broadway—only a few blocks from City Lights literary paperback bookshop. I had a second-hand typewriter, some cheap scratch paper. I began typing, not with the idea of writing a formal poem, but stating my imaginative sympathies, whatever they were worth. As my loves were impractical and my thoughts relatively unworldly, I had nothing to gain, only the pleasure of enjoying on paper those sympathies most intimate to myself and most awkward in the great world of family, formal education, business and current literature." To advertise the October 7 reading, Ginsberg distributed a typed postcard which listed the performers, promising "all sharp new straight-forward writing—remarkable collection of angels on one stage reading their poetry. No charge, small collection for wine and postcards. Charming even." By the start of the event at 8 p.m. on Friday night, over a hundred people, including poet/publisher Lawrence Ferlinghetti, had squeezed into the small gallery to find six chairs arranged in a semi-circle on a makeshift stage.

McClure continued: "Kenneth Rexroth introduced us that night, and Jack Kerouac showed up for the event. Allen read 'Howl' for the first time. That was my first reading ever. I read 'For the Death of 100 Whales,' which was probably the first reading of an environmental poem out in public like that. I also probably read 'Point Lobos: Animism' as well as several poems which did not make it into a manuscript. Gary read 'A Berry Feast' and maybe other poems. Philip Whalen that poem about being out on a limb and sawing that limb away ['Plus ça Change']. Phillip LaMantia read prose poems by a young junky poet named John Hoffman. Ginsberg read 'Howl,' and Jack was chanting, 'Go, Go, Go!' And we set up jugs of wine. It was a very powerful event.

"The art show in the gallery at the time was by Fred Martin. It was old wooden apple crates or orange crates that had been broken up and swathed in muslin or some kind of soft cloth, or it could have been plastic. I remember in introducing us, Kenneth Rexroth said that the artworks looked like furniture for Japanese dwarfs, which was not a bad visual description of it. It seemed to be both white heavy and white shivery and mystical; it reminded me in a way of the paintings of Morris Graves, and I thought in a way connected with Buddhism. I also read 'Poem':

> Linked part to part, toe to knee, eye to thumb
> Motile, feral, a blockhouse of sweat

"What I am getting to is that the poem contains references to physical anthropology, to biology, and to Buddhism, with 'The eye a bridegroom of torture' coming from 'The Fire Sermon.' Phillip Whalen was reading his Buddhist poems, Gary his nature poems, my poems being primarily nature poems. Looking back, I believe that we were, unknowingly, the literary wing of the environmental movement; what we were reading that night were primarily either poems of nature or poems of consciousness. When he says we're different, we're taking the intelligence, and the *intelligensis*, and the awareness of nature of all those people who were there before us, from anarchist-carpenters to philosopher-poets, and we're putting it into a new what is sometimes called 'postmodern' shape. But actually it's not a postmodern shape. I feel the shape we go back to—whether it's Gary Snyder's 'Riprap,' which has the beautiful aroma of Milton around it, or it's my work, which has to me a sense of Keats or Shelley about it, or Philip Whalen, whose poetry is so 18th Century in its lucidity, like Pope, except that it's so much more juicy than Pope—the mutation we are making , is a connection with the environmental movement, because so many of those first environmentalists were our friends, and also a connection with the English tradition, as well as with the work of Williams and Pound."

Just a year after the reading, in an article on "The Literary Revolution in America" co-written with Gregory Corso for an Amsterdam magazine, Ginsberg realized the impact of the event: "In the fall of 1955, a group of six unknown poets in San Francisco, in a moment of drunken enthusiasm, decided to defy the system of academic poetry, official reviews, New York publishing machinery, national sobriety and generally accepted standards to good taste, by giving a free reading of their poetry in a rundown second-rate experimental art gallery in the Negro section of San Francisco. Their approach was purely amateur and goofy, but it should be noted that they represented a remarkable lineup of experience and character—it was an assemblage of really good poets who knew what they were writing and didn't care about anything else. They got drunk, the audience got drunk, all that was missing was the orgy. This was no ordinary poetry reading. Indeed, it resembled anything but a poetry reading. The reading was such a violent and beautiful expression of their revolutionary individuality (a quality bypassed in American poetry since the formulations of Whitman), conducted with such a surprising abandon and delight by the poets themselves, and presenting such a high mass of beautiful unanticipated poetry, that the audience, expecting some Bohemian stupidity, was left stunned, and the poets were left with the realization that they were fated to make a permanent change in the literary firmament of the States."

June, 2024

In The Park

Jack Pulaski

"Herbie is a little slow," his mother, Sophie Mintz hollered, "and nobody should take advantage." And in case anyone should forget, as she tended to as the day wore on, she'd thrust her head from the fourth story window, and yell, "Herbie, Herbie." When he didn't respond, she shrieked, "Swifty, Swifty!"

No one could remember who named twelve-year-old Herbert "Swifty." None of the street's wits claimed credit. The nicknaming, a baptism, during which his head was doused with cream soda, flooded recall and Swifty had difficulty remembering that his name had been Herbert. This was a time when truth couldn't be veiled by euphemism, and on the same street lived Frankie-One-Eye, Sammy the Gimp, Moshe the Gonif, and Vinnie Pazzo.

Swifty's father, Sol, wasn't so much taciturn as overwhelmed by the one great truth of his life; to all questions he answered, "I make a living." The statement had sufficed for a marriage proposal, and if there were greetings or inquiries that required mouthing something more, he never noticed; but, when confronted with a question regarding a plumbing problem, his trade, he would describe in vivid detail, clogged pipes, and sewage flow, recreating, when words failed, the sound of unimpeded water, the flushing of a toilet.

Old Man Levine, weathered into the stone stoop, rested his head on his arthritic fist grasping the handle of his cane, and said to Sophie Mintz on various occasions, "Not to worry Sophie, Swifty lives in God's time." Swifty, lingering under the blows of astonishment, eyes and mouth agape, stared at the luminescent marble in the palm of his hand. The boy he was playing with crouched at the curb, one knee on the pavement, the other lowered on the asphalt, his shadow straddling the pavement and the gutter. He squinted, forefinger and thumb cocked, aimed, and shot his marble, a red jumbo. He looked up and called, "Swifty, yo Swifty." Swifty studied the marble in the palm of his hand. He heard faintly, "Swifty, yo Swifty," as his vision gathered in a mother further down the street squatting at the edge of the pavement and holding between her knees, a baby girl above the curb, the child's dress gathered up, panties around her ankles, the palms of the mother's hands cradled the undersides of the kid's thighs; the little girl's legs, from the knees down, dangled; her bare bottom hovered over the curb and she peed. The vision of the golden rivulet trickling down obscured Petey's claim on Swifty's attention.

Regarding stick-ball, Swifty could hit when he remembered to swing. One day he connected with what looked like a two-sewer home run; the ball flew high and arched, floating between roof tops and Swifty stood watching the ball chase a cloud. The other boys were shouting for him to run the bases. He stood and watched. A teammate shoved him. He stumbled, regained his footing and examined the sky. His teammates yelled. He heard a voice he was susceptible to, loped suddenly, and was nearly hit by a car. The vehicle veered toward the opposite curb and screeched to a stop. Swifty hardly noticed, never rounding third he continued to trot straight down the middle of the street and followed the cloud that had swallowed the ball until he and the cloud disappeared in the vicinity of the docks. When his mother remembered him, and cried, "Herbie-*oy*-Swifty," from the window, and there was no reply, neighbors pointed in the direction where Swifty had run until he was an illusion dwindling into the haze near the East River. Sophie charged down four flights of stairs screaming out of the building and searched for her son. Swifty perambulated in a mystery. Sophie and Swifty's circuits traversed, although they never met. Later at night, they encountered one another in the apartment. Sophie wept with relief, Swifty wept in sympathy.

On a Saturday late in the autumn the scent of snow could be detected among the smells of the shoe polish factory, the sugar factory, and the beer brewery. A group of boys had gathered to choose sides for a game of punch ball. Swifty wouldn't be chosen to play on either team. He stood, unperturbed, staring at Cosmo Leznick. Cosmo studying the dregs twisted his mouth in distaste, any selection foreordained defeat. Cosmo pointed to a boy staring at his feet, standing next to Swifty. Swifty, mouth agape, in what may have been taken for a smile, stood, his vision riveted on Cosmo. During the choosing of sides Cosmo had been scratching his crotch. He interpreted Swifty's smile as presumption, unspoken, but plain enough, and Cosmo wouldn't endure the insult alluding to his family's hygiene. He stopped scratching and popped Swifty. Swifty blinked and continued to stare. His nose throbbed and he stuck his tongue out to taste the blood. Sophie happened to be at the window. She appeared in the street. Cosmo had been about to lay down a flattened garbage can lid to serve as first base. She grabbed two fistfuls of his hair and yanked his head east and west, north and south. From the stoop Mr. Levine leaning forward on his cane, called to her in Yiddish saying she was creating a disgrace for the eyes of the gentiles. She ran back upstairs, locked herself in the apartment, and didn't appear at the window for the rest of the day. Cosmo's mother stood outside the locked door and spewed curses in Polish on the Mintz family. From that time on whenever Mrs. Leznick passed the Mintz family's door she paused to curse them; however as she knew they were already an accursed people, she also entreated Jesus to remember his responsibility and punish them.

Buzzy Demarco, a countervailing spirit to Cosmo Leznick, was often the captain of the opposing team: stoop ball, stick ball, punch ball, and all the variants of baseball. Buzzy's authority derived from a supernatural grace. A pink Spaulding bouncing off the roof of a moving car, gaining altitude would appear to halt in midair and wait as Buzzy's flight described the symmetry of larger winged birds, and obedient gravity brought the ball to his hand.

There was also the ritual of Buzzy's summertime beneficence. Buzzy's friends, admirers, and the envious would seat themselves on the steps of the stoop to watch. Old Man Levine mounted there, grimaced, watched the feral children and thought that surely the coming of the Messiah couldn't be far off. As Tony's ice truck slowed for a delivery, Buzzy trotting a car-length behind the truck, accelerated, and within three strides leaped onto the flat bed of the truck, and slid a cake of ice off the tailgate, which exploded shards all over the gutter. Tony slammed on the brakes, and shot out of the cab of the truck brandishing the ice tongs he swore would someday impale Buzzy's head. Buzzy was nowhere in sight. The ice man, who had once made an unwelcome advance toward Buzzy's widowed mother retrieved the largest piece of ice from the street and swore revenge against Buzzy, a maiming worse than death, and touched his crotch in analogous genuflection. Everyone knew Tony meant it, and Buzzy, a fugitive, most often in plain sight took this danger as just one more responsibility. When Tony and his truck were gone kids bounded from the stoop steps, grabbed the gleaming wet chunks from the black hot asphalt, and sucked the cold diamonds.

Swifty was among Buzzy's worshipers. Although Swifty couldn't speculate, as many did, on whether fourteen-year-old Buzzy, honing his extraordinary talent, would two years hence box in the Golden Gloves. Buzzy would reappear in the street as the kids bent to harvest the ice from the gutter. Swifty, always a little too late, never would have snatched a piece if it weren't for Buzzy, who handed Swifty the melting gem. Swifty licked it. His eyes fixed on the slits of Buzzy's eyes, shaped like smiles, the dark light of his irises shining in his umber tinted face. Swifty gaped, suckled by ice.

On a Sunday, church bells ringing, Buzzy, pinnacled on a scrap of floor jutting out of the side of a tenement recently destroyed by fire, called to his followers climbing through the charred ruin. The half dozen boys had progressed up above the fourth story and clung to the ladder and fire escapes attached to what had been the front of the building. Buzzy hadn't given Swifty permission to join in. He shook his head and said, "No Swifty, stay here, on the block," and pointed to a group of younger children gathered in front of Swifty's building. Still, Swifty tagged along, ambling a distance behind the group led by Buzzy. The game was "Follow the Leader" and it was up to Buzzy to determine the level of risk all would try to meet. Swifty followed the gang at a half block interval.

Three stories above the rubble piled in the street, Swifty opened a door to a chasm. The remains of the stairway that had shuddered under his weight trembled behind him, gaping space on either side of the steps. Suspended there, Swifty stretched his neck and looked below. Acrid wisps of smoke made his eyes tear. Looking down he saw the tenement's coal bin, like a jewel box, glowing. Others were calling from the ladder and fire escapes attached to one of the tenement's two remaining roofless walls. The wind moving the clouds surrounding the five story high wall made it appear to sway; the smashed windows dribbled ribbons of smoke. Vapors of mortar dust drifting from between the bricks blew in the air. The wall, and the fire escapes and ladder attached to it seemed to list in the wind.

Swifty heard them calling his name. He saw Buzzy riding the scrap of floor among the clouds, exhorting the boys below, frozen to the ladder and fire escapes. Buzzy hollered for them to continue the climb. A fragment of a vestibule made a narrow bridge between the two walls. A kitchen at the further end of the bridge rested on what looked like the outcropping of a giant, concrete mushroom, spawned from the blackened brick walls. The kitchen, with the four chairs and table was inhabited by pigeons strutting and pecking on the table. At the outermost lip of the kitchen floor one could view the East River and the Manhattan skyline; and hanging from below the concrete outcropping an entanglement of wire mesh, a network of girders and pipes the boys could climb down leaving a twelve foot drop to the sidewalk. But to reach the bridge the boys would have to continue their climb up the ladder and fire escapes to join Buzzy on the floating scrap of floor and then, one at a time, leap into the air.

Swifty stood in the doorway of sky. He was aloft as Buzzy was aloft, saying his name. Swifty couldn't remember how he got there, but he was comfortable as he was in the playground, standing on a swing, grasping the narrow links of chain on either side, bending his knees and pumping himself higher and higher into the sky. Now he bent his knees and rested the palms of his hands on the doorframe, navigating his flight. Buzzy was yelling, "Bennie, Joey, keep goin'." Swifty felt wind whoosh by his ears, the sound like Mama's lips at his ear pleading, "Give me loving." He'd reach his arms around her, far as they would go, hug her hips, his face sinking into the great cushion of her belly. "Give me loving," she wept. He'd maneuver his head so that he could breathe and repeat "loving," the tip of his tongue touching the roof of his mouth. Poppa only said, "Nah!" heaping food on his plate, and "Nah!" handing him a slice of bread. Sometimes Mama screamed, "Give me loving. Then Swifty was scared.

The prism of Swifty's seeing framed Louie falling from the ladder; the fathom of sky that framed him empty in the instant his cry dissipated. Louie would never walk again. People blamed Buzzy. The boys who had climbed the ruin of the burned building said that the fault wasn't really Buzzy's. They said everyone had become distracted by Swift in the doorway of sky; he had caused the accident. Swifty knew the word "accident." It felt like his mother's breath brushing his ear, when she pleaded, "Give me loving." Within weeks the boys' assertion that it was Swifty who had caused Louie to wind up in a wheelchair became the prevailing belief. Everyone said that Swifty had hexed Louie, not deliberately; but he was a jinx, susceptible to the *malocchio*, the tumult of cacodemons at play in the shadow of his dumb wonder. The gossip reached Sophie. She would have argued against it but her waxing unhappiness convinced her of the futility of opposing such talk. However, she did take the precaution of dropping a pinch of salt in Swifty's pants pocket to weaken the force of blaming.

Sophie under siege behind her locked door heard Mrs. Leznick curse, "*Paskuddniak!*" But Sophie knew her apartment was immaculate. She scrubbed the floors on her hands and knees. Stood on a ladder and washed the walls. The odor of disinfectant was the perfume of her home. The accusation and curse "Filth" that Mrs. Leznick spat at her door was ameliorated by Sophie's scouring, and knowledge of Sol's labor that kept faucets running and toilets flushing.

Sophie cried and confessed to the simmering pot roast that she couldn't remember Swifty every minute of the day. She considered tying him to his bed but decided that was too cruel.

As Swifty approached a group of boys, they faded and reappeared at a greater distance. Mothers pulled their children away when Swifty came near, and the distance between Swifty and other children remained constant. He saw the mothers' faces whispering, and knew it was about him. Only Old Man Levine mounted on the stoop made coaxing sounds. And it began to snow.

The bus was moving slowly through the slush, the chains on the tires ringing. Swifty thought he saw Buzzy. The runner outpaced the cloud of gas he was striding in and leaped onto the back of the bus. His feet resting on the rear bumper, he clung to the rim of the bus's oblong rear window, and bent his knees, riding the undulations, letting every bounce shape his posture. Voices from the stoop called out in scofflaw affirmation, "Hitchin' on the wagon, hitchin' on the wagon." And Swifty was off, chasing the bus as it slowed to a stop.

The wheels clanged. Swifty rode, clinging to the back of the bus, his legs flexing and thrusting like a swimmer riding the swell of a wave. From inside the bus a kid pressed his face against the rear window, the boy's nose flattened against the glass into a pig's snout; he rolled his eyes. The boy's cheeks ballooned and his eyes squeezed shut. The face gnashed teeth. Swifty looked away, up at the gray sky shedding snow. A surf of clouds raced along with the bus, invisibly tethered to Swifty's vision. The rooftops sped along, and a flock of pigeons rolled out of sight carried by the wind. And thick, wet snowflakes fell.

The boy clinging to the back of the bus wasn't Buzzy, and he jumped off after two blocks. Swifty tightened his grip on the metal rim that bordered the rear window. Gas fumes wafted around his head. The breeze buffed his cheeks. He thrust his head out of the cloud of gas and gulped air. A quivering radiated up his spine, humming the ride in his bones.

The knocking inside the rear window was urgent. The boy unpressed his face from the window, shouting warning, rapping on the glass. An old woman seated next to the boy scowled. Swifty knew what to do. The wheels hissed. The bus rocked to a stop.

He was halfway down the street when the bus driver gave up the chase several paces beyond the rear bumper, as was always the case; the driver stood, shouted warning and returned to the inside of the bus.

Swifty strolled along a street of neat brownstone buildings. Everything had turned white. He smelled something delicious. Under the rolled up awning the store front window of Ernie's Rib Joint was open. The savory breeze pulled a stream of brown men through the doorway. Swifty stood for a while in the mouth-watering aroma, and then wandered on. His hands hurt with the cold, he crossed his arms over his chest and sheltered his hands under his armpits.

"Hey snowflake, stop where you at." The three boys came up to him. Two were smiling. The one who wasn't smiling stood close to Swifty and said, "You woofin' at me?" Swifty looked at the two boys who couldn't stop laughing. The angry one grabbed the front of Swifty's jacket and said, "I ain't jokin', what you doin' paradin' your dumb ass on my street? Where you from, little ofay?" Swifty recited his address. The two laughing boys convulsed into a dance around Swifty. The angry one shouted, "I'm serious," and cuffed Swifty's ear. "Lemme see," the angry one said, "what's in your pockets." The two who had been laughing became attentive. Swifty turned his pants pockets inside out. From one pocket salt drifted down. Swifty raised the hand that had pulled out the pocket and tasted the tips of his fingers. The boys howled, "Nasty!" The angry one pantomimed a punch he didn't throw.

A stout, brown woman carrying a shopping bag stepped between Swifty and the boys. "What you up to here?" The angry one said, nodding toward Swifty, "He lookin' for trouble." One of the laughing boys said, "Sheeet, anyone can see he a born fool." The woman rested the clinking, shopping bag full of empty bottles on the sidewalk, and said, "Boy, when you talk around me you better mind your language." The boy said, "Sheeet" again. "Smell that," the woman said, and put her fist under his nose. The boy took a step back. "I was jus' sayin' anyone can see he dumb by nature." The woman studied Swifty's face. "Child," she said, "you can close your mouth." Swifty did. "And wipe your nose." Swifty raised his sleeve to his nose, and the woman said, "Wait." She opened her purse, removed a tissue and handed it to Swifty. She guided his hand with the tissue to his nose. "That's right," she said. "Now," she said, looking away from Swifty, standing there with his jacket and pants pockets turned out, "was you all gonna rob this child?" "We jus' playin' with him," the two who'd been laughing said. The angry one said, "Maybe he jus' some kind a runty nut, but he best keep to his home block anyways. He don't belong here." The woman took a closer look at Swifty as he appeared completely absorbed watching her. "Listen," she said, "whether he be a little simple or just carried away appreciatin' ain't no cause for robbery. Now you boys be on your way, and stay out a mischief, you hear?"

The stout brown lady told Swifty to stuff his pockets in and loaded three empty milk bottles in his arms. She pointed to a grocery store. Now, you give the grocery man these here empties, and he give you six cent, a nickel to ride, and a penny for what you want. You know your way home, child?" Swifty recited his address. The lady said, "Go now," Swifty lingered, wanting to stay in the warm eddies of the woman's voice. She smiled and pointed at the grocery. They stood looking at one another. She started to walk away and Swifty followed her. She stopped, turned and said, "Go on now" pointing, once more, at the grocery.

Seated in the bus Swifty watched the snow covered streets roll by. The rushing sky and rooftops lashed to his scrutiny by the thinnest membranes of light; again, he recited his address. A man seated across from him raised his head from a newspaper, looked at Swifty and ducked back behind the newspaper. The bus turned and went down a steep street.

Looking through his breath on the window he saw the faint reflection of the boy that was him, the falling snow, and two boys fencing with large, frozen fish. Passengers on the bus shouted, "Look." Boys all over the street threw fish at one another and whacked each other over the head and shoulders with fish. The bus maneuvered through the narrow street slowly. Fish were strewn all over the gutter; heads and tails, and glittering ice. A spiral of fish scales swirled, shining among the snow drops. A man seated in the back of the bus began to shout angrily in a language Swifty had never heard. Someone yelled back in English, "Believe me, the little bastards ain't orphans. It's the parents they should put in jail!" The bus driver said, "Amen to that." Snowballs thudded against the windows and sides of the slow moving bus. A woman passenger screamed and ducked her head toward her lap as a snowball splattered against the window where she was seated. Nuggets of ice and fish heads bounced off the bus. Swifty saw the boys take aim. Gleaming, somersaulting through air the fish guts flew like something alive, and smacked the window where Swifty stared. His head recoiled as though he'd been punched. The entrails slithered down the window. One round, stumpy *babushka* adjusted her kerchief, tightened the knot under her chin, and with a paper shopping bag hanging from her hand tottered to the rear door. "Stop," she wailed. The bus rocked to a halt.

She swayed. The doors whooshed open. "Leo!" she cried, "Leo!" The bus driver yelled, "Give it to him good! Warm his pants." A fish head landed on the floor near the *babushka*'s feet. She howled, "Leo, don't come home or you'll make me a murderer." All the passengers, except for the man reading the newspaper were yelling. The *babushka* stepped down and moved toward the melee. At the opposite curb there was a truck parked halfway up on the sidewalk, tilted to the driver's side, the right rear tire pancaked. Two boys stood on the tailgate and emptied bushel baskets of fish and crushed ice into the gutter. Swifty looked for Buzzy. Fish thumped off the side of the bus. The driver maneuvered the bus around the truck and the kids pounding each other with fish. At the corner the bus turned and picked up speed. Swifty reached up and pulled the cord. The bus didn't stop. He stood up, held onto a pole with one hand and with the other pulled the cord again. The bus sped on. Swifty looked toward the bus driver, he couldn't think of what to say. He saw unfamiliar streets flying by. At last the bus stopped. The rear doors opened. Swifty stepped down, off the bus.

The air was dense with snow. The corridor of trees, white. Next to a boarded up snow-domed kiosk was an entrance to a park. The paths and the benches were empty and white. Swifty had never heard such quiet. Except for his chilled feet he wasn't very cold. He tasted his salty fingertip, stuck his tongue out and lapped in the moisture. He looked behind him and saw the long trail of his footprints disappearing near the hedges where he'd entered the park. He walked in the quiet, following his shadow and exhaled little clouds of breath. The path turned, Swifty turned with it. Through the white flecked silence he heard wheezing. The sound grew louder. He came closer. He passed the breathing body heaped on the bench under a rug. The face had the pink sheen of a lollipop wrapped in cellophane. The lips trembled. The man's arms hung down, his fingertips sunk in the snow. Under the bench a brown bottle with a picture of three roses on it peaked a hillock of slush. The snow made all of the man white, except for his glistening pink face. Between the upright slabs of his shoes and the ragged cuffs of his pants, coils of newspaper squeezed out over his milky blue ankles. Swifty walked faster. The man's puling wheeze followed him. Swifty ran until he could no longer hear it.

Footprints in what had been the smooth expanse of snow appeared; he stopped, lifted his leg and placed his foot into the recess and his foot fit exactly. On either side of him the white sloping grounds swelled, untouched. His feet inside his sodden shoes were damp and chilled.

He walked in slow motion placing his feet in the indentations as if he'd made these footprints earlier, and now he was playing follow-the-leader, carrying himself somewhere he'd started trudging to long ago. Gingerly he lowered each foot into each footprint, following the trail laid out in front of him. After a while he strode less carefully, exploding the footprints into white dust, but kept to the path that led him toward the sound of barking.

The seal was perched at the top of a stone pyramid, head lifted, barking. There was no one else at the iron railing that encircled the pool of water. A breathing hump rose from the surface of water, floated for an instant and sank. The seal on top of the pyramid leaped, gliding in the air, it rode the arc it shaped down into the water, splashed and vanished. Swifty studied the water. The seal didn't reappear.

Beyond the pool and the cage with the largest black cat Swifty had ever seen was a towering cage with a giant tree inside it. Swifty studied the caged, birdless tree, walked on and thought he saw, not too far away, a uniformed park attendant disappear into a great stone house, from which came the sound of creatures he couldn't imagine.

It was getting near to dusk. He was shivering. Three boys walking toward him waved. He stood still, waiting for them to disappear, but they came nearer, gesturing for him to join them. As they turned into another path they called to him, whistling. Heavy footed in the snow, he trotted after them.

The tall one wore a leather aviator's cap, goggles, and was wrapped in a tent-like military coat, festooned with flaps, buckles, and brass buttons. The littlest one, in a red sweater, shivered. His eyes were watery, and he gnawed at his raw fist. The third was short, round, every part of him seemed swollen; he wore a flannel shirt, unbuttoned, corduroy pants, and sneakers. On top of his head, a baseball cap with the visor turned behind his head; he was sweating and smoking the stub of a cigarette. The tall one raised the goggles and placed them on his leather encased forehead. "You got a cigarette?" Swifty shrugged. The fat one said, "This little pisser got nothin'," The tall one said, "It's snowy Saturday and we own the joint, but don't worry we ain't gonna hurt you. You come to see the hellephants? Big sons of bitches ain't they?" Swifty looked beyond the railing down the deep stone incline that led to a trench filled with water; beyond it, a cobble stone hill climbed to a plateau, where two elephants raised straw in their curling trunks to their mouths. Behind the elephants stood their immense house. Swifty had never seen any living thing so large, so imperturbable.

The enormous fans of their ears moved slowly. Steam rose from their haunches. "Lissen," the tall boy said, "You're gonna trade your jacket for my brudder's sweater. Okay gimmee." Swifty watched the elephants. Monumental, they moved ever so slightly, like motion in the fluid tempo of a dream. The tall boy unbuttoned Swifty's jacket. Swifty turned obligingly. He pulled his arms out of the sleeves. For a moment he couldn't see anything as the sweater that the little guy had been wearing was pulled over his head. But then he saw the elephants again, the legs like tree trunks, enormity moving.

The snowball looped out of the sky. The littlest one wearing Swifty's jacket, took his bloodied knuckle from his mouth and pitched a snowball, high. The three were throwing. The snowballs curved in the sky, splashed into the trench of water, and plopped near the elephants, tranquilly eating. Swifty turned from the immense quiet of the elephants to the murderous faces of the boys: such concentrated vehemence in their intention, rehearsing slaughter they bellowed "Fuck! Bastard! Bitch!" and Swifty cried. As if the size and imperturbability of the beasts had offended them, the boys let go barrage after barrage and cursed. Swifty turned his head from the boys to the elephants, back to the boys; frantic, dizzy, his eyes retained the image of their ferocity; the turning of his head blurred the sight of the huge indifferent animals with the splotches of snowballs melting down their sides; Swifty at the center of the boys' war dance, they howled "Fuck! Bastard! Bitch!" Swifty's weeping wracked his body.

The tall one in the aviator's cap and goggles hollered "Cease fire!" The boys froze in place, grinning. "Look at that," the one in the goggles said to Swifty, "Look at that," he commanded, pointing to a purple Jelly Baby under the iron railing, sheltered from the snow. Next to the purple one was a yellow one, the size of a nickel. Slowly Swifty's tremors ebbed and he watched the boy peel the candy from the ground, kiss it, hold it up to the sky, and say, just before he put it in his mouth, "Kiss it up to God. He pointed to the yellow Jelly Baby and directed Swifty to do the same. Swifty held it in his hand. "Go on, go on. Kiss it up to God." Swifty kissed it and raised his hand with the candy above his head. "Yeah, awright, you can eat it now." Swifty put it in his mouth. It was sweet. "See you around," the boys said and marched away, while Swifty searched under the rail for more candy he could kiss up to God and eat.

The dark warmed him. When he looked up through the haze of falling snow he saw the white ball of the moon extricating itself from the tree's branches. Home was far away, and anyway he didn't want to go there. He walked deeper into the park, wading in the white dunes that had swallowed the streets and buildings, the billowing white going on and on until it was everything.

Pliny the Younger: A Balance Between the Public and the Private Persona

Peter Valente

The letters of Pliny the Younger offer the reader a rich and varied portrait of the administrative and personal life in the first century AD. In the letters we witness his shrewd negotiations as a lawyer, his love of an adoring young wife, his approach to the art of writing and the importance he gives to, among other things, the art of translation, and his disappointment at the indifference of an audience at a poetry reading. But he is not above jockeying for a place in the pages of Tacitus' histories. We might ask how much of what we read in these letters is truth and how much a façade. Of course, a letter is unlike an historical or scientific study that at least intends to strive for objective truth. Pliny had a distinguished career in government and thus all his actions, including these letters, published in several volumes in his lifetime, were visible to the public and to the emperor. So as we read we must also be conscious of this fact and not be over hasty in our judgment of Pliny's character. Upon first reading we can say he is humane and loving, politically shrewd and inquisitive. And this would be accurate. But we cannot know the extent to which he is "being himself." Is he hiding his real thoughts or simply adopting a kind of mask for professional purposes? His style, as opposed to Cicero's, which he followed early on in his career, is elaborate and less direct. Pliny's public persona is carefully balanced against his private thoughts. He is in fact writing his own biography. And who of us, in a similar position, would be completely truthful, even as we strove to be honest, in our expression of ourselves, if we knew that the entire world would read its pages. Indeed, it is for this reason, and also since many of his correspondents were famous in their own right, that the letters of Pliny the Younger are such a fascinating and unique document. So let us begin to examine these letters and see if we can create a portrait of Pliny the Younger carefully, remembering it is just as likely as not that he is showing us himself as he would like to be seen.

Regarding this theme of the public and private persona I would like to examine the following letter to the historian Tacitus. Pliny the Younger writes:

> I strongly predict (and about this fact I have no reason to doubt) that your histories will be immortal. Believing this sincerely to be the case, I all the more desire a place in them. If we are generally very careful to choose the best artist to do a portrait of our face then does it not stand to reason that one's actions ought to be celebrated by an author like yourself? And so in view of this, I would like to relate to you a story, which I'm certain you're already familiar with, as it was highly publicized at the time, yet still I'll repeat it now, that you may realize how valuable it is to me that my role in these events, well-known because of the dangerous circumstances in which I acted, may receive an additional luster from the pen of so bright a genius as yourself.

Here Pliny is creating a public image of himself. He asks Tacitus to record an event that relates how he defended a friend during the prosecution of Baebius Massa for extortion. Herennius Senecio, together with whom Pliny led the prosecution, sought to establish, after the case was over, a further "preventive measure" against Massa. Massa in retaliation accuses Senecio of having a "personal vendetta" against him and threatens to prosecute him in turn for "high treason". Pliny, witnessing his friend being threatened speaks to the court, ""Most noble consuls, I believe that for some reason Massa is implying that I have betrayed the interests of my client in this case, since he has failed to mention that he will prosecute me as well". He defends his friend by daring Massa to prosecute him as well. It is certain that Massa would not prosecute Pliny given his prestige and his association with the emperor. And so, he used his own power and influence to defend Senecio. He concludes the letter,

> The late Emperor Nerva (who in the days before he became Emperor would keep track of every worthy political event) wrote a very impressive letter to me, applauding not only myself but the Age that he said had produced such an orator who embodied the spirit (as he liked to call it) of the ancients.
>
> But whatever my action signifies, I know you will enhance and spread the glory of it; not that I require you to exceed the limits of reality. History should never depart from the truth nor does any noble act require any more than its truthful depiction.

The description of a "noble act" should not "exceed the limits of reality" because it should require no more than a "truthful depiction". Certainly, in this letter Pliny shows the importance of maintaining a certain kind of public persona. He is seeking a well-known historian to recreate that persona in his pages. He calls upon Tacitus to "enhance and spread the glory of it [his action]".

Pliny's letter to his young wife's aunt adds another dimension to his portrait. Here he writes about his wife, Calpurnia, who was fourteen years old when they married. Pliny was forty years old. She was his third wife, and he shows genuine affection towards her. The beginning of the letter is addressed to his wife's aunt. He writes,

> You stand out as an exemplary model of tender regard to your family in general and to your late brother in particular, whose feelings of affection and companionship you returned with an equal fervor, and you have not only exhibited the kindness of an aunt but supplied the warmth that a father shows to his daughter; and I am persuaded to say, with unwavering honesty, and pleasure, that she, in her capacity, behaves in a manner worthy of her father, her grandfather, and yourself.

He applauds the positive influence that she had on his young wife such that she, Calpurnia, "behaves in a manner worthy of her father, her grandfather, and yourself". In Pliny's description of his wife there is real tenderness and genuine love. A reader has no doubt that she also adored him and fully returned that love. He writes,

> She discriminates with the eye of one sure in her judgment, she is prudent, and her love for her husband is virtuous and bespeaks a chaste nature. Her affection for me has aroused her interest in literature, and she reads my compositions with pleasure, often memorizing them and afterwards repeating to me word for word the contents, she always has a copy ready in her hands. How attentive she is to my every argument when I am beginning a new case, curious about my line of reasoning. And she is as relieved and joyous as I am when the case has finally concluded. During the court proceedings, just as I've begun my opening arguments, she will quickly send for messengers to relay to her the impressions my case is making on the jurors, the amount of applause I receive, and the success, lastly, of my closing arguments. When I am giving a lecture in an auditorium, she hides behind the curtains at the back and peaks out at the audience and at me, listening, greedily, to my every word and following the logic of my argument. She adapts my lyrics to music and plays the resulting songs beautifully on her lyre. She has no other instructor in this but Love.

And he is sincere when he writes,

> But her devout nature is a product of your training and instruction and as she was growing up under your roof she was surrounded by all that was sacred and moral. And did she not learn how to love me as a result of your description of my character? You revered my mother as your own and it was you who shaped and encouraged my character from infancy, thus it is no mystery that I should have become the kind of man my wife is in love with.

It is a letter that shows Pliny was deeply in love with his new wife and that she returned that love. It is one of his most beautiful letters. And yet, if we are to keep in mind the intricate relation between the public and the private persona, we need to remember, that this is Pliny's portrait of his wife. And we must remember, also, that these letters were for publication.

Pliny the Younger's letters can be regarded as models of their form. They were used well into the 18th century as educational tools in writing and rhetoric. In this context, I would like to turn to the following letter to Fuscus, who had written to Pliny inquiring about "the method ... to use when pursuing [his] studies". Pliny begins by speaking about the importance of translation and then continues to elaborate on other helpful practices to improve one's writing. The beginning is worth quoting in full since so much of what Pliny says is now common practice for writers:

> Translation is a very important skill to develop and so I recommend (as many poets and writers in general do) translating from Latin into Greek or from Greek into Latin. This way you will learn many new and elegant expressions, a variety of colloquialisms, and forceful turns of phase. Also, to imitate authors allows you not only to invent after their manner but to become better acquainted with their language and little will escape you when translating: this method will improve your critical reading skills and increase your ability to judge the quality of a work.
>
> It may benefit you, also, when you have read enough of an author, such that you consider yourself fairly knowledge about his work, to hone your insights by carrying his ideas in your mind such that, after much thinking, you feel you now can consider him your rival by writing a composition on the same subject; now compare your work and his and minutely examine both his text and yours. You will feel that you achieved a great victory on points where you succeeded in bettering him in your exposition as you will suffer

humiliation if you find that his argument is logically sound on every point and immune to your critique.

You may dare to take the most brilliant passage from a work and try to better it yourself. This is bold indeed but as it is performed in secret and without an audience you cannot be accused of being presumptuous. And yet there are those with sufficient confidence who take on the task of adopting the voice of a great author only to better him in speech and they receive great applause, I might add, and because they dispense with being overly critical of their own work, they advance beyond those authors they thought brilliant enough to follow.

Pliny's suggestions here are especially useful when a writer is just starting out. The following reminds of something one might encounter in Ezra Pound's *ABC of reading*. Yet whatever one thinks of that text the advice Pliny offers is sound:

I know that your concern at present is forensic oratory and yet I would suggest that you not always take that line of reasoning and learn to vary your approach by exploring different subjects. A farmer rotates the various crops he plants to improve the quality of his land and so the mind is enriched by studying different subjects. Therefore it is useful to single out a brilliant passage from an historical text and then to practice writing letters with that text in mind. Often in pleading a case, one has recourse to both an historical style as well as a poetical style in developing one's argument and furthermore a succinct and polished style is cultivated by writing letters. It is also well to ease your mind by reading poetry and when I say this I do not mean a long and sustained work (for only men of leisure have the time to engage in this activity) but the short witty epigrams which serve to relieve your tensions and allow you to pass a few moments away from the more pressing work. These short poems are usually thought of as entertainments but these witty epigrams are often better known than longer, more serious poetry.

He concludes this letter with the following remarks on what to read:

Remember, when studying a topic, to read the best that was ever written on the subject; as the saying goes, "though we should know much, we should not read many books". I should not need to tell you exactly who those authors are, since they are generally well known. Though I have extended this letter far beyond the length I originally intended, nevertheless, if you follow my advice, you will find your own time spent studying considerably shortened.

It is a fascinating letter in which we read of the program of study suggested by a cultivated Roman gentleman of wealth in the first century AD, who would write, furthermore, in a letter to Arrianus, of the attitude one should adopt towards this study:

> Nothing, in my opinion, enables us to approach our studies with a graceful and genial air, as we do our manners, then to temper seriousness with good humor, since there is always the chance that the former may turn into arrogance and the latter is too close to frivolity.

Pliny the Younger wrote hundreds of letters, many of which survive and are of great historical importance to our understanding of the first century of the Christian Era. We must not be misled into thinking of these letters as intimate in the same way our own contemporary letters are considered intimate. They are not private; they were reworked for publication and their survival today is largely due to their popularity. They do not so much give us Pliny's "personality" (it would be wrong to use this modern word with all its psychological implications to speak of a Roman in the 1st century AD) as they do the public persona that he cultivated throughout his career. This is not to suggest that his opinions and his moral sense are somehow inauthentic. It is better to say that it is not quite Pliny "expressing himself" in these letters. Perhaps one can say the public and the private merge and are almost one and the same thing for Pliny the Younger.

He was born an aristocrat and rose through many imperial and civil offices, finally serving as the imperial magistrate under the emperor Trajan. We do not know much about his old age though it is thought that he died suddenly around 113 AD, during his appointment in Bithynia Pontus, a province of the Roman Empire on the Black Sea coast of Anatolia (Turkey), since nothing in his letters refers to later than that date. We do know that he made a will in which he called for the release of hundreds of slaves and established a fund to support them after his death. It is a great testament to the humane treatment that Pliny observed with those of a lower social status. The letters of Pliny the Younger offer the reader a fascinating portrait of Roman society in the first century AD as seen through the eyes of a cultivated Roman aristocrat. They are a unique document and as such we are fortunate that they have survived to this day.

To Cornelius Tacitus

I strongly predict (and about this fact I have no reason to doubt) that your histories will be immortal. Believing this sincerely to be the case, I all the more desire a place in them. If we are generally very careful to choose the best artist to do a portrait of our face, then does it not stand to reason that one's actions ought to be celebrated by an author like yourself? And so in view of this, I would like to relate to you a story, which I'm certain you're already familiar with, as it was highly publicized at the time, yet still I'll repeat it now, that you may realize how valuable it is to me that my role in these events, well-known because of the dangerous circumstances in which I acted, may receive an additional luster from the pen of so bright a genius as yourself.

The Senate had chosen Herennius Senecio and myself to serve as counsels for the province of Baetica, in their prosecution of Baebius Massa. He was eventually convicted, and his personal belongings were placed under official custody. Senecio, having heard that the counsels were ready to sit and hear complaints, motioned to me, and when I approached him, he said that we should, with the same fairness that we exhibited during the prosecution, propose to the consuls, in the form of an application, a preventive measure to ensure the safekeeping of Massa's belongings by those who were asked to guard them. I answered him, "As we were appointed to this case by the Senate you ought to inquire of them if there is anything else remaining that we ought to do with regard to this case or is it closed." He responded, "You may draw a limit to the extent of your involvement in this case, now that the conviction is won, but you don't have any connection otherwise with this province or its people except recently in your capacity as prosecutor; but this is not the case with me as I was born there and served as Quaestor among the people." I told him if such was his resolution then I would certainly support it and stand by his side so that he would not have to face alone whatever resentment was caused by these actions.

So, we approached the consuls; Senecio stated in no uncertain terms his proposition to which I added some remarks. We had barely finished speaking when Massa suddenly grew angry and complained that since Senecio had not acted out of loyalty to his clients but rather because of a personal vendetta against him, he would now prosecute him for high treason. The assembly was bewildered and became anxious to hear the outcome of this accusation. I immediately stood up and said: "Most noble consuls, I believe that for some reason Massa is implying that I have betrayed the interests of my client in this case, since he has failed to mention that he will prosecute me as well." My speech created conversation among all in the assembly and eventually the whole town was speaking about it. The late Emperor Nerva (who in the days before he became Emperor would keep track of every worthy political event) wrote a very impressive letter to me, applauding not only myself but the Age that he said had produced such an orator who embodied the spirit (as he liked to call it) of the ancients.

But whatever my action signifies, I know you will enhance and spread the glory of it; not that I require you to exceed the limits of reality. History should never depart from the truth nor does any noble act require any more than its truthful depiction.

Your intimate friend,
Pliny

To Calpurnia Hispulla 1

You stand out as an exemplary model of tender regard to your family in general and to your late brother in particular, whose feelings of affection and companionship you returned with an equal fervor, and you have not only exhibited the kindness of an aunt but supplied the warmth that a father shows to his daughter; and I am persuaded to say, with unwavering honesty, and pleasure, that she, in her capacity, behaves in a manner worthy of her father, her grandfather, and yourself. She discriminates with the eye of one sure in her judgment, she is prudent, and her love for her husband is virtuous and bespeaks a chaste nature. Her affection for me has aroused her interest in literature, and she reads my compositions with pleasure, often memorizing them and afterwards repeating to me word for word the contents, she always has a copy ready in her hands. How attentive she is to my every argument when I am beginning a new case, curious about my line of reasoning. And she is as relieved and joyous as I am when the case has finally concluded. During the court proceedings, just as I've begun my opening arguments, she will quickly send for messengers to relay to her the impressions my case is making on the jurors, the amount of applause I receive, and the success, lastly, of my closing arguments. When I am giving a lecture in an auditorium, she hides behind the curtains at the back and peaks out at the audience and at me, listening, greedily, to my every word and following the logic of my argument. She adapts my lyrics to music and plays the resulting songs beautifully on her lyre. She has no other instructor in this but Love. As I observe her gentle acts of devotion, my feeling is such that I hope the harmony between us increases with each day, and lasts for many years to come, for time does not so much impair my youth or my body as it does the luster of my glory of which she is enamored. But her devout nature is a product of your training and instruction and as she was growing up under your roof, she was surrounded by all that was sacred and moral. And did she not learn how to love me as a result of your description of my character? You revered my mother as your own and it was you who shaped and encouraged my character from infancy, thus it is no mystery that I should have become the kind of man my wife is in love with. Know then that we both thank you for giving us to each other and that you chose one for the other.

With affection,
Pliny

To Fuscus

You have inquired of me the method that you should use when pursuing your studies,

in that retirement you have enjoyed for a long time. Translation is a very important skill to develop and so I recommend (as many poets and writers in general do) translating from Latin into Greek or from Greek into Latin. This way you will learn many new and elegant expressions, a variety of colloquialisms, and forceful turns of phase. Also, to imitate authors allows you not only to invent after their manner but to become better acquainted with their language and little will escape you when translating: this method will improve your critical reading skills and increase your ability to judge the quality of a work.

It may benefit you, also, when you have read enough of an author, such that you consider yourself fairly knowledge about his work, to hone your insights by carrying his ideas in your mind such that, after much thinking, you feel you now can consider him your rival by writing a composition on the same subject; now compare your work and his and minutely examine both his text and yours. You will feel that you achieved a great victory on points where you succeeded in bettering him in your exposition as you will suffer humiliation if you find that his argument is logically sound on every point and immune to your critique.

You may dare to take the most brilliant passage from a work and try to better it yourself. This is bold indeed but as it is performed in secret and without an audience you cannot be accused of being presumptuous. And yet there are those with sufficient confidence who take on the task of adopting the voice of a great author only to better him in speech and they receive great applause, I might add, and because they dispense with being overly critical of their own work, they advance beyond those authors they thought brilliant enough to follow.

After you write a composition, put it aside for several months and then, when it's no longer fresh in your mind, come back to it and revise it; you'll retain sections of it and delete others; you'll rewrite certain passages, and insert new paragraphs, in order to sharpen the initial logic governing the composition; it is a tiresome and seemingly endless task to revise in this way, I know, and to have to rethink an approach after the initial inspiration has been checked and spent and finally to have to insert and alter and restructure the composition all the while keeping in mind and not significantly modifying the original plan; the very difficulty of this method will, I assure you, benefit you in the long run and increase your critical acumen.

I know that your concern at present is forensic oratory and yet I would suggest that you not always take that line of reasoning and learn to vary your approach by exploring different subjects. A farmer rotates the various crops he plants to improve the quality of his land and so the mind is enriched by studying different subjects. Therefore, it is useful to single out a brilliant passage from an historical text and then to practice writing letters with that text in mind. Often in pleading a case, one has recourse to both an historical style as well as a poetical style in developing one's argument and furthermore a succinct and polished style is cultivated by writing letters. It is also well to ease your mind by reading poetry and when I say this I do not mean a long and sustained work (for only men of leisure have the time to engage in this activity) but the short witty epigrams which serve to relieve your tensions and allow you to pass a few moments away from the more pressing work. These short poems are usually thought of as entertainments but these witty epigrams are often better known than longer, more serious poetry; and since I am speaking of poetry I shall attempt to be more poetical myself:

> As pliant wax is altered by our command,
> and shaped by obeying the Artist's hand,
> so now Mars' or virgin Minerva's form is put on,
> or the charms of Venus or her son.
>
> A single subject alone can't quench the raging flame
> except with the help of the sacred fountain stream
> sweetly winding through the abundant green
> spreading sweetness onto the happy scene.
>
> So if man's reasoning mind would be pliable as wax
> it should receive the impress of various arts nor be lax.

And so in this way the great orators, and the greatest men in history, used to either amuse themselves or exercise the mind or do both. You'll be surprised to find that there is pleasure, amusement and even possibly instruction in reading such things since they usually deal with courage, animosity, mercy, civility, and everything, in fact, that concerns daily life and even things that could be used in forensic oratory. Besides, one can derive a substantial benefit from reading these kinds of poems just as much as reading any other type of poem. And when you have written much prose, after spending so much time with the craft of poetry, you can judge more accurately which is the easier form of composition.

Perhaps I have satisfied your questions at this point; however there is one thing I forgot to mention: I did not tell you what books to read, though it should be apparent that I have implied which kinds those are by telling you what you should write. Remember, when studying a topic, to read the best that was ever written on the subject; as the saying goes, "though we should know much, we should not read many books". I should not need to tell you exactly who those authors are, since they are generally well known. Though I have extended this letter far beyond the length I originally intended, nevertheless, if you follow my advice, you will find your own time spent studying considerably shortened. Now go back to your writing tablets and either write something following one of my hints or continue on a composition you've already begun.

With affection,
Pliny

To Fuscus

You desire to know how I spend my days in the summer at my Tuscan villa. I wake after I am fully rested, and this is usually at sunrise; but often sooner and never later. When I am up, I generally keep the shutters of my windows closed. It is during this time, when all around me there is darkness and silence, that I feel most at peace and free from the distractions of the outside world, from all those objects and people that exhaust one's attention, and I am left with my own thoughts. Nor do I let my eyes wander but rather subject them to the force of my mind so that in the absence of any external objects I witness only the objects present in the mind's vision. If there is a composition that I've been working on, now is the time I choose to focus on it with regard to the general plan and even with respect to the style and tone, correcting and making final decisions as though I were actually writing. The amount of work that I can complete, in this way, depends upon whether the subject I am dealing with is difficult or not, and I retain a certain rhythm. Then I will open the shutters and call my secretary and dictate to him the result, after which time I ask him to leave for a while, and then ask him to come back and then dismiss him yet again. About ten or eleven (for I never observe the exact hour) according to the weather, I will either go to the terrace or the covered portico, and there I meditate and conclude my thoughts on the subject to my secretary. Afterwards, I get into my chariot and occupy myself in the same way as I did in my study or when I was walking such that the change of scenery restores and refreshes my attention. When I return home, I will rest for a while; then I'll go for a walk; and after that I will read aloud and with emphasis certain orations in Greek and Latin not so much to strengthen my elocution as my digestion; though the voice also, in this way, finds its proper tone. Then I go for another walk, am later anointed with oils in preparation for my daily exercises, after which I take my bath. At dinner, if only my wife is present or a few close friends, an author will read to us. After dinner, we are entertained with either music or a comic sketch. When that is finished, I go for a walk with my servants, some of whom are knowledgeable about literature, and we spend the evening in conversation; and even if the day felt long these hours go by quickly.

But on some days, I will go about things differently and my schedule will change. For example, on occasion I will sleep longer than usual or walk for a longer period of time; rather than using my chariot

I may ride on my horse; therefore, getting more exercise while losing less time. Visits from friends in neighboring towns takes up part of my day; sometimes it happens that they arrive, unexpectedly, and yet at the right time to provide a diversion and to relieve me of my stress. Now and then I amuse myself with the sport of hunting, but I always take my writing tablets with me into the field so that if I catch nothing I might at least bring home something. A part of my day is also spent listening (not as often as they would like I'm sure) to the complaints of my tenants: their rustic manner of speaking amuses me and yet truly I find a certain dynamic quality in their speech, a quality that I bring over to my own studies and also to those engagements of a politer sort.

Kind regards,
Pliny

To Cornelius Tacitus

Ah, you will laugh at me, and it is just as well, when I tell you that your old friend has taken up the art of hunting and has captured three boars. You'll say, "Pliny?, No that can't be". And yet I'm afraid it's true. However, you'll be amused to note that while I stood there with my nets, neither spear nor dart did I carry by my side but rather pen and tablet! My idleness follows me even here. So I took in the scenery and jotted some things down, feeling that if I didn't manage to catch anything yet I might have written something worthwhile. Perhaps you think I'm being contradictory. Not at all. Exercise fires up the imagination. Also, the countryside is pleasing to the eyes and so too the silence that one notices being so far away from the city. These things put me in a meditative mood. Therefore, my dear skeptic, let me advise you to take, when you're hunting, not only your basket and a bottle of wine but also your writing implements. You'll find that Minerva frequents the hills and forests as much as Diana.

With fond regards,
Pliny

To Attius Clemens

If there was ever a moment when the literary arts were at their peak it is the present and there are so many illustrious examples, I could provide you with, yet I will restrict myself to only one: the philosopher, Eurphrates. I first made his acquaintance when I was a young man and at the time, I was a soldier in the army in Syria and I longed to confide in him my as yet unformed thoughts. He was not exceedingly difficult to find and while making himself available to me, exhibited all the humanity and sympathy of which he speaks in his copious writings. To think that I achieved all that he thought me capable of and satisfied a certain image he had of me as a grown man, would make me exceedingly happy, as his own stature remains assured, and he has grown in prominence over the years. I understand now what I did not then about his writings though much still remains for me to discover, for one cannot estimate the value of an artist, painter, or philosopher unless one has advanced to a certain mastery of the subject. And yet, in so far as I have done so, I can say that Euphrates is possessed of so many talents, and so clear in the exposition of his ideas, that even one with little knowledge of the subject can glean the essence of his meaning. His reasoning cannot be disputed as it is conveyed with such force and eloquence, penetrating to the very heart of the matter, reaching such sublime heights and with such resplendent prose as to recall the works of Plato. His style is secure, his vocabulary rich and various, and his tone is at once sweet and inviting such that even an unwilling listener finds himself engrossed in the subject. His dress is impeccable. He is tall, with a friendly air, his hair is long and his gray beard is wide. Though these details seem somewhat accidental and insignificant yet all together they compose a figure of eminence. He is careful with his choice of words, never vulgar, somber and yet not austere. He commands respect but one never feels in awe of him. He lives a life of solitude but is comfortable in the city, his gaze is penetrating and yet his address is friendly. He speaks eloquently against the vices but never against mankind, he does not chastise the prodigal son but welcomes him home with open arms. His arguments are so sound and reasoned that you hang upon his every word; and even when you've followed his axioms to their necessary conclusion, and your heart is satisfied with their truth, yet you desire to keep listening, for the manner in which he reasons is so harmonious and of such captivating beauty. His family consists of three children, a daughter and two sons, all of which he educates with great attention to their evolving natures and with an eye to their future development and success in the world. His father-in-law, Pompelus Julianus, was a man who distinguished himself in all the facets of his own life, but particularly in this sense, that as a well-respected dignitary in his own province yet among the aptly qualified son-in-laws of the highest rank, he, to his great credit, chose one who had excelled in the pursuit of wisdom but of means was considered the less dignified. But what reason do I have to continue talking about this man whose conversation I have been unable to enjoy of late, unless it is only to increase my own frustration that I've no spare time in which to do so? Much, if not all, of my time is taken up in the various duties of a highly important and esteemed position and thus one of great inconvenience with regard to excess time; there are the arguments of litigants, prosecutors, defendants and the determining of causes; the signing of petitions; there are the passing of powers of attorney; and the writing of countless letters. On occasion, I complain to Euphrates (when indeed a moment is spared me to indulge myself) about the ways in which my time is spent, I dare say wasted, in these occupations. He does what he can to convince me otherwise by reminding me that to serve the public in this way, by hearing and determining the causes in a litigation, by articulating and affirming the laws, and passing judgment, all the while balancing the scales of justice, is an important part, if not the most important and noblest aspect of the Art of Philosophy as it puts into practice what her professors only speculate about in the classroom. He may be correct and yet on this point I will never be convinced: that the time spent in such endeavors can compare with his instructive and enlightening conversation. I urge you, if you have the time and can get away from Rome, which I hope you do (all the easier for me to visit you then), you will attend his lectures and benefit from the eloquence of his axioms and the refinement of his reasoning, the like of which has rarely been witnessed in our time. I am, you will see, not one of those people who envy others the happiness they cannot share in themselves. On the contrary, I enjoy a very sensible pleasure when my good friends are able to attend some event that I am excluded from for some judicial reason or other.

Very cordially yours,
Pliny

COVERED

Bob Arnold is the author of *On Stone, Yokel, Once In Vermont, I'm In Love With You, Who Is In Love With Me, Stone Hut, Start With the Tree* and other books of poetry & prose including the train traveling books *American Train Letters, Go West, Darling Companion, The Woodcutter Talks*. His newest collection of poems is *Heaven Lake*. He is currently working on childrens' books (for two granddaughters)—the most recent is *Rain Bear*.

In 1971 Bob Arnold founded Longhouse, as editor and publisher, under the original imprint Our Poets Workshop with various side venues: Scout, Poets Who Sleep, Love Thy Poet, and the small booklet series Just So Happens. He edited and published the final *Origin* (6th series, 2006) in celebration of Cid Corman, gathering poets and artists worldwide, released free online and now archived on CD. During 2015–2016 Bob edited and prepared for Longhouse new book titles by Lorine Niedecker, Janine Pommy Vega and as literary executor for Cid Corman *Of*, Volumes 4 & 5.

Jennifer Bartlett is the author of four books of poetry and *Sustaining Air: The Life of Larry Eigner*.

Until his retirement **Lee Bartlett** was Presidential Research Professor at the University of New Mexico. His many books include *William Everson: The Life of Brother Antoninus* (New Directions), *Kenneth Rexroth/James Laughlin, Selected Letters* (W.W. Norton), and *The Greenhouse Effect* (Lords of Language). He lives with his wife Anne in semi-seclusion near the Mexican border.

Kevin Bertolero is the founding editor of both Ghost City Press and *& Change*, a journal of gay poetry. He holds degrees in literature from Potsdam College and the University of New Hampshire, as well as an MFA from New England College. Kevin is the author of three collections of poetry, most recently *Love Poems* (Bottlecap Press, 2020), as well as a nonfiction book, *Forever in Transition: Queer Futurist Aesthetics in Gay Cinema* (Another New Calligraphy, 2021). His work has appeared in or is forthcoming with *Hanging Loose, The Cortland Review, Post Road*, and elsewhere. He lives in Portland, Maine.

Mary Bonina was finalist for the Goldfarb Fellowship from the Virginia Center for the Creative Arts, awarded several residencies, including one at the VCCA retreat, Moulin a Nef, in Auvillar, France. Previous publications include *My Father's Eyes: a Memoir*, two poetry collections—*Living Proof, Clear Eye Tea*—and the newly released collection Lunch in Chinatown, from Červená Barva Press. Her poems and essays have appeared in *The Lowell Review, Hanging Loose, Poets and Writers, Salamander, Mom Egg, Ovunque Siamo, Adelaide*, and many other journals. Her work has been included in several anthologies, including *Entering the Real World: VCCA Poets on Mt. Angelo* (Wavertree Press).

Daniel Bratton has taught Canadian and American literature at Toronto Metropolitan University, the University of Waterloo, and the University of Toronto, from which he received his PhD. He spent seventeen years in the Far East and was Professor in the English Department at Doshisha University in Kyoto, where Cid Corman and Will Petersen both taught. He is co-founder of the Elora Poetry Centre in Ontario.

Mairéad Byrne is the author of six poetry collections, *Nelson & The Huruburu Bird* (Wild Honey Press 2003), *Talk Poetry* (Miami University Press 2007), *SOS Poetry* (/ubu Editions 2007), *The Best of (What's Left of) Heaven* (Publishing Genius 2010/2019), *You Have to Laugh: New & Selected Poems* (Barrow Street 2013), and *Famosa na sua cabeça* (Dobra Editorial 2015); also nine chapbooks. Her poems have been published in anthologies including *Staying Human/ Staying Alive* (Bloodaxe 2020); *The Cast-Iron Airplane That Can Actually Fly: Contemporary Poets Comment on Their Prose Poems* (2019); *Women : Poetry : Migration* (2017); *Out of Everywhere 2: Linguistically Innovative Poetry by Women in North America & the UK* (2015); *If Ever You Go: A Map of Dublin in Poetry and Song* (2014); The Best of Irish Poetry 2007; *Krino 1986-1996: An Anthology of Modern Irish Writing* (1996); *Ireland's Women: Writings Past and Present* (1994); and *The New Younger Irish Poets* (1991); also a wide range of journals in the United States, Ireland, and the UK. For seven years, she co-curated couscous, a diverse poetry/performance event in Providence (USA) and Cork (Ireland). Along with Will Schutt and Miriam Grottanelli, she is the co-curator of Policromia, an annual international workshop and festival of poetry and translation across the arts, in Siena, Italy.

Leslie Cagan has worked in peace and justice movements for more than 60 years. From the Vietnam war to racism at home, nuclear disarmament to lesbian/gay liberation, from support of Palestinian rights to normalizing relations with Cuba, she's been a central organizer in many struggles. Her coalition-building and organizing skills have mobilized millions of people in many of the nation's largest demonstrations, including the 6/12/82 million-person Nuclear Disarmament demonstration in NYC; the lesbian/gay rights 10/11/87 march on Washington; massive mobilizations against the Iraq War from 2003 to 2007; the 9/21/14 People's Climate March in NYC; and the 2019 Queer Liberation March in NYC on the 50th anniversary of Stonewall. Her writings appear in 10 anthologies and in scores of print and online outlets.

Linda Dittmar, Professor Emerita, a Stanford University Ph.D., and Ron Schreiber's colleague, taught modern literature and film studies at the University of Massachusetts Boston (1969–2007). Winner of the Chancellor's Prize for Excellence in teaching, she had two Fulbright grants to India, one as Distinguished Chair, and taught at Tel Aviv University and the University of Paris. Her academic publications include *From Hanoi to Hollywood; the Vietnam*

War in American Film and *Multiple Voices in Feminist Film Criticism*. Her recently published memoir is *Tracing Homelands; Israel, Palestine, and the Claims of Belonging*.

Gregory Dunne is the author of three collections of poetry, most recently, *Other/Wise* (Isobar Press, 2019). He published a critical memoir on Cid Corman in 2014: *Quiet Accomplishment, Remembering Cid Corman* (Ekstasis Editions). He lives in Japan and is associate poetry editor at *Kyoto Journal*.

David Eberly is an original member of Good Gay Poets, which published his chapbook *What Has Been Lost* in 1982. He is co-editor of *Embodied Texts: Virginia Woolf and Trauma* (Pace 2007) and speaks and writes on narrative medicine. He is currently assembling *With Luck: Selected Poems* and writing his spiritual autobiography. He lives in Boston's South End.

George Evans has published poetry collections in the US, UK, and Latin America, including *The New World*, *Sudden Dreams*, and the bilingual *Espejo de la Tiera/Earth's Mirror* (Costa Rica). His poetry, fiction, essays, and translations have appeared in magazines and anthologies in the US, Australia, Costa Rica, England, Ireland, France, Japan, Mexico, Nicaragua, and Viet Nam. His literary awards include two poetry fellowships from the US National Endowment for the Arts, a writing fellowship from the California Arts Council, two Lannan Foundation Literary Fellowships for poetry, and a Japanese government Monbusho fellowship for the study of Japanese poetry. He edited *Charles Olson and Cid Corman: Complete Correspondence*; cotranslated, with writer Nguyen Qui Duc, The Time Tree by Vietnamese poet Huu Thinh; and translated *The Violent Foam: New and Selected Poems*, by his wife, renowned Nicaraguan poet Daisy Zamora. They live in San Francisco.

Michael Franco is a poet, playwright and artist. His publications include: *The Marvels of David Leering* [Pressed Wafer 2017], *A Book of Measure Volume One: The Journals of the Man who Keeps Bees* [Talisman House 2017], *The Library Of Dr Dee* [dromenon press for Pressed Wafer 2006], *How To Live* [Zoland, Cambridge Ma. 1998]. He was the founder of the Word of Mouth Readings Series in Cambridge Ma. and is a board member for the Pioneer Valley Poetry Festival. He is currently a Visiting Writer for the University of Coimbra, Portugal and curator of the Xit The Bear reading series in Somerville, MA.

Kirk Glaser is a poet and fiction writer whose work has been nominated twice for the Pushcart Prize and appeared in over fifty publications, including *The Threepenny Review, Nimrod, Chicago Quarterly Review, Catamaran, The Cortland Review*, and elsewhere. Awards for his work include an American Academy of Poets prize, C.H. Jones National Poetry Prize, University of

California Poet Laureate Award, Gertrude Stein Fiction Award Finalist/ The Doctor T.J. Eckleburg Review, *New Millennium Writings* Contest Finalist, and Richard Eberhart Poetry Award/*Southeast Literary Review*. His poetry collection *The House That Fire Built* will be published in 2025 by MadHat Press. A Teaching Professor at Santa Clara University, he serves as Director of the Creative Writing Program and Faculty Advisor to the *Santa Clara Review*. He is co-editor of the anthology *New California Writing 2013*, Heyday.

Kirk grew up in Connecticut, attended Dartmouth College in New Hampshire, and then lived in Vermont for a number of years. While he still finds those forests a spiritual home, the forests and coast of Central California have claimed him. He has lived in California since attending U.C. Berkeley, where he earned a M.A. in creative writing and PhD in English (in contemporary American poetry and American eco-literature), He has been a resident of Santa Cruz for over three decades. For many years, he lived with his wife and daughter in the Santa Cruz Mountains, under oaks, madrones, redwoods, and Douglass firs. Their home on top of the mountain adjoined a wilderness that swept from their ridge top at 2500 feet down to the ocean. After the second fire and two homes destroyed, they finally moved to the edge of town.

Kirk has had the honor and pleasure of teaching at Santa Clara University for over twenty-five years, many of those mentoring the creative and passionate students who run the *Santa Clara Review*. He also started (over a dozen years ago) and runs the Writing Forward Reading Series on campus, which brings world-renowned and emerging writers from diverse backgrounds to campus to share their writing, skills, and knowledge with students.

Kirk has regularly practiced Vipassana meditation, as taught by S.N. Goyenka, since 1992, when his future wife took him to his first ten-day silent retreat. An unforgettable experience, one which he thought he would never repeat (it was hard!). Since then, he has done a ten-day retreat at least once a year, as well as volunteer work, and has traveled with Vipassana meditators to sit at many sites in Northern India and Nepal where the Buddha was born, enlightened, taught, and died. Vipassana retreat centers have spread around the world and are offered completely free of charge—you just have to agree to stay and practice, silently, living the life of a bhikkhu or bhikkhuni for the ten days. A pearl of great price.

Olena Jennings is the author of the poetry collection *The Age of Secrets* (Lost Horse Press, 2022) and the novel *Temporary Shelter* (Červená Barva Press, 2021). She is a translator of collections by Ukrainian poets, Kateryna Kalytko, together with Oksana Lutsyshyna, Iryna Shuvalova, together with the author, and Vasyl Makhno. Her translation, together with the author, of Yuliya Musakovska's *The God of Freedom* was released in May 2024 from Arrowsmith Press. Her translation of Anna Malihon's *Girl with a Bullet* is forthcoming from World Poetry Books. She founded and curates the Poets of Queens reading series and press.

Burt Kimmelman's recent books include *Zero Point Poiesis: George Quasha's Axial Art* (2022), *Steeple at Sunrise: New Poems* (2022), and *Visible at Dusk: Selected Essays* (2021). He is a distinguished professor of Humanities at New Jersey Institute of Technology

Michael Londra writes poetry, fiction, reviews, and essays. His work has appeared or is forthcoming in *Asian Review of Books*, *The Arts Fuse*, *Restless Messengers*, *The Fortnightly Review*, *The Blue Mountain Review*, and *Boog City*. He lives in Manhattan.

Dick Lourie co-founded *Hanging Loose* magazine, the oldest independent literary journal in the country, with Ron Schreiber, Emmett Jarrett, and Robert Hershon, in 1966. (Hanging Loose Press grew from the pages of the magazine a few years later). He remained Ron's close friend and colleague for the next 38 years until Ron's death in 2004, and is still active with Hanging Loose. A poet, editor, and blues musician, he travels frequently to the Mississippi Delta, and has lived in the Boston area (Somerville, Chelsea, Rockport) for more than forty years. His most recent collection is *Jam Session and Other Poems*.

Ron Padgett was born in 1942 in Tulsa, Oklahoma, where he attended public schools. His father was primarily a bootlegger who also traded cars, his mother primarily a housewife who also helped with the bootlegging. Around the age of 13, young Ron began scribbling his thoughts and poems in spiral notebooks. This practice followed hard on the heels of his having read, for the first time, "serious" literature. In high school Ron discovered contemporary literature and started a little magazine called *The White Dove Review*, along with his friends Dick Gallup and Joe Brainard. In its five issues (1958–1960) the magazine published Allen Ginsberg, Jack Kerouac, Robert Creeley, LeRoi Jones, Ted Berrigan, and others. In 1960 Padgett moved to New York to attend Columbia College, where, over the course of four years in the pursuit of English and Comparative Literature, he was fortunate to study under teachers such as Kenneth Koch, F. W. Dupee, Andrew Chiappe, and Lionel Trilling. After his junior year, Padgett married Patricia Mitchell, whom he had known in Tulsa and who had also immigrated to New York. Other Tulsa émigrés during this period included Brainard, Gallup, and Berrigan. During his college years, Ron published his work in a number of "underground" literary magazines and gave readings of his poetry in New York City. In 1965–66 Padgett was able to spend a year in Paris on a Fulbright, studying and translating 20th-century French literature. The following year, Ron and Pat's son Wayne was born. The three set up house in a bohemian apartment in New York in what is now called The East Village, where the parents have lived ever since.

Beginning in the mid-1960s the Padgetts visited Kenward Elmslie and Joe Brainard at the former's house in northern Vermont each summer for fifteen years. Then they constructed their own abode nearby. In the late

1960s a spate of Padgett's books appeared: *Bean Spasms*, in collaboration with Berrigan and Brainard, from Kulchur; a translation of Apollinaire's *Poet Assassinated*, illustrated by Jim Dine, from Holt, Rinehart & Winston; and *Great Balls of Fire, poems*, also from Holt. In January of 1969 Kenneth Koch talked Ron into teaching poetry writing to children, which he did for the next nine years. Padgett also served as Director of the St. Mark's Poetry Project 1978–1980. Then he took the position of Publications Director at Teachers & Writers Collaborative, the nonprofit organization that specializes in teaching imaginative writing to children. There he edited and wrote books on that subject for 20 years.

Mark Pawlak has been a co-editor of the Brooklyn-based literary press Hanging Loose since 1980. He is the author of ten poetry collections, most recently *Away Away* (Arrowsmith Press, 2024), and the memoir *My Deniversity: Knowing Denise Levertov* (MadHat Press, 2021). His poems have been translated into German, Japanese, Polish, and Spanish; and have been published widely in such places as *The Best American Poetry*. He taught mathematics at the University of Massachusetts Boston (1979–2016), where he was Director of Academic Support Programs and received the Chancellors Achievement Award. He lives in Cambridge.

Jenny Penberthy's editions and writings about Lorine Niedecker brought her into contact with Cid Corman and in turn with Kamaike Susumu. Currently, she is working on an edition of previously unpublished Niedecker letters and a book about Fulcrum Press.

Jack Pulaski grew up in the Williamsburg section of Brooklyn, New York. Pulaski's authored two novels, *Courting Laura Providencia* and *Chekhov Was a Doctor*, and two short story collections, *The St. Veronica Gig Stories* and *Love's Labours*. His stories have appeared in *Agni*, *The Iowa Review*, *Ohio Review*, *Ploughshares*, *MSS.*, and *The New England Review*, as well as in two anthologies:, *The Pushcart Prize I* and *The Ploughshares Reader*. He is the recipient of fiction awards from the Coordinating Council of Literary Magazines, the Pushcart Prize, and has received the Special Merit Award in the Nelson Algren Short Fiction Contest twice. Pulaski currently resides in Vermont.

Hoyt Rogers is an award-winning translator, essayist, poet, and novelist. He has published many books; he has contributed poetry, fiction, essays, and translations to a wide variety of periodicals and anthologies. His latest works are a poetry collection, *Thresholds* (MadHat Press); the novel *Sailing to Noon* (Spuyten Duyvil), book one of *The Caribbean Trilogy*; a chapbook of prose poems, *Canvases* (Mudlark); a translation of Yves Bonnefoy's *The Wandering Life* (Seagull Books); and a translation of Marco Simonelli's *Will: Shakespearian Sonnets* (Spuyten Duyvil). For more information, please visit his website, hoytrogers.com.

Guy Rotella is Professor of English emeritus at Northeastern University, where, for twenty-six years, he edited the Morse Poetry Prize. His books include *Castings*, on monuments and monumentality in postmodern poets.

Betsy Sholl's tenth collection of poetry is *As If a Song Could Save You* (University of Wisconsin Press, 2022). Her ninth collection of poetry is *House of Sparrows: New and Selected Poems* (University of Wisconsin, 2019), winner of the Four Lakes Prize. Other awards include a Maine Book Award for Poetry, The Felix Pollak Prize, the AWP Prize for Poetry. She teaches in the MFA in Writing Program of Vermont College of Fine Arts and served as Poet Laureate of Maine from 2006 to 2011. She was a founding member of Alice James Books.

Tracy K. Smith is a Pulitzer Prize-winning poet, memoirist, editor, translator and librettist. She served as the 22nd Poet Laureate of the United States 2017–2019, during which time she spearheaded *American Conversations: Celebrating Poetry in Rural Communities* with the Library of Congress, created the American Public Media podcast *The Slowdown*, and edited the anthology *American Journal: Fifty Poems for Our Time*.

Smith is the author of five poetry collections: *Such Color: New and Selected Poems*, which won the 2022 New England Book Award; *Wade in the Water*, which was awarded the 2018 Anisfield-Wolf Book Award; *Life on Mars*, which won the 2012 Pulitzer Prize; *Duende*, winner of the 2006 James Laughlin Award of the Academy of American Poets; and *The Body's Question*, which received the 2003 Cave Canem Prize. Her memoir, *Ordinary Light*, was a finalist for the 2015 National Book Award in nonfiction. She is the co-translator (with Changtai Bi) of *My Name Will Grow Wide like a Tree: Selected Poems of Yi Lei*, which was a finalist for the 2021 Griffin Poetry Prize; and co-editor (with John Freeman) of *There's a Revolution Outside, My Love: Letters from a Crisis*. Her memoir-manifesto, *To Free the Captives: A Plea for the American Soul*, was a *Time* magazine and *Washington Post* Best Book of the Year, and a *New York Times Book Review* Editors' Choice.

Among Smith's other honors are a Guggenheim Fellowship, the Harold Washington Literary Award, the Academy Fellowship of the Academy of American Poets, the Harvard Arts Medal, the Columbia Medal for Excellence, a Smithsonian Ingenuity Award and an Essence Literary Award. She is a Chancellor of the Academy of American Poets and an elected member of the American Academy of Arts and Letters, the American Academy of Arts and Sciences, and the American Philosophical Society.

Patrick Sylvain is a poet, writer, social and literary critic. Twice nominated for the Pushcart Prize. Published in several creative anthologies, journals, periodicals, and reviews including: *African American Review, Agni, American Poetry Review, Callaloo, The Caribbean Writer, Chicago Quarterly Review, Ep;phany,*

Magma Poetry, Ploughshares, Prairie Schooner, and *Transition*. Sylvain has degrees from the University of Massachusetts (B.A.), Harvard University (Ed.M.), Boston University (MFA), and Brandeis University (PhD). Sylvain is an Assistant Professor at Simmons University, and he is also on faculty at Harvard University's History and Literature Division. Sylvain's poetry chapbook, *Underworlds*, is published by Central Square Press (2018). Sylvain is a featured poet on Benjamin Boone's Poetry and Jazz CDs *The Poets are Gathering* and *Caught in the Rhythm* (Origin Records, Oct 2020, Nov 2023). Sylvain is the leading author of *Education Across Borders: Immigration, Race, and Identity in the Classroom* (Beacon Press, Feb 2022). His latest bilingual collection, *Unfinished Dreams // Rèv San Bout* (JEBCA Éditions, Jan 2024).

Peter Valente is a writer, translator, and filmmaker. He is the author of nineteen full-length books. His translation of Nanni Balestrini's *Blackout* (Commune Editions, 2017) received a *Publisher's Weekly* starred review. Recent books include a translation of Gérard de Nerval, *The Illuminated* (Wakefield Press, 2022), a translation of Artaud's notebooks, *The True Story of Jesus-Christ: Three Notebooks from Ivry (August 1947)* (Infinity Land, 2023), *The New Revelations of Being & Other Mystical Writings by Antonin Artaud* (Infinity Land Press, 2023), and his translation of *Nicolas Pages* by Guillaume Dustan (Semiotext(e), 2023)). Forthcoming is his *Selected Essays (2019–2023)* (Punctum books, 2025) and a book he edited on the work of the filmmaker Harry Smith, *The Occult Harry Smith: The Magical & Alchemical Work of an Artist of the Extremes* (Inner Traditions, 2025). Twenty-Four of his short films have been shown at Anthology Film Archives.

Cornelia Veenendaal was a faculty member at U Mass–Boston, and one of the founders of Alice James Books. Retired, she now lives in the North Country of New Hampshire. Her books of poetry include *The Trans-Siberian Railway, Green Shaded Lamps* (Alice James Books), *What Seas What Shores* (Rowan Tree), and *An Argument of Roots* (BlazeVox {Books}).

www.ingramcontent.com/pod-product-compliance
Lightning Source LLC
Chambersburg PA
CBHW031312160426
43196CB00007B/495